Dedication

This book is dedicated to all those who in the face of considerable pressures over the past thirty years kept faith with democratic principles and values and ensured the preservation of civilized society in Northern Ireland. May their faith and labours continue to flourish.

D1615720

CONTENTS

ACKNOWLEDGEMENTS

We are deeply indebted to many who rendered us invaluable assistance in completing this work. We are indebted in the first instance to our respective institutions, the University of Ulster and Rosemont College from which we both received encouragement and support to enable us maintain our trans-Atlantic contacts throughout the period of research and writing.

To the librarians in the many locations where we researched our sources we wish to acknowledge their expertise and professionalism.

We are particularly indebted to Professor Bob Welch of the University of Ulster and to Colin Smythe, our publisher, both of whom provided considerable help and guidance. To Marc Ross of Bryn Mawr College we are especially grateful for his many insightful comments.

We are also deeply grateful for the support and assistance provided by our families, especially to our wives Patricia and Alie. Ronan and Niamh Farren deserve our special thanks for their work during the final stages of preparing the text for printing.

Sean Farren and Robert Mulvihill

INTRODUCTION

This book comes from an awareness that numerous peacemaking and other political initiatives, large and small, have been advanced to deal with Northern Ireland. People have been interested in what has sustained the conflict, but not with a theoretical and critical analysis of the various efforts to resolve the conflict. If there are underlying patterns associated with past failures, and we would contend there are, then it seems foolish indeed to ignore them. There is now a substantial literature dealing with intense and persistent conflicts, but it has not yet been extensively applied to the Northern Ireland conflict. This book involves a systematic application of a segment of the conflict studies literature to the Northern Ireland conflict.

A principal contribution of our discussion lies in an attempt to integrate theories of conflict and strategies of conflict resolution, on the assumption that the failure to do so dooms many attempts at peacemaking. If most of us are 'naive scientists', our theories of conflict remain implicit and untested. And yet, it is from these incoherent theories that our plans for resolving conflicts are drawn. This book aims at making these connections explicit, especially in the minds of policy makers with responsibility for dealing with conflict.

A second major contribution of this book lies in its particular contribution to the study of intense and persistent conflicts. We are aware, as everyone familiar with Northern Ireland is, of the importance of dealing with the history of the conflict. We are, however, also aware that the uncritical recitation of conflict history adds little to the understanding of the conflict and is, itself, often little more than an apology for a particular interpretation of the conflict. We wanted to find a way to integrate the historical residues into the contemporary experience of the conflict and to examine how historical memory influences the interpretations of conflict and the relationships that bind conflict.

Third, we know that most studies struggle to deal with the multilateral structure of conflict, preferring instead to focus on the seemingly more economical bilateral approach. This observation has led us to the work on family systems of Murray Bowen, the late professor of psychiatry at Georgetown University. It is our view that Bowen's work is a highly innovative and comprehensive approach to the study of conflict, inclusive of elements of structural and psychocultural perspectives, and with clear implications for peacemaking. We believe that the Anglo-Irish Agreement of 1985, for example, provides an excellent test of the Bowen approach.

The Bowen systems approach is vitally important because it gives us insight into how to, in the language of game theory, 'invade' the strategies that conspire to maintain intense levels of conflict over long periods of time. Many people would argue that conflicts such as Northern Ireland's end only when one party is subdued or expelled. We think that such a view is shortsighted and empirically shallow.

The test is not whether conflict ends, but rather whether it can be transformed in ways that allow for the peaceful development of cooperative relationships between all the involved constituencies. Clearly, neither of the two main communities in Northern Ireland has been, or is likely to be subdued. The Good Friday Agreement of 1998 and its validation in the joint referenda held in both parts of Ireland has given the people of Northern Ireland along with the people of the rest of Ireland and of Britain, an historic opportunity to build just such relationships.

The first four chapters describe essential features of the relationships between the major sections of society as these have evolved over a long period of time, relationships which continue to influence the behaviour and interpretation of the major actors in Northern Ireland's drama. The final four chapters employ the natural systems framework to explain the transformation of the conflict, a transformation that took shape in the New Ireland Forum of the early 1980s and found its first significant expression in the Anglo-Irish Agreement of 1985.

That the political agenda has been transformed by the Good Friday Agreement does not make the task any less formidable. Building sustainable democracy in deeply divided societies is a work in progress in many corners of the world. We hope that studies such as ours will add to the development of a comparatively based understanding of these problems useful to the policy makers whose responsibility it is to build democratic institutions.

Sean Farren,   Robert F. Mulvihill,
University of Ulster,   Rosemont College,
Coleraine   Philadelphia

ONE

DIVISIVE THEMES

In the spring of 1968, a Catholic family was evicted from a house in Caledon, not far from Dungannon, in County Tyrone. The family squatted in the house which had been allocated by the local council to a nineteen-year-old unmarried Protestant woman, secretary to the local Unionist parliamentary candidate. Austin Currie, a young nationalist member of the Northern Ireland Parliament, organized a sit-in at the house to protest on the family's behalf and then raised the issue in parliament. Currie went further and helped organize the first major civil rights march, from Coalisland to Dungannon, designed to focus attention on the generalized pattern of housing discrimination practised against Catholics.

If any one event could be pointed to as the precipitant of the contemporary conflict in Northern Ireland, it was most likely this housing dispute. The housing problem evoked images of the historic settlement of Ireland by English and Scot, Anglican and Presbyterian, and the displacement of Catholics from the land they had long occupied. Centuries-old attitudinal and behavioural patterns had moulded the ways in which Catholic and Protestant conceived of each other. One a constant and violent threat, the other a righteous and arbitrary usurper. At Caledon, questions about these two major Northern Ireland communities – how they imagined one another and their relationships with each other, both contemporary and historical – were once again pushed to the surface in one jarring event.[1]

Three hundred years of isolation and anxious togetherness define the ways in which the respective traditions gather communally. Northern Ireland was, and still is, a largely segregated society.[2] Segregated in housing, schooling and in most of their social activities, the people of Northern Ireland have nursed suspicions of each other that fuel their politics, Protestants with a defensiveness for what the

1

settlers have built and Catholics with a corresponding sense of dispossession for what they have lost. It was not surprising, therefore, that
the allocation of public housing evoked fresh images of settlement and
dispossession.

The housing dispute at Caledon provides, therefore, an apt instance
through which to understand the conflict in this deeply divided society.
As the Northern Ireland conflict unfolded, housing estates were sites
of communal intimidation and migration. House searches by security
forces reached staggering proportions – over 80,000 by the end of the
1970s.[3] Northern Ireland, already a largely segregated society in 1968,
became even more so. The house was not merely a private residence
but rather a marker of communal identity in a deeply riven society.

The protest at Caledon threatened the barriers, structural, cultural, and
emotional that had sustained the embattled communities over three
centuries. No accident, then, that the protest was sufficient to ignite a
long-awaited explosion.[4] According to Padraig O'Malley 'in 1968 occu-
pations, squattings, marches, might appear the simple mechanics of the
international student protest; but within Ulster they represented
symbolic invasion of ancient territory, and the assertion of an illegiti-
mate right to "walk".'[5] Across the region, in towns, villages, and especially in housing estates, walls, parades, marches, flags, all marked
identity, Protestant and unionist in the majority, Catholic and nationalist
in a minority, and simultaneously invited trespass.

Ireland's long history of unrest emanating from its close and
complex relationship with its powerful British neighbour, was about to
repeat itself, this time with a ferocity that would shock the world. Why
the English effort to incorporate, or at least pacify Ireland, and later
Northern Ireland, failed has, of course, been the object of much historical scrutiny. Our purpose in this chapter is less to review that history
than to consider how the failure itself has contributed to the persistence and intensity of the conflict. Seen from this perspective, two
major factors, settlement-dispossession and covenant, combined to
establish the fundamental relationships that have been at issue since
the seventeenth century and which had frustrated many efforts to end
the conflict. These relationships established a geography of suspicion
and resentment most intense in the north-east of the country where the
greatest concentration and mix of native Catholics and Protestant
settlers existed. As a result, Catholics and Protestants could be said to
have lived 'alone together'[6] since the beginning of the seventeenth
century.

SETTLEMENT

While Anglo-Norman efforts to control Ireland in late medieval times had gradually resulted in the assimilation of settler to the native society, post-reformation Elizabethan Ireland witnessed a significant change. The English crown, by then Protestant, seeing the native and still Catholic society as a threat to its security, determined that the governing and control of Ireland would most effectively be achieved, as Ian Lustick argues, through 'the planting of colonies of settlers from England and the pale'.[7] The manner in which the plantation or colonization of Ireland took place was in the mainstream of colonial endeavours throughout the world. Large numbers of settlers, of differing cultural and religious backgrounds to those of the native population, came or were sent to Ireland in the sixteenth and seventeenth centuries to consolidate English rule over Ireland. The settlers walled themselves off, literally and figuratively, from 'natives', who were thoroughly dispossessed.[8] As Foster and others have argued, this dispossession was the single most important factor influencing the evolution of relationships within the Irish-English system.[9] The historic record clearly shows that efforts to Anglicize Ireland, to extirpate the native Gaelic culture and to establish the legitimacy of English authority over Ireland failed, resulting in the establishment of a political system, in which historical emotions are embedded that substantially define the continuing conflict in Northern Ireland.

The fear of Catholic insurrection, of course, was first tied to the manner in which Ireland had been settled and land distributed. Despite early expectations of resistance, land was seized from the native population at an alarmingly rapid rate. As Roy Foster puts it, confiscation of land 'took the form of massive expropriation of estates and transplantation of native inhabitants. This was the Irish revolution, and its social effects were arguably more long-lived than any other inheritance of the Cromwellian era.'[10] Natives were forced off the land, banished to remote parts of Ireland, or retained in feudal-like labour arrangements. The extent of land confiscation, shown in the following table, demonstrates that the native Catholic population had become nearly landless in their own country:

Table 1.1 Proportion of land owned by Catholics[11]

1641	61%
1688	22%
1703	15%
1776	5%

Over the years, the Crown gave confiscated land to civilians and soldiers, in repayment of debts, and to new settlers, both English and Scottish. Natives were expelled, genocide contemplated but rejected in favour of retaining cheap labour, and conditions created that excluded all but the considerably reduced Catholic gentry from any productive role in the country.

Catholics and Protestants became natural enemies in a political system forged by the vast and rapid confiscation and plantation of land. The Catholic uprising in 1641, and the massacres of settlers in its early stages, reinforced the view of Catholics as enemies. Whether the threat from Catholics was real or not, the country was, as David Miller says, 'full of Catholics',[12] a fact which no doubt reinforced Protestant fear. Protestants lived in an embattled state, one which was, in their own minds, chronically in danger of attack. The events of 1641 were seen by Protestants as a clear warning of things to come if the Catholic population were not thoroughly suppressed. The Cromwellian wars established that oppression and solidified the patterns of communal isolation and togetherness that were and are still so influential in the history of Ireland, North and South.

The conquest of Ireland was incomplete, however, and this incompleteness established itself as permanent not only in the Protestant mentality but in the system of relationships between settlers, natives and the metropolitan power that describes Ireland's political history. Catholics were enemies, 'heretics and traitors' according to Conor Cruise O'Brien[13], and a system of stereotypes developed which helped maintain these relationships. As Ned Lebow has carefully argued, these stereotypes enabled the otherwise decent people of England and the settlements to do indecent things, expropriation and harassment for the most part, to the natives.[14] Once the land expropriation by the settlers had begun, it was no longer a question of political or religious loyalty that needed to be demonstrated. Instead, the assumed Catholic drive to re-gain the land confirmed their seditious intent. The Catholic refusal to affirm the legitimacy of the settlement was reason enough, as O'Malley points out, in settler eyes, for their insecurity.

Insecurity and the fear it breeds are, of course, permanent parts of the local Protestant mentality. The Protestant colonizations of northeastern Ireland in the early seventeenth century were partial. At all times the new settlers lived in scattered enclaves and under precarious circumstances. Surrounded by a dispossessed and hostile native Catholic population, they were always vulnerable to attack.[15]

The walls which surrounded the settler enclaves and figured so prominently in historical mythology formed emotional cul-de-sacs that defined relationships between all the parties.

Most notorious among the mechanisms designed to subjugate the native Irish and maintain settler privilege were the penal laws. The maintenance of these settler prerogatives and privileges required subjugation of the Gaelic Irish that was achieved by depriving them of civil and religious rights, most especially rights to property. While the penal laws were not always vigorously enforced, they nevertheless acted to remind Catholics daily of their subjugation and exclusion from participation in the governance of Ireland. As Edmund Burke wrote about these laws in his famous letter to Hercules Langrishe:

Their declared object was to reduce the Catholics of Ireland to a miserable populace, without property, without estimation, without education. The professed object was to deprive the few men who, in spite of those laws, might hold or obtain any property amongst them, of all sort of influence or authority over the rest. They divided the nation into two distinct bodies, without common interest, sympathy or connexion.[16]

According to Liam de Paor, the pernicious long-term effects of these laws were in:

. . . erecting a formidable barrier between the privileged colonials and the excluded natives. Poverty, in spite of increasing general prosperity, not only remained widespread and squalid but tended to increase as the population grew. There was a deep structural fault. No tradition of ancient dependency tempered the alienation of tenants from their landlords, of Catholic artisans and merchants from protestant placement, over most of the country. The thousand petty humiliations of a resentful subservience could be met only with the glib deference and the placating comicality that masked hatred.[17]

Throughout this entire period, there remained, as Foster puts it, the 'special condition of Irish politics: could reform accommodate Catholics?'[18] The issue is not that efforts to reform the native-settler relationship were not attempted, but rather that these efforts were either obstructed by settler opposition, or were frustrated by the failure of the British to sustain the reforms.

Reform attempts aimed at integrating Catholics into the English state can be observed from the 1600s on, and they appear again and again right through to the Home Rule legislation of the late 1800s. As Lustick points out the plantation of Ulster had amongst its objectives the conciliation of the Catholic population. As he points out, in 1603:

James received a plan from Bacon urging the conciliation of Irish Catholics as a means to guarantee the political unity of England and Ireland . . . James hoped to implement the settlement of Ulster in ways which would generate royal revenue but still protect native rights . . . In practice, however, not only in Ulster but elsewhere in Ireland, early seventeenth-century settlement efforts led to sweeping expropriations of native land, aggressive segregationist policies toward Catholics, and greater hostility to English-rule among both Gaelic and Anglo-Irish Catholics.[19]

The Treaty of Limerick, which ended hostilities in 1691 and which had been consented to by King William, contained commitments to religious tolerance and to upholding the property rights of Catholic landowners, which were omitted when the Irish parliament ratified the treaty six years later.

Religious conversion might have served as an alternative to the civic incorporation of Catholics but Catholic conversion was ever only half-heartedly attempted. In a society increasingly influenced by Calvinist beliefs about predestination, conversion was more often due to initiatives from English - than Irish-based missionary societies. Foster argues that:

Ideas of wholesale conversion were circumscribed, not only by uncertainty as to what doctrines were officially acceptable, but also by a deep-rooted idea that the Irish nation was too steeped in guilt to be worth much bother. Despite an effort to proselytize in Irish, the conversion of Catholics was never really attempted, though there were some who crossed over, evidently from fairly cynical motives.[20]

Despite efforts, some quite significant in scale, to convert the Catholic population, the failure to engage in full-scale evangelization of Catholics may seem puzzling given the otherwise strong commitment of Irish Protestantism to evangelization. As Protestantism underwent a change from what Miller calls a prophetic to a conversionist emphasis in the nineteenth century, a consensus developed that Catholics were 'not among the elect'.[21] So, whether it was their own reluctance to convert, or the unwillingness and inability of the Irish Protestant community to successfully evangelize them, Catholics remained religiously far apart from Protestants. As Lustick points out, 'Indeed the settlers quickly and naturally developed an interest in preserving religious distinctions between themselves and the native Irish. They took more pains . . . to make the land turn Protestant than the people.'[22]

Religion and property division combined, therefore, to reinforce the feelings of isolation and togetherness that maintained communal distinctions. In Ulster where Presbyterianism was particularly strong and, within it, the notion of the 'elect' widely held, Catholics were not regarded as being among that number precisely because of their refusal to convert and their consequent rejection of salvation. There was not only no need to evangelize among Catholics, there was an increasingly positive obligation to avoid Catholics.[23] The separation theme received positive endorsement, and the system of governance increasingly moved towards a form of apartheid.

It was the failure of the metropolitan power to involve the Irish native elite in the governance of the island that distinguished the Irish experience from other colonial relationships. The Irish experience is distinctive in colonial and state-building terms insofar as few sustained efforts were made by the metropolitan power to involve native elites in the governance of the island. Lustick compares the Irish situation to the French-Algerian one in which native elites were incorporated on a far wider scale than in Ireland, with far different results.[24] In Ireland, however, Catholic elites were not recruited to serve in the colonial administration and the general opportunity of participation was never extended to the native public. As might be expected, restricted opportunities to participate insured that only settler interests received the consistent attention of the colonial administration. This was nothing new. Attempts at such exclusion of the native Irish had long pre-dated the reformation period and, though unsuccessful during Anglo-Norman rule, had been central to state policy in Ireland for several centuries. As far back as the Statute of Kilkenny in 1366 the plan was to enact 'separation from "the Irish enemy"'.[25] The Protestant reformation together with the confiscation and plantation of Catholic owned land gave added justification to this policy. As a result, the state did not begin to fully legitimize Catholic participation until well into the nineteenth century.

Lustick explains this failure by pointing to the distinctive characteristics shared by the settlements of Ireland and Algeria.

In each of these cases the settler community was physically close enough to the core territory, and politically close enough to core elites, to enjoy protection from, and support against, the natives at whose expense the colony was established. The settler colony was also large enough relative to the native population to be able to use core support to achieve and maintain its local dominance. Yet these settlers were too weak relatively at least to the potential for native political mobilization, to cut their ties to the core territory and still preserve their ascendancy in the outlying region.[26]

In an interesting twist, policies pursued by both settler and English tended to be contradictory. Such policies resulted not only in maintaining divisions within Ireland between settlers and natives, but not infrequently produced serious divisions between both and the English, as Lustick also highlights.

Whereas settler commitment to the permanence of the tie with the metropole combined with their fear of native opposition, will lead them to emphasize the symbols of metropolitan rule and the integrity of the ties binding the peripheral area to the metropole, an equally strong commitment to their own local ascendancy will lead settlers to oppose policies and processes which, by effectively integrating the native population into the metropolitan political system, would thereby undermine settler hegemony in the peripheral area.[27]

The first element in the system was grounded in the dependence of the settlers on the metropolitan English authorities. As John Fitzgibbon, Lord Chancellor of Ireland 1789-1802 and determined opponent of Catholic emancipation, reminded 'the gentlemen of Ireland that the only security by which they hold their property, the only security they have for the present Constitution in Church and State, is the connexion of the Irish Crown with, and its dependence upon, the Crown of England'.[28] The very policies they endorsed, for example the penal laws, deepened their insecurity and consequent reliance on England's government. An equally compelling reality was that integration with the native population was not deemed possible. 'Patriot nationalism', as it came to be known, 'remained exclusive: the rule of an enlightened elite'[29] and was, in the end, nothing less than the politics of separatism. Reform and inclusion were not possible, in the minds of most settlers, without jeopardizing their hold on land, privilege and power. A tense relationship existed between settler dependence on the core and the imperative of retaining local dominance over a restive and inevitably explosive population. If the core were to insist on a regime which 'by effectively integrating the native population into the metropolitan political system, would thereby undermine settler hegemony in the peripheral area',[30] the dominance of the settlers would be imperiled. The settlers were too few in number and too isolated to retain control in the face of native resistance and metropolitan abstention.

As F.S.L. Lyons points out, the settlers were, in effect, caught between two worlds, neither of which fully accepted them, and neither of which they fully accepted.

Deserted by the Tories, insulted by the Whigs, threatened by the Radicals, hated by the Papists, and envied by the Dissenters, plundered in our countryseats, robbed in our town houses, driven abroad by violence, called back by humanity, and, after all, told that we are neither English nor Irish, fish nor flesh, but a peddling colony, a forlorn advanced guard that must conform to every mutinous movement of the pretorian (?) rabble – all this, too, while we are the acknowledged possessors of nine-tenths of the property of a great country, and wielders of the preponderating influence between two parties on whose relative position depend the greatest interests in the empire.[31]

The language is frighteningly contemporary.

Elite cooption and the extension of participation[32] might, as it had in several other colonial situations, have modified the separatist tendencies by establishing the kinds of cross pressures that would have created multiple loyalties. The essential element of what Lustick calls the cooperative bargain 'is the state's trade of protection of local prerogatives and influence over centrally allocated resources for the legitimization of its authority, for loyalty, and for access to local resources'.[33] Incentive patterns, economic and political, would have helped to moderate polarizing tendencies. The multiple loyalties induced by these arrangements might have overcome the built-in tendencies toward isolation and togetherness characteristic of ethnocentrically divided and anxious societies. Instead, the settlement of Ireland succumbed to these tendencies, leading to the kind of us *vs.* them and essentialist thinking that White describes as the 'diabolical enemy' syndrome. It is a syndrome that allows people to 'torment themselves by imagining a monster-like enemy, or at least imagining that their human enemies are more monster-like than they actually are'.[34]

In an important sense, however, Britain was never absent. According to Foster, 'It is, in fact, the British connection that should be stressed: for Irish parliamentary politics continued to react to changes in England, and English politicians continued to see Ireland as an appropriate area for intervention'.[35] From the mid-sixteenth century to the present day, we see a pattern in Britain's relationship to Ireland repeated time and again. Reforms calculated to improve the lot of Irish natives are conceived and subsequently implemented only partially or abandoned altogether. And this almost always in the face of settler resistance to reform. 'The cycle of native unrest, central state intervention, attempted reform by the metropole and settler blocking of the reform continued', Lustick writes in commenting on the seventeenth century.[36] For most of the eighteenth century, there was little need or opportunity for native resistance, since the majority native population fell into what can be called a state of political quiescence, and so, appeared to acquiesce in its own domination. When, however, the Catholic population pressed its grievances, or when the British government, for its own reasons, decided to advance the native case, settler resistance proved insuperable. Sometimes for economic, sometimes for political reasons, the British both advanced Catholic reform and retreated from it.[37] In all this, the settler relationship with both native and English was never resolved. 'Constitutional insecurity ruled out political imagination: another enduring theme in Anglo-Irish relations'.[38] Perhaps the most enduring theme.

Over time, social structures evolved which not only subdued but isolated the native Irish from the political, professional, and commercial life of the country. That the ascendant English and settler classes did not succeed one hundred per cent in achieving their objectives matters little in terms of the pyschological impact of the messages it conveyed to the majority of the native Irish. In periods of crisis these dominant

Protestant groups could rely on the 'metropole' to help ensure the subjugation of the natives; in periods of calm they resented any intervention from London, especially if that intervention suggested reform which might benefit the native Irish and threaten settler control. In only one period, roughly 1780-1799, did a major breach emerge in the ascendancy-settler alliance. Then, influenced by the liberalism of the age, leading Protestant intellectuals from both the ascendancy and settler communities, together with some politicians, made common cause with the emerging leadership of middle-class Catholics in a campaign for the repeal of the penal code. Successful to a considerable extent, the alliance did not survive the atrocities perpetrated against Protestants in the course of the 1798 uprising and the Act of Union which abolished the Irish Parliament and created the Union of Great Britain and Ireland in 1801.

Thereafter, the fear of Catholic insurgence, especially in Ulster, and the spectre of Catholic political power that might attempt to undo the land settlement all over Ireland and suppress the Protestant religion, spurred an ever closer alliance between the Protestant ascendancy and descendants of the settler community. As 'emancipation' and reform advanced Catholic political influence in the nineteenth century and especially once Catholics began to campaign for the return of an Irish parliament and a degree of autonomy for Ireland, the alliance tightened, hardening attitudes toward the native Irish. Nowhere was this alliance to be more evident than in the country's north-eastern counties where Protestant numbers were most heavily concentrated. No longer able to prevent the extension of civil liberties to the native Catholic Irish, this coalition of Protestants was determined to frustrate any attempt on the part of the government in London to grant independence or even home rule to Ireland.

The fear of encroachment by the Irish and abandonment by the English led Protestants to rely on their own forms of self-help, mostly in the form of volunteer vigilantism known as banding, in order to protect their status in Ireland. Protestants, in Ireland and later Northern Ireland, were constantly under siege. Means had to be devised which would maintain access to British protection against the increasingly discontented Catholic population on the one hand and which would promote Protestant hegemony throughout Ireland on the other.

COVENANT

If all ideas presume sociologies, then the 'covenant' was the idea in which the Ulster Protestant settlement was embodied. This Protestant covenant had its origins uniquely in the Old Testament 'covenant' and was particularly expressive of the Presbyterian tradition.

At the heart of the scriptures is a deal, hard and clear. This is the covenant between Yahweh and his people . . . If Israel will be his people, Yahweh will be their God. This though easily stated, is as profound a commitment as any set of human beings can make. This is the opposite of the Faustian deal, but it has one element in common with it. Whereas the covenant is a collective, not an individual bargain, and it is with the Almighty rather than the devil, it is identical in this regard: once you sign on, you belong to him. The contract is Israel's perpetual enlistment in the divine army; it binds the entire nation and does so generation after generation from time unto eternity. This is a very big deal indeed.[39]

Historians agree that, as time passed, a substantial element of convergence around core elements of Calvinism developed between Presbyterians and Anglicans, bringing more and more Anglicans into the covenantal fold. In 1638, the National Covenant was compiled by the General Assembly of the Anglican Church and it implicitly adopted the covenantal framework. This commitment, made first by Scottish Presbyterians and later embraced in varying ways by most other Ulster Protestants, was at the heart of Protestant persistence and togetherness:

We promise and swear by the GREAT NAME OF THE LORD OUR GOD, to continue in the profession and obedience of the foresaid religion; and that we shall defend the same, and resist all those contrary errors and corruptions, according to our vocation, and to the uttermost of that power that God hath put in our hands, all the days of our life.[40]

As Donald Akenson puts it, 'There is an implicit if-then clause in the National Covenant: if the monarch follows the ways of God, we will be allegiant to him. Otherwise no'.[41] The ways of God phrase, of course, begs the question of what are the 'ways of God'. While its origin was scripturally inspired, the covenant's expression in Ireland was as political as it was religious. In the Northern Ireland case, the ways of God were highly politicized and had to do as much with sustaining Ireland, ultimately Northern Ireland, as a Protestant state as they did with sustaining individual Protestants. The covenant embraced the underlying political ambivalence of the settlement and sought reassurance in a conditional reciprocity between Britain and the settlers.[42]

Indeed, the covenant took on aspects of the contract theory of politics prevalent in England during the seventeenth and eighteenth centuries. In the English-Irish context, 'The Whig notion of political obligation – that the people were bound to support the regime only so long as the regime fulfilled its undertaking to protect their rights (primarily rights of property) – was in any event practically the same whether the undertaking was regarded as a contract or a trust'.[43] As Miller points out, it was not an agreement of mutuality. The people or community had rights, largely property rights, and the sovereign had duties to protect these rights. Failure to do so forfeited the contract. So long as the settlement distribution of land remained, enforcement of the contract was the key to understanding settlement politics. According to Miller:

> The fact that the landed elite of Ireland should strive to place their relationship with authority on a contractual footing analogous to the arrangement their English counterparts believed themselves to have achieved in 1689 is wholly unremarkable. The eighteenth century was an age in which educated men throughout the Atlantic world thought about political authority in terms of original contracts, of which the Irish 'Constitution of 1782' might be called a textbook example. Whereas in England the contractarian myth rested upon the social reality of the gentry's special role in maintaining public order, however, and really defined only their political obligation, in Ulster it rested on a different reality. In Ulster each Protestant irrespective of social position was assumed to have a special role in the maintenance of order in a special situation where massive disorder was traditionally expected from one source: the Catholics. The public band was the ad hoc community defined by that role and while the community was not a claimant to sovereignty, banding did have the character of a primeval social contract seeking to place its relationship with the sovereign power on a contractual basis or, perhaps more exactly, to get the sovereign power to acknowledge the terms of its trusteeship of authority. The community's essence was that its members could trust one another, and no one else. It stood uneasily between those who could never be trusted (the Catholics) and a sovereign power which might be trusted only within limits. The sovereign power – in the seventeenth century the king, in the eighteenth the Westminster regime – should be compelled to agree to very explicit terms.[44]

The band, or self-organization tradition, simultaneously populist and nativist, provided powerful incentives for widespread participation in the defence of settler privilege. The band dealt with the problem of collective action by identifying participation as a duty and then collectivized that duty in various 'volunteer' organizations, most notably the Orange Order, founded in 1795. The Orange Order's feverish anti-Catholicism was fed by the nearly universal Protestant fear of a Catholic effort to re-take the land. The Order bridged the gap, intensified by economic modernization, between lower-class and upper-class Protestants and between Presbyterians and Anglicans. Indeed, as Miller points out, 'Orangeism sustained for Protestant workers in town and country the sense that the most important feature of the old structure – a special relationship between them and their Protestant betters – still obtained'.[45]

The Orange Order preserved and enhanced the special 'conditional' nature of the covenant. The Order's position 'is significant because it reflects the popular conception that the proper relationship between the public band and the constituted authority is a contractual one'.[46] Both the Orange oath and Orange practice allowed Protestants to think of themselves as being apart from the British national community. The consequence was not trivial in terms of its future significance to the individual: 'In many situations his essence was still his social position, i.e., his Protestantism'.[47]

In his work, *The Politics of Unreason*, Seymour Martin Lipset describes a concept of preservationism which refers to tendencies to call for a restoration of a past, imagined or real, in which an imperiled group was dominant. In his elaboration, class differences are blurred for the sake of communal solidarity.[48] Preservationists provide an unusually high degree of support for violence for reasons of social control. From the early bands to the institutionalized Orange Order, to the locally recruited members of the 'B Specials' in Northern Ireland, this tradition of popular willingness to defend its own community has been a major force in Protestant political life. The banding tradition operated as a social mechanism independent of any particular threat from Catholics. Given the insecurity, not only of land tenure, but of rents, the band was easily called into action, as much to promote owners' interests as to defend against native unrest.

The framework of preservationism influenced reform policy throughout the eighteenth century and was jeopardized by the pace of reform in the nineteenth century. It more recently was embraced in 1912, and then again, though less formally in 1974 and 1985-86. In 1912, responding to the threat of home rule being granted by Westminster, Ulster Protestants produced the Solemn League and Covenant, which read in full:

Being convinced in our consciences that Home Rule would be disastrous to the material well-being of Ulster as well as of the whole of Ireland, subversive of our civil and religious freedom, destructive of our citizenship and perilous to the unity of the Empire, we, whose names are underwritten, men of Ulster, loyal subjects of His Gracious Majesty King George V . . . humbly relying on the God whom our fathers in days of stress and trial confidently trusted, do hereby pledge ourselves in solemn Covenant throughout this our time of threatened calamity to stand by one another in defending for ourselves and our children our cherished position of equal citizenship in the United Kingdom and in using all means which may be found necessary to defeat the present conspiracy to set up a Home Rule Parliament in Ireland. And in the event of such a Parliament being forced upon us we further solemnly and mutually pledge ourselves to refuse to recognize its authority. In sure confidence that God will defend the right we hereto subscribe our names. And further, we individually declare that we have not already signed this Covenant.[49]

The defiance promised in the Solemn League and Covenant (signed by 218,206 men and 228,991 women) combined with the 'Poor People's' budget (the first major British social welfare plan, opposed bitterly by

Conservatives, and ultimately by the House of Lords) to produce a major constitutional crisis in Great Britain. Politicians and military officers threatened mutiny against the government if Home Rule were granted to Ireland. Only the onset of World War I prevented, or more accurately, delayed, a major crisis.[50]

In 1974, the Sunningdale and power-sharing accords appeared to offer an end to the conflict in Northern Ireland. A coalition of Unionists and Nationalists was actually in power when extreme Unionists, usually refered to as 'Loyalists', called a general strike which threatened to deprive Northern Ireland of all of its public ultilities. Faced with this opposition and the British government's refusal to place these ultilities under military control, the power-sharing experiment collapsed.[51] More recently, in covenantal form, Protestants proclaimed that they rejected and would resist the Anglo-Irish Agreement of 1985. Among other things, the agreement allowed the Republic of Ireland to have a formal, consultative role on a range of matters, including security, affecting Northern Ireland. For many Protestants, it was an acknowledgment by the British government of the legitimacy of the Republic's claim to the North. A banner running across the front of Belfast City Hall, and duplicated across the province, said very simply, 'Belfast Says No'. Critically, unionist opposition was not successful on this occasion though their determination to be rid of the agreement remained implacable.

The covenant clearly conveys the idea that loyalty to the government is contingent upon the government's support for the maintenance of a Protestant state and people in Northern Ireland. Allegiance was conditional and 'not a matter of national feeling, but a bargain whose only sanctions are honour and interest'.[52] Many Ulster Protestants, especially those of Scottish background, never did develop a feeling of 'co-nationality'[53] with the British state because neither the British state nor the British people could be fully trusted. The only sure guarantee was to be found in the loyalty of the Ulster Protestant community. British nationalism was not cultivated in Protestant Ulster where inhabitants looked to Britain primarily for protection against the expected native insurrection. In return, Ulster Protestants would join in defence of the Empire.

The covenant was less importantly a characteristic of Ulster Protestants than it was a system that defined relations between settlers, natives and the English. The covenantal grid, while not the religious expression of most Anglicans, eventually came to embrace, as did the Orange Order, the entire Protestant community. Having taken root in the political, economic and religious insecurity of the settlers, the covenant came to define a political reality that was embodied in the complex web of relationships that defined the Northern Ireland conflict. Chief among its characteristics are three that lay the groundwork for the relationships that have dominated the evolution of politics in Ireland.

First, and most important was the fact that, as Miller points out that for Protestants, 'the ultimate ground of human experience in the scriptures is this deal, the covenant, hard, inflexible, comprehensive'.[54] Far from being a religious principle, the covenant was a brokered deal. Its terms were adhered to only if there were reciprocation. This was a distinctive kind of reciprocity, however. In the covenant, reciprocity never led to a final resolution of the relationship. Instead there was a continuous and conditional struggle to gain reciprocity. In the Irish case, the relationship between settler society and the English state was always in doubt, the function of a tense and insecure set of commitments. From time to time, this loyalty would be demonstrated in vivid terms and celebrated just as often, e.g., in both World Wars. So when, in 1987, an IRA bomb killed eleven mourners in Enniskillen at the annual commemoration of the dead of both world wars, for Protestants it was among the worst examples of nationalist treachery.

Second, the covenant was an interlocking defensive structure, designed to protect against the perfidy and disloyalty of Catholics and against the instability of a commitment from either the British Parliament or the British people. At issue, of course, was the settlement itself, and it was the covenantal system that was to secure the settlement. The defensive quality of the covenant meant that even the smallest concession was to be resisted lest it lead to the undoing of the entire edifice. 'Not an inch' was not an idle exclamation but rather the defiant exhortation of a besieged people. We might refer here to Freud's 'narcissism of minor difference' because it is precisely the minor differences in people who are otherwise alike that form the basis of feelings of strangeness and hostility between them. It would be tempting to pursue this idea and to derive from this 'narcissism of minor difference' the hostility which in every human relationship we see fighting successfully against feelings of fellowship and overpowering the commandment that all men should love one another. Vamik Volkan applies the concept to the Northern Ireland problem in a useful manner given the importance of the housing issue:

In Northern Ireland, Catholic villages distinguish themselves from the Protestant ones by a subtle colour code to which every member of the village adheres; Catholics paint their front doors and gates green, Protestants paint theirs blue. There is no direct correspondence between the two colours and the two religions; the colours are simply unalterable minor differences that separate the two groups and that each group preserves under the influence of tradition.[55]

These attachments are of great significance to core concepts such as self-esteem, especially in and among people who fear extinction, cultural and physical. As Volkan points out, a person's sense of self rises and falls with the progress of the group with which they identify. Markers seemingly as trivial as colour indicate not only community but survival.

Third, the covenant was a corporate structure, defined by the organic bonds that Isaiah Berlin finds at the heart of nationalism.[56] As Miller again points out, 'surrounded as they were by hostile natives the Ulster-Scots assumed something of a corporate personality'.[57] He explains the implications of this when he refers to the idea that 'in Ulster each Protestant irrespective of social position was assumed to have a special role in the maintenance of order in a special situation when massive disorder was traditionally expected from one source: the Catholics'.[58] Miller raises the question as to whether or not it was true that Catholics could not be trusted, but in part at least, the question seems to miss the point. The combined settler-covenant framework created a self-fulfilling prophecy of oppression and exclusion within which Catholics were defined as disloyal, a designation confirmed by their religious exclusion.

A. T. Q. Stewart has described the Ulster loyalist patterns as 'sedimented' in the Northern Irish political landscape and political culture since the seventeenth century. The geography of settlement has created the Protestant town or city encircled by Catholic districts, as well as the inter-penetrating settlement patterns which raise fears of 'traitors in our midst'.[59] It is these patterns and perceptions that nurture militant Protestant volunteerism and vigilantism. Ulster Protestants were corporate in another well-known respect, i.e., they regarded themselves as a chosen people. Being chosen, however, was as much a burden as it was a blessing. Being 'chosen' intensified the contract dimension of the covenant, requiring, much as in Hebrew Law, that the contract had to be observed in strict terms. 'To keep the deal, that is the covenant, a society must be uncompromising, adamantine, self-centred'.[60] Where compromise is a virtue and an art in British politics, it was something to be avoided by a significant number of Ulster Unionists. The 'Chosen People' syndrome is a projective concept, establishing Catholics as radically other. Protestants were 'one people', religiously and politically. Catholics were outside. In this context, neither compromise nor inclusion could be permitted, lest the status of Protestants be threatened and their ability to maintain their privileged status be undermined. The Chosen People dynamic reinforces the we-they opposition which in turn sustains the insecurity of the siege mentality established by 'settlement patterns'.

On the eve of the creation of Northern Ireland in 1921, the Protestant elite was very anxious. Events seemed to be moving in Catholic directions. During the preceding decades Irish nationalism had been gathering force and a Gaelic cultural revival sustained it. The Home Rule movement, the Easter Rising of 1916, and the bitter Anglo-Irish war which had commenced in 1919, all seemed directed at extirpating the remnants of Protestant privilege. It was in this environment that the Protestant state of Northern Ireland was born. The bitterness of its birth was most profoundly expressed in fierce inter-communal strife which coincided with the IRA (Irish Republican Army) campaign from the summer of 1920 and lasted for almost two years. This strife was especially bitter in Belfast with Catholic workers being forced out of the shipyards, hundreds of homes burnt and a total of over four hundred from both communities killed.[61] Northern Ireland 'was founded morally on the terms of the Ulster Covenant and pragmatically on the promise that it would be a Protestant state for a Protestant people, a Chosen People'.[62] With an unreliable English ally, an apparently ambitious Irish Free State, and a disloyal Catholic population in the Six Counties, Protestants committed themselves to a state of hyper-vigilance. It was in this frame of mind that many Protestants once more banded together to resist the demands for change in the late 1960s.

DYSFUNCTIONAL RELATIONSHIPS

Northern Ireland was, therefore, from its inception, deeply divided in virtually every aspect of communal life, its deep patterns of segregation most readily identifiable in terms of religious affiliation. In housing, education and employment, perhaps the three most important markers of inter-community division, separation was such as to ensure that for long social contact across any of these boundaries was minimal. Each community was endogamous, while the region's political institutions, rather than providing meeting places in which conflict could be resolved, merely reinforced division at every level. From 1921 until the Northern Ireland parliament was abolished in 1972, the Unionist Party usually held forty of the fifty-two seats in its House of Commons, the Nationalist (Catholic) Party the remainder. Excluded from any meaningful role in either government or administration, the latter played only a desultory role in parliament, attending with little regularity and participating most vigorously only when issues affecting its own community were under discussion, such as education, housing and the partition of Ireland.[63]

Despite its numerical dominance throughout the fifty years of its control of Northern Ireland's affairs, the Unionist Party, like the unionist community generally, behaved as if under perpetual siege. It feared the nationalist community inside Northern Ireland and the wider nationalist community throughout the rest of Ireland. Fuelling unionist fears was the continued existence, outside of parliamentary politics, of militant nationalism in the form of the Irish Republican Army (IRA) and its political wing, Sinn Fein ('We Ourselves'). The level of support for both from within the Catholic-Nationalist community varied over the years after 1921 and while the IRA had been very active in the turbulent years surrounding the state's inception, thereafter its campaigns were, until the 1970s, characterised more by farce and incompetence than by any realistic prospect of success. By the early 1960s following a poorly organized and very ineffectual campaign which had lasted from 1956-62, support for the IRA was at a low ebb.[64] Fears that nationalist Ireland, as represented by the new state in the South, might threaten the North's separate existence were based more on the possibility that some British government might be persuaded, or tricked into abandoning the North to the South, than on any real prospect of the South, on its own, subverting unionist control.

Relationships between unionist administrations and the British government throughout this period tended to be distant, exactly as the Unionist Party preferred, and as the British themselves were happy to allow. The arrangements reached with Irish Nationalists and Irish Unionists in 1920-21 whereby each had obtained a form of home rule for the part of the country in which it enjoyed majority support, appeared to have provided the ideal solution. In the period 1921-68 successive British governments declined to make any representations to the government in Belfast whenever questions were raised about the latter's behaviour on the grounds that to do so would constitute improper 'interference'.[65] London maintained, therefore, the traditional distance which is generally evident in metropole-settler relationships during periods of political calm, respecting its side of the covenant into which it had entered with Unionists in 1921.

North-South relationships had become even more distant as both parts of Ireland grew steadily apart in the years following the country's partition.[66] The South, preoccupied with building its own Catholic-Nationalist state imbued with a Gaelic-Irish cultural ethos, found little energy and less inclination to address divisions between both parts of the island other than in rhetorical flourishes and much less to address the problems of fellow Nationalists in the North. With only a relatively small Protestant-Unionist population, less than ten per cent in 1922 and declining, the South quickly became characterized by the influence of the Catholic Church over many aspects of its public life and by the considerable efforts made to revive the Irish language and to have it replace English as the country's vernacular.[67] Both features of southern politics were frequently represented by Unionists as evidence of the fate that would have awaited Protestants in a united Ireland. Added to these were the decisions by the Dublin government, one, to adopt a new, more overtly republican style of constitution in 1937 and two, to declare the South 'neutral' at the outbreak of World War II.[68] The latter was interpreted by Unionists as motivated essentially by the South's Anglophobia and as marking a contrast with the North's very active contribution to the war against fascism and a further justification of its continued attachment to Britain.

Three articles in the 1937 Irish Constitution fuelled unionist fears, two of which were regarded as particularly objectionable – Articles 2 and 3. These two articles which, by appearing to declare the Irish state synonymous with the Irish nation and by declaring the jurisdiction of the former to extend over the whole of the island amounted, in unionist eyes, to a claim of sovereignty by the South over the North. This view was eventually confirmed in a 1990 judgement by the Irish Supreme Court to the effect that these articles amounted to 'a constitutional imperative' on Irish governments to pursue the unification of Ireland.[69] Despite successive Irish governments' declarations that in seeking Irish unity they are bound by a further article in the same constitution to do so by 'pacific means', Unionists have continued to point to Articles 2 and 3 as clear evidence of a hostile intent on the South's part towards the very existence of Northern Ireland – a justified reinforcement of their siege mentality. Until its deletion from the Constitution in 1974, a third article, Article 44, contained a clause which spoke of the 'special position' of the Catholic Church in Ireland because it is the church of the majority of the people.[70] This too was frequently pointed to as further evidence of the power and influence to which Protestants would be subject should they ever find themselves trapped into a united Ireland.

To protect their own state against perceived internal dangers, successive Unionist governments permitted and actively connived at a range of discriminatory practices aimed at diminishing as much as possible Catholic-Nationalist political influence, while at the same time consciously developing a sense of Britishness about life in Northern Ireland to mark it off as much as possible from its southern neighbour. Measures taken to achieve the former included the abolition of proportional representation in local government, the gerrymandering of electoral boundaries to favour majority unionist areas, the allocation of

housing to favour unionist constituents and the manipulation of employment opportunities in both the public and private sectors to favour applicants from a unionist-Protestant background.

Political and religious divisions in Northern Ireland were, therefore,
mutually reinforcing. Religious division was characterized by deep
suspicions and antagonisms between Catholics and Protestants, not just
at communal level, but frequently at the level of church leadership as
well. Contacts between the churches were minimal with communities in
each being encouraged to socialize as much as possible with 'their own'
and as little as possible with the 'other side'. Recreational and cultural
pursuits mirrored these fundamental divisions while denominational
segregation in schooling served to strengthen communal bonds along the
same religious and political divides.[71]

Most important in terms of the spark which ignited the conflict in the
late 1960s was the fact that, as a result of many of the above practices and
attitudes, housing patterns were indicative of how communities imagined
each other and how they understood their relationships with one another.
Housing, especially public housing, became largely segregated along
denominational lines. Many areas are predominantly Catholic, while other
areas are predominantly Protestant and today, thirty years after the
Caledon incident, the extent of this segregation is even more pronounced
than previously.[72] So, in 1968, all the physical and emotional barriers, with
the weight of their historical burdens that sustained segregation, were
threatened by the Caledon protest. It was no accident, therefore, that it was
a dispute over housing that ignited the conflict.

Both in terms of Northern Ireland's creation and in the manner in which
it developed over its short history until 1968, the themes of 'settlement',
'siege mentality', 'penal laws' and 'deprivation' were plainly evident. But
in so evolving, Northern Ireland could not establish either the means, or the
conditions for an inclusive, reconciled or even a permanently stable political society. On the contrary, both in the manner of its inception and of its
evolution, the seeds of its own destruction were gradually ripening. The
incident at Caledon in 1968 signalled the beginning of that destruction, but
to be replaced with what is now, thirty years later, only being determined.
The 1998 Good Friday Agreement[73] is the most hopeful challenge to the
view that Northern Ireland is unable to achieve a satisfactory settlement.

TWO

SIMMERING CONTENTION:
THE O'NEILL PERIOD

What happens when a political system undergoes serious change or the threat of change? Donald Horowitz maintains that, among other things, as the shape of the polity is about to change, anxiety will increase, with serious consequences for political alignments and behaviour.[1] This is precisely what happened when the process of change was stimulated in Northern Ireland by Prime Minister Terence O'Neill in the mid-1960s. O'Neill was forty-eight when he took office as Prime Minister of Northern Ireland. He had, by then, already served in Parliament since 1946, where he had been a member for the Bannside constituency – a seat rarely contested since it contained an overwhelming unionist majority. Before becoming Prime Minister, he had served his predecessor as Minister for Finance and was already associated with progressive thinking within the Unionist Party. This chapter tells the story of the political and economic initiatives taken by O'Neill at a time when Northern Ireland was enjoying growing prosperity, peace, and an apparent reduction in traditional animosities.

O'NEILL TAKES OFFICE

Terence O'Neill took office as Northern Ireland's fourth Prime Minister in 1963, at a time of considerable change across the western world. However, no one expected O'Neill to promote the changes that would lead to the dissolution of the Northern Irish government in less than a decade. In the United States John F. Kennedy was president and the demand for civil rights dominated the national agenda; in Europe, the drab post-World War II years were being left behind as the European Economic Community developed with much discussion of its possible expansion to include the United Kingdom and Ireland; in religious

21

terms, an ecumenical spirit was abroad as the Second Vatican Council met to re-invigorate and modernize the Roman Catholic Church and to develop more open and extensive relations with other Christian churches.

Just as O'Neill took office, the first signs of real change in Northern Ireland were becoming apparent, both in the religious and political domains.[2] With respect to the former, greater tolerance and inter-church respect were emerging as a result of deliberations within the Vatican Council on the Catholic side and as a result of a growing spirit of ecumenism on the Protestant side. O'Neill sent an unprecedented message of condolence to the Catholic churchmen of Ireland on the occasion of the death of Pope John, in the summer of 1963. On the same occasion, Belfast City Council, not renowned for fostering cross-community relations, allowed the Union Jack to be flown at half-mast from the City Hall in another gesture that was deeply appreciated by the Catholic community.

An inching toward change was also evident in the political sphere. The end of the IRA's totally ineffective campaign of violence in the late 1950s and the decision of its political leadership in 1962 to pursue Irish unity by promoting social change, must have seemed a turning point for the militant tradition of Irish nationalism. This coincided with changes in constitutional nationalism, marked by a longstanding debate on the role nationalist politicians should play in Northern Ireland. Nationalist politicians whose largely abstentionist roles were based on the negative policy of anti-partitionism, came to be challenged by a new generation of young political activists. At Queen's University, Belfast, the New Ireland Society became a significant forum within which such questioning took place. The society's lively political debates reached and influenced a wide audience.[3]

An early, if limited effect of this changing atmosphere was the government's decision in late 1963 to formally recognize the Northern Committee of the Irish Congress of Trade Unions as the representative trade union body with which to deal on labour-related matters. Previous governments had strongly opposed recognition of the Northern Committee of the Irish Congress on the grounds that the Irish Congress was a southern-based organization. Recognition would entail unionist governments having to deal with an all-Ireland body, and this had been regarded as politically unacceptable to many unionist representatives and to their supporters. O'Neill's decision that the Northern Committee of the Irish Congress should be recognized was significant, though not one which had any deep political significance.

As far as relationships with the Republic of Ireland were concerned, O'Neill was to be assisted by the fact that considerable changes were already underway there. The Taoiseach, or Prime Minister, of the Republic since 1958 was Sean Lemass, a close associate of the revered Eamon de Valera, but a man whose republican convictions were coloured by a strong political pragmatism. Since assuming office, Lemass came to represent the economic revival underway in the Republic since the late 1950s. He was seen, therefore, as a modernizing force, as a political leader who wished to lead his society away from the dogmatism of the past and into an era when the Republic would become a fully modern European state, a member of the new European Economic Community with an outlook reflecting the general spirit of the age rather than a society looking inward on itself as it had been over the preceding decades. O'Neill and Lemass found themselves looking simultaneously beyond their respective borders, and they appeared to be doing so with broadly similar perspectives.

O'NEILL'S PHILOSOPHY

O'Neill was never given to much philosophising about the internal divisions that beset Northern Ireland's society. He preferred to speak about modernizing his society rather than committing himself to any detailed programme for resolving inter-community differences. On one important occasion, however, in the early years of his premiership, he did offer his reflections on the topic. In a speech entitled 'The Ulster Community', O'Neill attempted to deal with fundamental aspects of community division and constitutional allegiance in Northern Ireland.[4] The timing of the speech was not without some irony. It coincided with the fiftieth anniversary of the 1916 Easter Rising in Dublin, which for Unionists, coming as it had during the First World War, symbolized one of the worst betrayals of Irish nationalism.

The speech began by acknowledging the coincidence of religious and political divisions in Northern Ireland. O'Neill then proceeded to identify as the core issue affecting community relations, disagreement about the very existence of the state and the absence of allegiance to it from a large section of the population. While many Nationalists might well have agreed with him in this diagnosis, they most strongly rejected his proposed resolution of the problem, namely that Nationalists had an obligation to give their allegiance to Northern Ireland. Their failure to do so was, according to O'Neill's analysis, the reason that community relations were fraught with tension and suspicion.

Elaborating on his contention, O'Neill argued that the state had a right 'to call upon all our citizens to support the Constitution'.[5] Since only the nationalist community was withholding this support, the solution to Northern Ireland's fundamental problem, as defined by O'Neill, lay almost exclusively with the Nationalists. There was no suggestion of any need for fundamental reform on the part of Unionists. Adding to the responsibility which he was placing on the nationalist community, O'Neill commented that if the Catholic Church would cease to insist upon its own school system, then another major step towards the integration of Northern Ireland's society would be possible.

O'Neill highlighted what he regarded as signs of progress in Northern Ireland: the success of his economic policy in attracting new industries, the development of the infrastructure, and the decision to establish a new university. Improving community relations would be a highly desirable and necessary addition to this list of achievements. Fearing the consequences of failure to achieve this objective O'Neill sounded a warning, one profoundly ominous in retrospect: 'I believe that only two things can possibly stand in the way of full realisation of that promise (of an integrated society – author's addition). One of these – a serious economic set-back for the United Kingdom as a whole – is not a matter within our control . . . The other – which is very much within our control – is the danger of self-inflicted wounds'.[6] O'Neill's words were prophetic. Isaiah Berlin notes the 'explosive power generated by the combination of unhealed mental wounds, however caused, with the image of the nation as a society of the living, the dead and those yet unborn'.[7] O'Neill's own analysis of the problem, which placed most of the blame for division on the nationalist side, ignored the accumulated wounds of Nationalists.

THE O'NEILL APPROACH

O'Neill's approach provides insight into how liberal, well intentioned Unionists envisaged change taking place in Northern Ireland and into the interpretations that would influence their responses to the demands for change coming from the nationalist community. Given the covenantal commitments of its supporters and its majority, devolved status, the unionist government had never been required to elaborate an alternative vision. The initiatives undertaken by O'Neill suggested what was acceptable to significant elements of the unionist community, and they clearly marked the boundaries of acceptability. It would not be long before their limitations would become apparent.

The initiatives came in two very broad areas. The first dealt with issues of economic development and modernization, including a new period of functional, cross-border cooperation between Northern Ireland and the Republic of Ireland, symbolized by the first meetings between the respective heads of government since the 1920s. The second dealt with issues relating to community relations and the sources of mutual antagonism within Northern Ireland itself. Taken together, the two elements disturbed traditional expectations and aroused old apprehensions and created new aspirations.

ECONOMIC DEVELOPMENT

Economic development was the most important of the two reform efforts from O'Neill's perspective. It was the one with which he obviously felt more comfortable due, in all likelihood, to having served as Minister for Finance prior to becoming Prime Minister and having witnessed considerable improvement in Northern Ireland's economic situation over the preceding ten years. Indeed, his first major speech in parliament as Prime Minister contained not a single direct reference to community divisions, or to any policy for improving community relations. His speech was entirely devoted to the policies of economic and general infrastructure development on which his government was embarking and which he hoped would bring positive results to all of the people in Northern Ireland.

O'Neill relied heavily on economic modernization to alleviate conflict by lifting everyone to prosperity. Intuitively, he believed that modernization would make people more alike in values and desires, and that this would reduce communal differences (he even argued at one point that Catholics could become like good Protestants if they had a good job!). But O'Neill failed to understand that in a deeply divided society, the drive to modernize could intensify inter-communal conflict. As Eric Nordlinger points out, 'individuals come to rely heavily upon their communal identities and resources' in pursuing the economic rewards of modernity and dealing with the dislocations wrought by economic change.[8] Northern Ireland is what Horowitz calls a ranked society,[9] one in which social class and ethnic identity coincide and, therefore not a society for which modernization could be expected to heal wounds and promote reconciliation.

Economic development was also the plank on which O'Neill sought to justify and foster contact between Northern Ireland and the Republic of Ireland. He believed that both parts of Ireland would have much to gain from developing economic and social links, and in Sean Lemass he found a willing counterpart. Soon after his entry into the premiership of the Republic, Lemass declared that coercion could not be the basis of a policy to unify both parts of Ireland.[10] Good relations and cooperation based on a mutuality of interests were the messages Lemass conveyed. He made no significant headway with O'Neill's predecessor, Lord Brookeborough, who had declined to meet him. O'Neill, however, took a different line and, in 1965, he invited Lemass to visit Stormont for what was to be the first in a series of inter-governmental contacts.[11]

The meeting received a mixed reception from the public in Northern Ireland. Many Unionists welcomed it, but others, notably Ian Paisley[12] and his followers, expressed deep opposition. These critics bitterly attacked O'Neill, accusing him of a 'sell-out' and claiming that such contacts would mark the beginning of a move along the slippery slope of unification. In general, Nationalists were pleased with the meeting, signalling, as it did, a more positive recognition of relationships with the South. The Nationalist Party itself indicated its satisfaction by finally agreeing to accept the role of 'official' opposition in the Northern Ireland parliament.

COMMUNITY RELATIONS

Much as O'Neill may have wished to concentrate on economic development and cross-border relations, he could not ignore the issues and realities affecting relationships between the nationalist and unionist communities. O'Neill's elevation to the premiership coincided with the first rumblings among Nationalists for a new civil rights protest that gathered pace over the following four years. Eventually, street violence and inter-communal rioting combined with the developing civil rights campaign to push O'Neill to act.

Northern Ireland's civil rights movement gave a new impetus and direction to nationalist politics. For the first time since 1921, a movement would embrace people of different political persuasions and aspirations in an attempt to address a range of social and political inequities and establish a more just social order. Ultimately, however, it embroiled the region in the disturbances, riots, and disorder which brought British troops onto the streets and precipitated the events leading to the abolition, in 1972, of Northern Ireland's government and locally elected parliament.

CIVIL RIGHTS

The civil rights movement developed out of the Homeless Citizens League[13], formed to protest against what was judged to be the unfair allocation of houses by the local council in Dungannon, County Tyrone. The League accused the unionist-controlled council of favouring Protestant applicants for public sector housing, with the result that many Catholic families remained in over-crowded, unsanitary accommodation. So successful was the League in highlighting these grievances that it became the basis from which a wider campaign against similar injustices elsewhere was launched in 1966, under the banner of the Campaign for Social Justice[14] in Northern Ireland. The campaign was initially conducted through the publication and widespread circulation of information and statistical data highlighting allegations of discrimination against the Roman Catholic-Nationalist community in employment, public housing allocations, and electoral law and practices. Discrimination in employment was alleged to be most rampant within the services operated by local authorities, and the figures produced for several authorities demonstrated that there was a clear case to be made. Allegations about electoral practices focused on the law by which business people and property owners could enjoy plural voting rights, the restriction of the local franchise to ratepayers and the manner in which electoral boundaries were drawn to ensure a particular kind of balance on local councils.

Unionist and government circles attempted to ignore or dismiss the campaign 'as typical of the scurrilous propaganda put out by a small section of the community whose avowed intention is to overthrow the Constitution of Northern Ireland'.[15] Responses from the Conservative government in Britain to the campaign's earliest initiatives merely urged that anyone with a grievance should pursue it through the local courts. The new Labour government in Great Britain followed the line of its Conservative predecessor almost to the letter, arguing that since allegations of injustice pertained to matters under the direct jurisdiction of the Northern Ireland government, it would be improper for the British government to intervene. Prime Minister Harold Wilson's Private Secretary, made this point quite bluntly in reply to correspondence with the campaign when he wrote in 1965: 'The matters about which you allege discrimination are falling within the field of responsibility of the Northern Ireland Government and Parliament. This being so, he thinks it would be wrong for him to seek to intervene.'[16] This had been the pattern since partition created Northern Ireland in 1921. It was consistent with the British response to northern Protestant insistence on autonomy and protection since the seventeenth century.

O'Neill appeared oblivious to danger signals looming ever larger as both demands from the nationalist community and resistance from the unionist community intensified. Even when decisions were made which evoked extremely negative and hostile responses from the nationalist community and beyond, O'Neill appeared not to appreciate their implications. Instead, he seemed to consider his achievements significant and hoped that dividends would soon be reaped. After all, he was pursuing an economic policy that was succeeding in attracting considerable investment to Northern Ireland; he had opened doors to the political leaders in Dublin and he appeared to be opening doors to the Catholic-nationalist community in Northern Ireland itself. Finally, he hoped that his many visits abroad would create a new, outward-looking image for Northern Ireland.

Although O'Neill allowed himself a degree of satisfaction in his early years of office, trouble was brewing, not just in the issues already identified by civil rights activists, but in decisions taken by his own government which would add significantly to communal tension. One such decision was to develop a new town, to be named Craigavon, after Northern Ireland's first Prime Minister, in the east between the existing towns of Portadown and Lurgan. This decision was immediately regarded as a snub to the west and in particular, to the predominantly Catholic city of Derry, already suffering from very high unemployment and a lack of development.[17] The second decision, seen as a further snub to western areas, was to locate a new university in Coleraine, a predominantly unionist and Protestant town, and not in Derry, although that city already contained a small university college which many believed should have formed the basis for an enlarged institution.[18] Both decisions caused deep resentment in nationalist circles. In the case of the university decision, nationalist and unionist opinion in Derry united in a massive protest demonstration that drove in cavalcade from the city to the parliament buildings at Stormont outside Belfast.

Communal relations were further affected during this first period of O'Neill's government by events surrounding the commemorations held in nationalist communities for the fiftieth anniversary of the 1916 Easter Rising in Dublin. Although most of these events took place without incident, tension mounted in the weeks preceding them when Ian Paisley decided to organize counter-demonstrations to highlight unionist opposition both to the commemorations themselves and to what they represented – a commitment to Irish unity on the part of a substantial segment of the population of Northern Ireland.

Paisley had gradually gained prominence in Northern Ireland over the preceding decade as a result of his very public stand against the increasing number of inter-church contacts as well as for his very pronounced anti-Catholic views. During the 1964 general election campaign, he had played a significant role in provoking an incident in the West Belfast constituency from which serious disorder followed.[19] On that occasion Paisley and the Unionist candidate from West Belfast succeeded in forcing the government to order the police to remove nationalist emblems which they claimed were 'aimed to provoke and insult loyalists in West Belfast'.[20] Confrontation between the police and the nationalist crowds which gathered to protect their emblems led to several nights of rioting.

Paisley and his followers represented an element in the unionist and Protestant community which was deeply opposed to Irish unity and to almost any kind of contact between North and South. Many of them were bitterly anti-Catholic, and events which celebrated either the aim of Irish unity or contacts with the Catholic Church were likely targets for those associated with this element of Protestant-Unionism. Paisley's counter-demonstrations against the 1916 commemorations in 1966 testified to the tension that lay close to the surface of community relations and which was easily and quickly inflamed when the circumstances were right. Many of those who participated were rigid 'covenantal' people who insisted on loyalty to Britain only insofar as Britain was loyal to a Protestant, as opposed to a British, Northern Ireland.

One glaring issue which O'Neill might have addressed, given his call for allegiance, was Catholic membership in the Unionist Party. Catholics had never held any significant positions within the Unionist Party, nor had many ever joined. Yet encouraging them to do so might have been one very obvious way of demonstrating that Northern Ireland was not inherently hostile to their interests. Indeed, one leading member of O'Neill's government, Bill Craig, Minister for Home Affairs, did express hope at the time that his own party 'will receive increasing support from the Catholic community .... I see no reason why a Catholic should not join the Unionist Party or even become, eventually, a member of the Cabinet'.[21] Craig was severely criticised for his remarks in an editorial in the leading pro-unionist daily *The Newsletter*[22] and received no public endorsement for his views from his Prime Minister. Some years later, at the height of his political crisis, O'Neill still equivocated when the possibility of a Catholic being accepted as a parliamentary candidate was proposed. Yet, following his resignation in 1969, O'Neill blamed, in part, the lack of widespread support from Catholics for his weakened electoral position.[23]

There is no evidence that O'Neill tried to further his understanding of the situation by consulting with the political or religious leaders of the nationalist community in Northern Ireland. Reform did not mean inclusion, though some of the blame for this must also rest on the shoulders of these nationalist leaders themselves. These leaders did not rigorously challenge O'Neill on his pronouncements, or on his whole strategy, and there is no evidence that they sought in any concerted way to offer him advice as to how he might proceed, except to criticize those decisions of O'Neill's government with which they disagreed. Indeed, they appeared too often to feel that the very general goodwill which O'Neill expressed was sufficient to promote more positive community relations.

DARKENING CLOUDS

Despite these ominous signs, as 1967 drew to a close, O'Neill appeared quite happy with his achievements since taking office. In addition to the successes mentioned above, he had withstood a bungled attempt by some backbenchers in his own party to have him replaced as Prime Minister in late 1966. More significantly, he had led his party to a very significant electoral success in 1965, when Unionists in Belfast had regained seats lost in the previous elections to the Northern Ireland Labour Party. Also, the events of Easter 1966 had passed with relative peace despite Paisley's threats, while relationships with the Republic of Ireland were developing in a positive direction.

A note of warning was, nonetheless, being sounded within nationalist circles that the time had come for action rather than gestures. Austin Currie spoke in Derry in October 1967 of the hopes and expectations which O'Neill had raised. At that time, Currie warned that the Prime Minsister had but twelve months to show that he could 'weed out injustice and intolerance' and that, if he failed, a 'growing militancy' would develop within the nationalist community.[24] O'Neill himself dismissed Currie's remarks as 'a very ugly . . . a very intolerant and potentially a very dangerous speech'.[25] Indeed, O'Neill may also have felt that he was already effectively and adequately responding to the issues Currie and other nationalists had in mind. Far-reaching legislation to effect electoral reform was being prepared for both the regional parliament and local councils; legislation to reform electoral law was being put into place and reforms were being planned to allow higher levels of funding to be made available to voluntary, mainly Catholic schools. Yet, for all that, 1968 was to prove a turning point in O'Neill's premiership and a watershed in the history of Northern Ireland; civil rights protests intensified and the first signs of a determined counter-protest began to take shape within the unionist community.

STREET PROTESTS FOR CIVIL RIGHTS

1968 is remembered in many European and American cities as the year of student demonstrations in favour of university reform and in opposition to the war in Vietnam. It was also the year of the Prague Spring in Czechoslovakia and the subsequent Soviet invasion of that country in August. In Northern Ireland, 1968 was the year when civil rights became a mass movement and took to the streets demanding reform of local government, fair allocation of public housing, an end to discrimination in employment, and the repeal of the special legislation which vested the police with considerable powers of search, arrest, detention, and control over public demonstrations.

From as far back as January 1966 the civil rights movements began to coalesce. There were many different local bodies, including prominently, the Campaign for Social Justice. Most of these local bodies retained their separate identities, but an umbrella group, the Northern Ireland Civil Rights Association (NICRA),[26] was set up to coordinate and strengthen the campaign. Throughout 1966 and 1967, NICRA continued the propaganda and representational tactics of the Campaign for Social Justice with little success. It was not until the spring of 1968, when civil rights protests in the United States were being widely publicized in Europe, that NICRA began to consider a change in tactics. Even then, however, a spark was required to fuel a more direct protest strategy; that spark was provided by the events in Caledon. The house in Caledon from which the Catholic family had been evicted was taken over by civil rights protestors, among them Austin Currie. The ensuing debate within civil rights organizations led to the first protest march from the town of Coalisland to Dungannon, whose council was responsible for allocating the Caledon house, in August 1968. A foretaste of things to come was evidenced that day when Ian Paisley organized a counter-rally among Unionists to protest against the civil rights demonstrators. He did so knowing full well the deep historic connotations associated with marches and demonstrations.

Marches are not simple political demonstrations in Northern Ireland. Rather, they are emotionally-charged, historical re-enactments of communal triumph and suffering. The insistence on being allowed to march through the other's neighbourhood reveals the territorial and defensive nature of marching. In particular, the many traditional Protestant marches which annually celebrate the victories of King William are highly offensive to the Catholic population since the marchers are affirming their Protestant solidarity against the alleged Catholic threat. The civil rights marches evoked such sentiments and inevitably provoked the age-old responses.

O'Neill, on holiday in England at the time, remarked revealingly in his autobiography that 'Had we all known it, that . . . Civil Rights march was to be the start of something which would shake Northern Ireland to its foundations, split the Unionist Party, and initiate more reforms in two years than I had thought possible in ten'.[27] The representations of the Homeless Citizens League and of the Campaign for Social Justice over the preceding years had, in his own admission, made little impression on him or his unionist colleagues, but a civil rights march had.

Events began to move rapidly as the civil rights movement gained momentum and a growing number of adherents. The Dungannon march was followed by an even more significant march in Derry that October. Plans for the march were carefully laid by NICRA and other participant organizations. Particular attention was paid to ensuring the widest possible media coverage. The plans included travelling along a route traditionally followed by members of such Protestant organizations as the Orange Order and the Apprentice Boys of Derry. In what was to become a familiar pattern, a second march for the same day and route was announced by the Apprentice Boys. Once this announcement had been made, the Minister for Home Affairs issued an order banning the latter and placing restrictions on the former as to the parts of the city in which participants could march, prohibiting them from entering the mainly Protestant districts. The civil rights groups under NICRA's banner decided after considerable debate, however, to go ahead with their demonstration as planned and thereby defy the order.

The rationale behind NICRA's decision was that civil rights marches were non-sectarian by their very nature, seeking to vindicate the rights of all, irrespective of religious or political views; NICRA should not, they argued, be prevented from marching in any section of any town. Conversely, and despite the fact that a number of prominent figures from outside the nationalist community had been attracted to the cause, leading unionist politicians were casting the civil rights movement in a subversive role. One strategy employed by Unionists was to call attention to the presence in civil rights organizations of people with IRA or 'strong' nationalist views and people with allegedly communist leanings.[28] Even without such comments, its very origins within the nationalist community inevitably meant that the civil rights movement would be perceived by large sections of the unionist community as predominantly nationalist. That meant it could only be seen as subversive of unionist control of Northern Ireland in its intent. For civil rights marches to proceed through unionist areas was, therefore, in the eyes of the police, an open provocation and a threat to public order.

The Derry march ended in violent confrontation with the police, who attempted to prevent the marchers from gaining access to the prohibited sections of the city.[29] Marchers were baton charged, many demonstrators and non-participants were injured, and the violence that followed throughout the evening and night set a pattern for similar events that would take place over the next few years. That October Saturday in Derry was, however, significant not just for the violence which erupted, but more so because it took place in the presence of television cameras and many reporters from outside Northern Ireland. The result was that images and stories of the events reached a very wide audience, with grave consequences for O'Neill's government and his policy of very gradual reform and modernization. Another crucial outcome was that the conduct of the police, seen as representatives of the majority community, became a major civil rights issue. Demands for an inquiry into the behaviour of the RUC at Derry went, not unexpectedly, unheeded by O'Neill's government.

The most important short-term result, and the one which exposed the fundamental weakness of Northern Ireland's political institutions, was the summons, some weeks later, from Prime Minister Harold Wilson to O'Neill and two of his senior colleagues to meet him in London. The four discussed the evolving crisis and agreed to a package of immediate reforms.[30] The significance of this meeting lay in the fact that it underlined the subordinate nature of O'Neill's government and its accountability to London. By that very fact the autonomy of the settler-covenant arrangement had been called into question. From that meeting on the initiative for reform passed slowly from the control of unionist politicians in Belfast to the government in London. Not surprisingly, unionist apprehensions were raised by this meeting in London and were evident in reactions from unionist MPs at Stormont, who expressed more concern about what they regarded as unwarranted interference in Northern Ireland's affairs by the British government than about the contents of the reform package. In effect, their reaction betrayed a recognition of the underlying constitutional reality that Northern Ireland was not a sovereign entity, however much Unionists had striven over the preceding fifty years to give it that appearance.

REFORM PROMISED

The reforms agreed to by O'Neill and his colleagues and eventually endorsed by his ruling party included:[31]

(i)   the appointment of an Ombudsman to investigate complaints of discrimination of any kind;
(ii)   the creation of a points system to determine the allocation of housing;
(iii) the abolition of Derry City Corporation and its replacement by a Development Commission;
(iv)   a review of the Special Powers Act; and
(v)   the abolition of plural voting in local government elections.

The government also announced that it intended to proceed with its previously declared goal fundamentally to reform local government. The one issue missing from the package was a clear commitment to grant a universal franchise for local authority elections, instead of restricting that franchise to ratepayers. Since proportionately fewer Catholics than Protestants were either householders or owned business properties, they were considerably under-represented in elections to local authorities in which only ratepayers could vote. Perhaps it was expected that the commitment to fundamental reform of local government would have been sufficient to assuage concerns at that stage. However, the absence of an explicit reference to the possibility of adopting 'one man, one vote' local elections turned out to be a very serious omission from O'Neill's reform package.

Aside from the issue of the local franchise, the package did address the major demands of the civil rights campaign. The hope in many quarters was that the campaign would now end since there appeared to be little left for which to campaign. Those who held such hopes had not reckoned with the overriding importance of communal loyalties, the heightened expectations of the nationalist community, and the growing level of reaction within the unionist community, especially within O'Neill's own Unionist Party. In short, they had not considered the legacy of three-hundred years of settler-native relations. The challenge to O'Neill was led by Minister Bill Craig, one of the two who had accompanied him to the meeting with Prime Minister Wilson. In a widely reported speech, Craig criticized some of the recently announced reforms, and, in clear contradiction of views expressed only two years earlier, suggested that Catholics were incapable of acting in accordance with democratic principles.[32] He went on to raise the unionist community's traditional red flag by claiming that the civil rights movement was essentially a front for the IRA. It would seem that Craig was incensed by the British government's intervention in Northern Ireland's affairs when he criticized the infringement of 'our powers', and when he declared that 'It is in the Parliament and Government of Northern Ireland that our future will be decided'.[33] Once again, a leading unionist politician seemed to be saying that loyalty to the British constitution was a secondary matter when unionist hege-mony in Northern Ireland was questioned.

O'Neill resisted immediate calls from several quarters for Craig's dismissal. However, when Craig persisted in his criticisms and especially when he challenged remarks by O'Neill on Northern Ireland's position within the United Kingdom by suggesting that interference from the British government might have to be opposed, O'Neill felt obliged to dismiss him. In the meantime, disorder manifested itself again during civil rights demonstrations in several towns throughout Northern Ireland. In the face of increasing tension and polarisation, O'Neill decided to make a television address in which he would present the people of Northern Ireland with a stark choice between reform and anarchy.

CROSSROADS

Known as his 'Crossroads' speech[34] because it began with the statement 'Ulster stands at the crossroads', O'Neill claimed that he had been trying over the preceding five years 'to heal some of the deep divisions in our community'. He appealed to the civil rights campaigners and to those who were resisting reform to pause and consider the effects of their actions. He claimed that reform was on its way and could not be with-held. He reminded his audience that Northern Ireland was a subsidiary region of the United Kingdom, and dependent on the British government for financial aid and support; it could neither contemplate going it alone, nor defy Westminster. He asked for an end to street demonstrations and condemned those who attempted, with 'bully-boy tactics', to defend the union with Britain.

Initially, O'Neill's address appeared to achieve its desired effect. He won praise from leaders in both sections of the community and NICRA announced that it was suspending its demonstrations. However, praise was not universal and it was in the wake of this address that Craig continued his programme of speeches criticizing features of the reform package and denouncing British government interference. Craig was only the most prominent of unionist parliamentarians who were increas-ingly unhappy with the nature and pace of change under O'Neill. Others were joining in the criticism, some openly but many others in the privacy of Unionist Party committee rooms. So, despite considerable public support evoked by his address and his policies, it was clear that O'Neill had not managed to persuade enough of his colleagues to endorse fully the proposed reforms. The views of those who were uneasy with the style and substance of his government only served to reinforce the more extreme elements of unionism represented by Ian Paisley and his followers.

Within the civil rights movement, on the other hand, there were groups determined to continue pressing their demands publicly. One such group, the Queen's University based People's Democracy (PD),[35] decided that despite the general suspension of civil rights demonstrations by NICRA they would embark on a march across Northern Ireland from Belfast to Derry at the beginning of January 1969. Given the small numbers involved and the actual nature of the march it was not banned despite the fact that it would have to pass through or close to a number of predominantly unionist towns and villages. As the march made its way from Belfast to Derry it encountered several very hostile counter-demonstrations, culminating in one very vicious attack during its final stages. During this clash, several marchers were beaten and severely injured by a Protestant mob that ambushed the marchers at Burntollet, while the RUC merely looked on.

Severe criticism was levelled at the police for their handling of the march, while the sympathy and support won by the marchers encouraged the PD organizers to hold other marches and demonstrations in the weeks that followed. These also resulted in violence, putting further strain on police-community relations and on the government. Under pressure to show that he was dealing with the situation, O'Neill adopted a widely used tactic which he felt could diffuse the situation: in an attempt to please all sides, O'Neill proposed that a commission of inquiry be set up to investigate the violence and disturbances of the previous months. On the one hand, O'Neill hoped the establishment of the commission would show civil rights campaigners that the government was prepared to heed an objective view of the disturbances and their causes. On the other hand, O'Neill also hoped that an authoritative inquiry would clearly demonstrate to his unionist colleagues in government and parliament, and to the community generally, the need for reform and so make it easier to accept.

Once again O'Neill was to have his hopes dashed. The decision to hold an inquiry precipitated the resignation of two of his ministers, the more important of whom was Brian Faulkner, a politician who had frequently been seen as a strong rival to O'Neill for leadership of the Unionist Party and who eventually was to assume that role. Faulkner resigned because, he claimed, the commission was 'a political manoeuvre and to some extent an abdication of authority'.[36] It would appear that he had also had reservations about the pace of political reform in response to a civil rights campaign many of whose members he regarded as intent on subverting Northern Ireland's constitutional position. The immediate effect of Faulkner's resignation was increased pressure on O'Neill to demonstrate that he was still in control. In response he decided to call an election in February despite having only recently declared that he would not.

THE 'O'NEILL ELECTION'

The election campaign was a bitter one, with the future of the Unionist Party the real issue. Many unionist candidates were selected by their constituency organizations on the basis of whether they supported or opposed O'Neill. Several constituency associations had declared their opposition to O'Neill's reform package while others had accepted its necessity. The election campaign also witnessed the nomination of many civil rights activists, several standing in opposition to long-serving nationalist MPs. In his own constituency, O'Neill faced opposition not only from a prominent civil rights campaigner, but also from the formidable Ian Paisley. O'Neill retained his seat, but only by a very slim margin over Paisley. His narrow local victory was a significant factor in his decision, two months later, to resign.

The outcome of the election marked a significant change in both nationalist and unionist politics.[37] For the nationalist community, the electoral success of several young civil rights activists – notably John Hume, who defeated the then-leader of the Nationalist Party in Derry, Eddie McAteer – signalled the virtual demise of the Nationalist Party. Other civil rights candidates, although not ultimately victorious, earned significant support in a number of constituencies. A realignment in nationalist politics was evident, and the need for a more cohesive and effectively organized political party became obvious. Within a year, that party, the Social Democratic and Labour Party, was in existence founded by several prominent civil rights activists.[38]

If positive for Nationalists, for Unionists the shift in the political climate was essentially negative. The Unionist Party emerged from the elections with none of its difficulties resolved. O'Neill was faced with two particular problems: hostility from a sizeable section of his party and the formation of a splinter group of extreme Protestant-unionists rallying to Ian Paisley. While Paisley's formal entry into parliamentary politics did not take place until the following year when he was elected, first as MP to Stormont to succeed O'Neill in Bannside and then as MP at Westminster for the constituency of North Antrim, during the British general elections, [39] he was already a formidable threat.

At the time, O'Neill himself knew that the end of his premiership was in sight. As he wrote later, 'I knew in my bones that the game was up . . . . Why should I soldier on in this impossible situation?'[40] His decision to resign was hastened by continued street violence and, much more sinister, bomb attacks against public utilities. Street violence was associated with civil rights marches which were renewed in March after the election campaign, while the bombs exploded in April, damaging electricity power stations and water installations. At first, these explosions were thought to have been the work of the IRA, but it was eventually revealed that they were perpetrated by an extreme unionist paramilitary group, the illegal Ulster Volunteer Force (UVF), whose aim was to create the impression that the IRA was active again and using the civil rights campaign as an excuse for renewing activity.[41]

Following the elections, O'Neill tried to play one final card to maintain his position. He indicated to his cabinet that if proposals to concede 'one man, one vote' for local government elections were not endorsed, he would resign. The cabinet endorsed his recommendation, but a senior minister resigned, the man who was to be O'Neill's immediate successor, James Chichester-Clark. At Stormont, the Unionist Party supported O'Neill, but only by the narrow margin of twenty-eight – twenty-two.[42] With his support in parliament so obviously in decline and with further bomb attacks damaging Belfast's water supply, O'Neill felt he had no option but to resign. This he did on 1 May 1969.

THE LEGACY OF THE O'NEILL YEARS

There can be little doubt that the O'Neill years marked a profound change in the history of Northern Ireland, the effects of which are still clearly evident today. A challenge to the status quo was issued by O'Neill himself and by many others, but it was issued in ways which put the consequences far beyond the control of those responsible for that challenge. The essential weakness in the challenge was the substantial absence of any coherent strategy to determine or even guide its course. A sense of goodwill which in essence glossed over and ignored the underlying tensions, even when acknowledging their existence, proved an inadequate and insufficient basis for a strategy aimed at creating a more cohesive and integrated society in Northern Ireland.

Success in such a task must involve all sides to the divide in a careful reconsideration of their position and, above all, it requires the cautious construction of institutions acceptable to and agreed to by all. Since O'Neill did not show that he had any real appreciation of the nature of the task he had attempted to address, it was not surprising that the means he adopted were totally inadequate.

O'Neill is not the only one who can be judged inadequate in this period. The civil rights movement was, to some degree, naive in not acknowledging that its demands for reform and for a clear commitment by government to uphold civil rights, did not contain profound political implications. As events turned out these implications became increasingly evident. Consequently, in a short period after O'Neill's departure, politics would emerge as the real arena for reform to achieve what O'Neill had rightly identified, but not addressed, as a central issue, namely, how to create institutions which would attract the support and allegiance of both sections of the community.

There were also many inadequacies evident in the nationalist community's leadership as it attempted to respond positively to O'Neill. Its responses were often as incompetent as his gestures. The Nationalist Party's assumption of the role of official opposition in the Northern parliament, for example, was, in reality, as superficial a gesture as O'Neill's visits to Catholic schools.[43] In this role the Nationalist Party was in effect moving from a position of informal political impotency to one of formal impotency and had they remained in that position would have been seen as even more impotent than they had previously been. Indeed, by not accepting the role of official opposition the party had made a much more powerful statement about the political realities of Northern Ireland than it did in its brief period as the official opposition.

Missing from the Nationalist Party's analysis, as from that of the civil rights movement, was any clear idea as to the kind of political institutions, or even broad political framework which might accommodate the different and apparently mutually exclusive allegiances held by the communities in Northern Ireland. The desire by many within the nationalist community to play a positive role in public life in Northern Ireland had not yet found clear expression. Participation in and then reform of existing institutions seemed the most obvious first steps, but since reform was proving difficult, if not impossible, the need to have these institutions replaced was beginning to dawn on some, but with what was by no means at all clear yet.

Finally, the O'Neill legacy contained important implications for North-South relations in Ireland. His meetings with the Prime Minister of the Republic and subsequent meetings involving a number of his ministers with their southern counterparts seemed a genuine breakthrough with the result that some joint endeavours were undertaken and others were planned. However, once the disturbances associated with civil rights demonstrations broke out and persisted, relationships between both governments cooled. Taoiseach Jack Lynch, Lemass' successor, publicly criticized the manner in which the authorities in Northern Ireland dealt with the civil rights demonstrations and pointed out that the disturbances merely underlined Northern Ireland's inherent political instability and, therefore, the failure of the 1920-21 settlements by which Ireland had been partitioned.

As O'Neill handed the government over to his successor, Northern Ireland was effectively on the brink of a major political and social crisis. Relationships between the communities in Northern Ireland were worsening and with them the bridges which he had so hopefully attempted to build with the South. It must have seemed to O'Neill himself as if all of the efforts over the previous six years were having effects opposite to those which he had intended.

THREE

ESCALATING FEARS AND HOPES:
FROM STREET RIOTS TO
DIRECT RULE

This chapter examines the escalation of the conflict from street riots to a full-scale political crisis and military confrontation between the IRA, the British Army and Protestant paramilitary forces, eventually resulting in the imposition of Direct Rule by the British government. An important outcome of the crisis was the British government's emergence as a central participant in the conflict. The more distant but increasingly significant role of the Irish government will also be noted in anticipation of its involvement in the first major attempt to resolve the crisis within a new framework.

FROM CIVIL RIGHTS TO ANARCHY

1969 witnessed the rapid deterioration of political order in Northern Ireland and its gradual redefinition in political terms from a focus on civil rights reform to a questioning of fundamental relationships within Northern Ireland and between Northern Ireland and Britain. Before the need to examine those relationships was acknowledged, a period of virtual anarchy was to exist in some parts of the region; paramilitary forces emerged within both communities, most particularly the IRA in the nationalist community and control of events rapidly slipped away from Northern Ireland's political authorities. Terence O'Neill's resignation as Prime Minister did nothing to stabilize the situation, nor did the election of his successor and cousin, James Chichester Clark, who proved quite ineffectual in dealing with the rising tide of street protests throughout the summer of 1969.

The immediate focus of the civil rights protests in 1969 was the

behaviour of the Royal Ulster Constabulary and of its reserve force, the
B Specials. Policing had succeeded housing as the predominant item on
the civil rights agenda after the Derry demonstration in October 1968,
and the attacks on the People's Democracy marchers earlier in 1969.
Indeed, it was the only major civil rights issue which remained to be
addressed, all of the others, including 'one man one vote', having been
conceded.[1]

POLICING AND SECURITY

Police behaviour was, however, more than a simple civil rights issue. In
Northern Ireland's divided society, policing was also a highly political
matter wherein the police defended the interests of the unionist community against the threats, real or imagined, of the nationalist community.[2]
The origins of the police force itself lay in the pre-1921 Royal Irish
Constabulary which had been more a *gendarmerie* than a local police
service, serving as it had as the eyes and ears of the British administration in Ireland. The RUC had continued this tradition and whenever
the IRA was active, the RUC and its civilian auxiliary force, the B
Specials, led the effort against it. In this respect, the RUC operated as a
counter-insurgency force fulfilling a semi-military role. Its members,
almost all were Protestant (the B Specials were exclusively Protestant),
were permanently armed and it was equipped with armoured vehicles.

Given its role and its composition, sympathy within the police force
for civil rights protesters, the majority of whom were from the Catholic
community, was almost inevitably limited and declined further as the
civil rights movement began focusing its protests on the police itself.
Feelings within the nationalist community towards the police were either
openly hostile, or quietly critical but never really very favourable. Only
small numbers of Catholics had ever joined the RUC, and it was rare to
find any expression of open support for the police coming from authoritative nationalist sources. Policing has been one of Northern Ireland's
most fraught public issues given the demands for communal loyalty
which emanate from both sides. For Unionists, the killing of a police
officer was seen as a direct attack against the unionist and Protestant
community. For Catholics, police behaviour daily reminded them of
their inferior status while joining the RUC was tantamount to participating in the oppression of one's own people.

As the events of 1969 unfolded, it was to become increasingly clear
that policing Northern Ireland would have to be one of the fundamental
issues to be addressed if a political order acceptable to both communities

was to be established. The civil rights campaign revealed the inherent weaknesses and underlying instability not only of the existing political system but of the police force established to protect it. The streets of Northern Ireland, always the paths of communal antagonism, were tense in the summer of 1969. In attempting to contain the anger, the police were increasingly under pressure from both sides of the community; with their natural sympathies inclined toward one side of the conflict events would prove them unable to cope. Their failure to resolve or control the situation brought British troops on to the streets, revealing in full the true, underlying dimensions of the conflict.

A WICKED SUMMER

Summers in Northern Ireland are characterised for many by a series of traditional parades, the majority organized within the Protestant-Unionist community to commemorate the Williamite Revolution of 1689-90.[3] In 1969, however, to the traditional parades were added those of the civil rights movement. Rioting frequently punctuated the parades, as rival demonstrators clashed either with each other, or with the police. July and August witnessed particularly destructive and vicious violence, and, in Derry, the events that have come to be known as the 'Battle of the Bogside' took place.[4]

The 'Battle of the Bogside' began as demonstrators from the Catholic Bogside area of the city became embroiled in violent exchanges with participants in the annual march of the Apprentice Boys of Derry.[5] As the police became involved, the situation rapidly dissolved into a confrontation between police, Apprentice Boys marchers and the people of the Bogside. The latter retreated into their own area, erected barricades, and for three days in the middle of August attacked the police from behind barricades with petrol bombs, sticks, stones and any other form of weapon they could lay their hands on. Trouble also erupted in other parts of Northern Ireland, as police in Catholic-Nationalist areas came under attack and as Protestant mobs, especially in Belfast, burst into Catholic areas in retaliation for what had been perceived as provocative civil rights marches and demonstrations.

Seven people were killed in the violence that August; hundreds of houses were destroyed and thousands of people in religiously and politically mixed areas fled their homes to seek refuge within safe ghettoes. The authorities, least of all the police, were unable to contain the situation on the ground. Under pressure in several places at once, the RUC, even with the B Specials fully mobilized, quickly became an exhausted and then a very demoralized force. Faced with growing anarchy and a lack of resources to cope with the situation, the government in Belfast felt that it had no option but to seek assistance from London. Chichester Clark contacted Prime Minister Wilson, and British troops were dispatched to undertake patrol duties ostensibly alongside and in support of the RUC. Given that authority over the army lay exclusively with the government in London, its involvement would inevitably precipitate the opening of a new phase in the conflict, a development which, however, was not immediately apparent.

At a further remove, but also waiting to become a more significant participant, was the government in Dublin. The deepening nature of the crisis evoked expressions of grave concern from the Irish government. During the rioting in Derry, the Taoiseach Jack Lynch declared that his government could not 'stand idly by.'[6] To give meaning to his words, Lynch dispatched army field hospitals to the border near Derry to treat any injured who, out of fear of arrest, might not wish to use hospitals in the city. The move lacked any immediate impact, but it served two important purposes. First, it was a signal to the nationalist community in Northern Ireland that, however impotent Dublin might be to intervene directly, there was a sympathetic neighbouring audience outside of the United Kingdom. Second, it served to remind the British and Northern Ireland authorities that the Irish government felt it had a direct, and in its view, legitimate, interest in what was happening in Northern Ireland.

WHOSE RESPONSIBILITY?

With troops committed in Northern Ireland, the British government now found itself with a direct responsibility for events there for the first time since 1921. Control of the British Army rested exclusively with the government in London and could not be delegated to any subordinate authority. As long as the RUC had appeared potentially able to manage the situation, the British government had been reluctant to become involved. Once this potential evaporated, as it did in the Bogside in 1969, authority over Northern Ireland's destiny began to shift, however slowly, from the devolved, local administration into the hands of the London government.

The introduction of British troops was to be a mixed blessing. Troops on the streets of Northern Ireland touched upon old wounds and exacerbated anxieties which threatened each community. However benign the army's initial purpose might have been, the appearance of troops reminded many Nationalists of what they took to be the unfinished business of Irish freedom. For Unionists, the possibility of direct London control did not make itself immediately apparent, but the fear of losing autonomy was not far beneath the surface.

A BREATHING-SPACE – THEN A VACUUM

The arrival of the troops provided a breathing space which, in retrospect, might have been used more positively to address issues at the heart of the political problem. The British, through the energetic intervention of Home Affairs Minister James Callaghan, who had been given cabinet responsibility for dealing with Northern Ireland, set about insisting that reform measures be adopted and implemented immediately. To many in the Catholic community, it seemed a transformation in their situation was about to take place, and on a visit to Northern Ireland, Callaghan's welcome in most Catholic areas 'was close to triumphal'.[7]

A report addressing concerns about policing was prepared by a commission under the direction of Sir John Hunt, of the London Metropolitan Police. The report recommended that the existing force be reorganized, disarmed, and the B Specials disbanded in favour of a locally recruited army regiment, the Ulster Defence Regiment (UDR). In addition, a package of further reforms was also agreed recommending that all basic civil rights demands be endorsed; that an ombudsman be established to deal with complaints of misconduct and poor administration (i.e., discrimination in employment, etc.); and that an independent Community Relations Commission be set up together with a new Ministry of Community Relations.[8]

The scene should have been set for a new and more positive beginning for the people of Northern Ireland. However, despite a general welcome for the pace and nature of the reforms from 'moderate' leaders in both communities, two important developments prevented that from happening. First, the appearance of a British government minister, James Callaghan, who was actively engaged in the reform effort in Northern Ireland, was unacceptable to most unionist politicians, and they lost no time in protesting his involvement. Traditional majoritarian interpretations of democracy heavily influenced their appeals that the autonomy of Northern Ireland's government and parliament were at stake by virtue of Callaghan's interference. Outside the Unionist Party, the most notable opposition to British interference came from Ian Paisley and his followers; within the party William Craig and Harry West voiced their objections.[9] West and his supporters organized the West Ulster Unionist Council as a forum for outspoken opposition to some of the reforms introduced, while he and Craig travelled throughout Northern Ireland speaking to unionist audiences and denouncing 'British' interference. Such pressure had an inhibiting effect on those Unionists who were inclined to give reform a greater welcome and provided a rallying point for those uncertain of its merits, or who were totally opposed to it.

The second development was the gradual emergence of the IRA in Catholic-Nationalist ghettoes throughout 1970. The IRA first proclaimed itself as a force to defend the ghettoes against any further attacks by police and loyalist mobs, and later it became the self-appointed 'freedom force' which would finally drive the British out of Ireland. To some community leaders in Catholic areas, the need for a form of self-defence had been accepted after the events of August 1969, had demonstrated the unacceptability of the RUC. The leadership of the newly formed Provisional IRA was determined to re-assert a military option as a means of achieving a solution to the problem. To them, British intervention in the deteriorating situation only confirmed their definition of the conflict as essentially a colonial or imperialist one. It provided a very appropriate opportunity to renew their struggle for Ireland's 'freedom' in the manner they preferred.

Early in 1970, elements within the IRA in Belfast who were anxious to exploit the situation through military action split from the majority in the organization.[10] The latter wished to continue to pursue the policy of social reform through political agitation and did not favour an offensive military campaign. Called the Provisional IRA (Provos), the break-away group soon enjoyed a rapid growth in membership. With funds flowing in from sympathisers in the United States and in the Republic of Ireland, arms and explosives were acquired in preparation not for defensive purposes, as originally suggested, but for a 'war of liberation'. The Provos were determined to redeem themselves of the charge baldly represented in the slogan, 'IRA-I Ran Away', which appeared on gable walls in several nationalist areas after the events of 1969.

DESCENDING INTO THE ABYSS

As evidence of the IRA's increasing strength and activity accumulated, starting in early 1970, the army and police stepped up counter-measures to curb the organization's movements. Such measures, involving house searches, road-checks on motorists and pedestrians, more aggressive patrolling, especially in densely populated urban areas like Belfast, almost inevitably resulted in conflict with the civilian population in the nationalist areas, which were the main targets of these measures. Serious inter-communal disturbances in the Ballymurphy area of West Belfast in April resulted in confrontations between civilians and the army in which petrol bombs were thrown at troops. As a result, the British Commanding Officer issued a statement in which he said that people throwing such bombs risked being shot.[11] In an effort to establish itself as the defender of the nationalist community, the IRA announced its intention to target any British troops shooting at members of the nationalist community.[12]

Further serious rioting took place at the end of June. During that time, what many regard as the opening shots of the IRA's campaign were fired. Six people were killed and several hundred wounded. The deteriorating relationship between local people and British troops deepened as a result of the 'Falls Road curfew', when a substantial area in nationalist West Belfast was sealed off for a period of thirty-four hours to enable intense house searches to be conducted by the military. The manner in which the curfew was imposed and the searches conducted produced a deep sense of resentment and effectively removed whatever remained of nationalist willingness to cooperate with the army. In October, rioting in the loyalist Shankill Road area directed specifically against the army revealed just how complex and dangerous the situation had become and just how volatile were relationships between the army and both communities. Less and less was the conflict defined in strictly Catholic and Protestant terms; instead, the old and complicated settler-covenantal relationships between the British and both local communities were resurrected.

The disturbances earlier in the year led to the introduction of new 'law and order' legislation, the Criminal Justice Act which considerably strengthened police and judicial powers in dealing with rioters and persons 'likely to cause a breach of the peace'. Introduced by a unionist government, with no indication that fresh political thinking was needed, this new legislation merely reinforced a 'them' and 'us' outlook in nationalist minds and suggested that a security rather than a political response to nationalist grievances was being adopted. Its harsh measures had no appreciable influence in eliminating disturbances, much less in deterring the IRA, so it did nothing to reassure the unionist community itself that its political leaders could resolve the crisis. The situation had all the characteristics of the 'security dilemma' in which one side's efforts to protect its own security only makes the other side feel more insecure and thus likely to take 'protective' measures of its own. In fact, on the latter point, the level of criticism of the leadership within the Unionist Party increased as 1970 drew to a close, and it began to appear more and more likely that Chichester-Clark's days as Prime Minister were numbered.

Clark's only recourse was to demand more support in the form of increased British Army involvement in countering the IRA, but the more he sought refuge in this policy the more he threatened that part of the settler-covenant arrangement Unionists held most dear – Protestant autonomy. The inability to maintain order, a main ingredient of the Protestant-Unionist ethos, exposed Unionists to excessive reliance on Britain though the full implications of this dilemma were, however, not to become evident for another year. The new British government was slow in its evaluation of the crisis and reluctant to take decisive measures while Clark's own rather hesitant demeanour suggested that a more decisive local figure might be able to deal with the situation. By March 1971, Clark's ability to influence events in any decisive manner had vanished and he resigned, to be replaced by the Minister for Development, Brian Faulkner, who had the reputation of being a no-nonsense, direct and pragmatic politician, a clear contrast to the country-gentleman background of his immediate predecessors.[13]

When Faulkner took office he immediately launched a programme of further reform. The first sign of Faulkner's style and of his determination was his appointment of a leading Northern Ireland Labour Party member and former MP, David Bleakley, as Minister for Community Relations. Faulkner recognized that this sensitive area required someone who would be seen as less partisan than unionist politicians had traditionally been.[14] Bleakley's appointment marked the first overt indication by Faulkner that government in Northern Ireland required a base broader than that provided by the unionist electorate and, as such, was to become increasingly significant over the next two years. It has to be noted, however, that Faulkner balanced his appointment of the moderate Bleakley with the recall to the cabinet of the hardliner Harry West, who had been deeply critical of what he claimed had been Chichester-Clark's failure to deal effectively with the IRA.

Despite his determination to restore 'law and order', Faulkner's assumption of office made no apparent impression on the IRA, and throughout the spring and early summer of 1971, its campaign intensified. Easter was particularly vicious as rioting and shooting, resulting in several deaths, broke out on the occasion of Orange Order parades in Belfast. Openly defying the authorities, the IRA mounted a major demonstration at the funeral of one its members killed in an encounter with British troops. Over 1,000 IRA members paraded through West Belfast in a display of strength which was intended to indicate a new source of authority for a large section of the population of the city. To the unionist community as a whole, but especially to its extremists, it was a blatant provocation, illegal and threatening.

Faulkner's political initiatives were not directly aimed at encouraging the IRA to abandon its violent campaign. Any attempt to directly address the IRA, other than by security means, would have been out of the question. Rather, Faulkner hoped to engage the mainstream leadership of the nationalist community who had declared themselves opposed to violence and committed to the democratic process. Since 1969, changes of a significant kind had been taking place in political alignments outside of the Unionist party, which must have given Faulkner hope that reform of the existing political institutions might be possible without disturbing in any way the existing constitutional framework.

NEW PARTIES

By the close of 1969 constitutional nationalist politics were in the process of significant change. The traditional nationalist definition of the situation rendered its existing leadership completely unprepared to deal with the reformist implications of the civil rights movement. The Nationalist Party had adopted a wishful and symbolic role in advancing the cause of Irish unity. In the 1969 election, several of the nationalist politicians, including Eddie McAteer, the long-time leader of the Nationalist Party, had been replaced by much younger men.[15] Most of these younger candidates had been activists in the civil rights movement, men like John Hume in Derry, Paddy O'Hanlon in South Armagh, and Ivan Cooper in Mid-Derry. Individually and collectively, these new politicians, together with Gerry Fitt and Austin Currie who already had been in Stormont for several years, performed remarkably well in arguing the case for change and in articulating the grievances of the nationalist community. Nevertheless, they lacked the impact which membership of a single coherent political party would have given them.

For some time there had been talk of building a new nationalist party, or of a realignment which would bring together a number of small parties like the Northern Ireland Labour Party, Republican Labour and the Irish Labour Party. In the end, the initiative was taken by seven leading nationalist and civil rights politicians elected to Stormont, who announced in August 1970 the establishment of the Social Democratic and Labour Party (SDLP). The party declared that it would be a non-sectarian, left-of-centre party with the aim of working for Irish unity by consent.

Another new political party also appeared on the scene in 1970, the Alliance Party of Northern Ireland (APNI).[16] The party was the product of a discussion group called the New Ulster Movement, which had been active over preceding years in trying to promote debate on political issues that might lead to enhanced cooperation between people of different religious affiliations in Northern Ireland. The most significant characteristic of the Alliance was its cross-community membership, in a denominational sense, a characteristic which suggested that, for the Alliance Party, the defining division between people in Northern Ireland was religious. Hence, its founders argued, if cooperation could be developed across that divide, it might be possible to create new political institutions for Northern Ireland that would win the support of both communities. The Alliance Party stated that the union with Britain should remain as long as this was the wish of a majority of the people in Northern Ireland.

While the Alliance Party attracted some members who had previously been associated with the Unionist Party, and a few who had been involved in nationalist politics, more notably it attracted members who had no previous active political involvement. Unlike the SDLP, however, which included from the outset several leading politicians in the Northern Ireland parliament, the Alliance Party had to await the 1973 elections before its real electoral strength could be assessed. The establishment of the Alliance Party of Northern Ireland, which effectively was a moderate unionist party, underlined the divisions that had been gradually tearing the Unionist Party itself apart. Not only was there some shifting of membership from the Unionist Party to Alliance, but a more concerted challenge emerged from the religious right of the party with the election of Ian Paisley to Stormont in April 1970.[17] One of Paisley's leading associates, William Beattie, also won election, an achievement to be followed in June by Paisley's victory in the British general elections. The fragmentation of the unionist political movement was underway just as Faulkner was about to attempt political reform, leaving him with an increasingly unstable base from which to launch his reforms.

Ironically, it was in the course of celebrations marking Northern Ireland's fiftieth anniversary that Faulkner announced his main political initiative. He proposed the establishment of three new parliamentary committees, two of which he believed should be chaired by members of the opposition.[18] As he proposed them, these committees would scrutinize government in its entirety and, in addition, would have input into policy making and into the preparation of legislation. Faulkner hoped that such a development would provide an important role for nationalist members of parliament and reassure them that their interests would be taken fully into account both in the framing and the execution of government policy. Building on the point of view which Bleakley's appointment had signalled, he argued that in Northern Ireland 'we must aim to govern with the consent and acceptance of a far wider majority than is constituted by those who elect the governing party.'[19] The implications of what could be accomplished by trying to achieve this wider consent were, however, by no means clear. Faulkner's proposals were certainly innovative in the context of Northern Ireland and were regarded by many as a brave first step towards seeking a new consensus. Yet, the SDLP leadership remained cautious. John Hume, the party's deputy leader acknowledged the reform that had been accomplished, but wondered if 'we should not be discussing the system itself rather than tinkering with it any further'.[20] Nonetheless, Faulkner's proposals were sufficient to entice members of the non-unionist parties to open discussions with the government in order to explore what possibilities they might contain.

In a pattern familiar to students of ethnic politics in the Middle East, Sri Lanka, and elsewhere, inter-party talks commenced in early July but after only one meeting collapsed, victim to the violence of the streets. From 1971 on, the option of using violence to disrupt the political process was indulged by the IRA.[21] The key factor was not so much the IRA's use of violence as it was the response of democratic party leaders from both communities to the violence. As G. Bingham Powell argues, 'the accumulated grievances and hatred caused by so many deaths and attacks made development of cooperative democratic action that much more difficult'.[22] He goes on to argue that 'it is hard to escape the conclusion that the reactions of the democratic parties are at least as important as the terrorist strategies or military sympathies'.[23] Many within the unionist community either condoned or ignored extremist violence against the nationalist community while in the latter, democratic leaders found it difficult to always condemn violence which appeared to be committed in its defence.

In Derry, when two young men were killed following clashes with troops the SDLP demanded a full inquiry into the circumstances surrounding their deaths. These demands were rejected and the party withdrew not only from the talks but from the Northern Ireland parliament itself and announced the establishment of an alternative assembly. Faulkner's hopes of achieving a new understanding with the nationalist community within the framework of existing structures had received an irreversible set-back. Just how irreversible would become obvious within a month, when the decision to intern without trial large numbers of IRA suspects would be taken.

INTERNMENT

Internment of IRA suspects had been widely discussed for some time, but when Faulkner became Prime Minister, his predisposition to its use led to intense speculation that it would be invoked sooner rather than later. It was a measure which had been used during all previous IRA campaigns, from the 1920s to the 1950s and to Unionists had appeared effective in reducing and helping to end violence. Although it has since emerged that Faulkner had opposed internment when it had been discussed in O'Neill's and Chichester Clark's cabinets, he did not flinch from deciding to use it when convinced that it was necessary. As the violence rose to unprecedented levels in the early summer of 1971, preparations for internment were undertaken. Faulkner managed to convince London that internment, drastic as it would be, was the only option available to stem the IRA tide.[24] That he could order it, albeit with the consent of the British, confirmed that while the Northern Ireland government's authority over security was diminished, it still retained some power.

Following consultation with the British government, Faulkner decided that internment should be introduced on August 9. Early on the morning of that day, over 300 men were detained by troops and police, taken to a number of interrogation centres for questioning, and later imprisoned in detention camps without trial. In the course of his press conference later that day, Faulkner asked 'those who will quite sincerely consider the use of internment powers as evil to answer honestly this question; is it more of an evil than to allow the perpetrators of these outrages to remain at liberty?'.[25] Any hope he had of the question being answered in a manner supporting his decision was destroyed by the treatment of those detained and interrogated. By the nature of its execution, internment was interpreted as being aimed exclusively at the nationalist community, and for the most part it was. Intelligence data was vague and imprecise, having been gathered in an atmosphere suggesting that all Catholics were possible terrorists.[26] It was an old theme but one invoked with disastrous consequences on this occasion.

Indeed, even before news of the 'inhuman and degrading treatment'[27] meted out by the British Army interrogators to those questioned reached the public, the IRA was giving its verdict on the streets of Northern Ireland. In Belfast and elsewhere in nationalist areas, reaction was swift and deadly. Fierce gun battles raged over several days, barricades were erected, and rioting broke out. Seventeen people died violently in the two days following the introduction of internment, many more were injured, and thousands of pounds worth of damage was caused. In addition many thousands fled from nationalist areas in Belfast to the Republic, where they were accommodated in hastily prepared army camps. Contrary to the government rationale provided for internment, violence increased almost immediately. In one year, deaths attributable to the violence went from 174 to 467, the highest number by far, of deaths recorded in any year since 1968.[28]

At a political level, nationalist politicians found themselves in an impossible position with little but extreme rhetoric to invoke and negative protest actions to recommend. Nationalist councillors across the North decided to withdraw from city and town councils, while many other Nationalists withdrew from positions on public bodies. The SDLP declared that it would not participate in political talks for as long as internment lasted. The Irish government demanded an end to partition as the only viable solution! Internment pressed Nationalists of all views, moderate and extreme, closer together. In the United States, leading Irish-American politicians initiated Congressional hearings on Northern Ireland to which they invited SDLP and other nationalist spokespersons to give evidence. United Nations intervention was sought by the SDLP's Leader, Gerry Fitt. In Britain itself the Labour leader, Harold Wilson, broke the delicate bi-partisan approach to Northern Ireland which had existed since the recent civil unrest and terrorism first broke out and produced a detailed plan aimed at achieving Irish unity. While such gestures brought no immediate redress to the situation, they were not without long-term influence, most especially on the British government's thinking about the conflict.

The British government's first reaction was to offer its fullest support to Faulkner, but as the pressure under which it was coming both at home and abroad intensified, it gradually began to undertake a fundamental re-assessment of the whole situation. The view was gaining ground in government circles that the crisis had been transformed and was unlikely to be contained without substantial and even radical structural reforms. The immediate political objectives were to find ways of opening up the political process to expanded Catholic-nationalist participation, and to cooperate with the Irish government in countering IRA terrorism. Searching for ways to achieve both, but especially the former, absorbed much time and energy in the Autumn and Winter of 1971. It was not until another critical development forced the pace and level of British involvement that fresh possibilities eventually emerged.

CHASING AN INTERNAL SOLUTION

In public, Faulkner remained opposed to any greater involvement by nationalist representatives than that proposed in June 1971 and since the SDLP was insistent that there could be no talks until internment was ended, there was no opportunity locally to probe Faulkner's intentions further. His argument was based on the traditional unionist attitude towards Nationalists, i.e. that, since their objective was to end partition, they could not be afforded a role in the government of the region whose separate political existence they wished to end. Faulkner did hold out several other carrots in an attempt to entice the SDLP back into discussions.[29] He suggested the possibility of using a sytem of proportional representation in elections to the Northern Ireland parliament and the possibility of enlarging the House of Commons and of giving the much smaller and insignificant senate an enhanced role. Demands for proportional representation to ensure a fairer reflection in parliament of community representation had emerged as an important SDLP demand. Apparently under pressure from the British government, Faulkner agreed that a proposal be made to Nationalists whereby 'an active, permanent and guaranteed place in the life and public affairs of Northern Ireland shall be available both to the majority and minority community'.[30] Such an offer contained the suggestion that radical reform of the government of Northern Ireland might be in the offing. In the immediate aftermath of internment such suggestions were ignored by the SDLP in favour of what it and the nationalist community generally perceived to be the immediate and greater need of ending internment. Internment, by radicalizing substantial elements of the Catholic population and stimulating violence, threatened to undo the centrist role pursued by the SDLP. Internment was by then the great injustice. A role in government, especially in a government responsible for that injustice, could not be contemplated.

For Faulkner to have appeared any more generous towards Nationalists was extremely difficult given not only the SDLP's terms for discussions, but also the growing militancy evident among extreme Unionists, more frequently referred to as Loyalists. By mid-autumn 1971, a newly formed Loyalist Association of Workers (LAW) was organizing in Belfast to demonstrate for tougher measures against terrorists with considerable support from politicians like Bill Craig and Ian Paisley.[31] Even from the moderates within his party Faulkner was under constant pressure for even more stringent measures.[32]

ANGLO-IRISH RELATIONSHIPS

Anglo-Irish relationships became very brittle following the imposition of internment. The British government resented Dublin's criticism of what its subordinate regional government in Northern Ireland was doing, especially when that criticism was vehemently expressed abroad, particularly to powerful and sympathetic politicians in the United States. Nevertheless, a recognition that Dublin's assistance was vital to suppressing the IRA and to moving the SDLP towards a compromise forced Prime Minister Heath to see the wisdom of inviting his Irish counterpart to a meeting with himself and Faulkner in September 1971. At this stage, despite the optimistic developments of the mid-sixties, the Dublin government's only fixed position on Northern Ireland was that it should not exist. Hence its reaction to internment had been no more than to call for an end to partition, though subsequently it used the evidence of ill-treatment of those detained to indict the British government for grave human rights violations before the European Court of Human Rights.

Instead of addressing the wider and underlying political issues, the first meeting involving the heads of government from the Republic of Ireland, Northern Ireland, and the United Kingdom in over fifty years concentrated almost exclusively on the security situation. Heath and Faulkner sought maximum cooperation from Lynch by trying to persuade him to introduce internment in the Republic and to extradite fugitive offenders from the North. Internment would have been politically impossible in the Republic at this point, not least because of the manner in which it had been introduced in Northern Ireland. In addition, the outrages suffered by the nationalist community had, in the eyes of some sections of the population in the Republic, given the IRA a degree of justification to act as 'defenders' of that community. The fact that no Loyalist suspected of terrorism had been detained, despite clear evidence of terrorist activity by Loyalists, justified the claim that internment had been deliberately one-sided. As far as extradition was concerned, the government regarded it as a matter for the courts, whose responsibility it was to administer and interpret the relevant extradition legislation.[33]

BLOODY SUNDAY – THE ABYSS

As the Winter of 1971 closed in, there was no sign that anyone was prepared to break the stalemate. Internment, and the communal loyalties it invoked remained the burning issue for Nationalists and for Unionists. Responding to the deep resentment concerning internment, the Civil

Rights Association announced that, despite a ban on marches and demonstrations in force since the previous August, it would organize a number of public demonstrations. Whatever wisdom might be gained about this decision in hindsight, it represented at the time an attempt to avoid leaving all the protests to the IRA gunmen. The results were, however, tragic, bringing Northern Ireland to the brink of civil war and drawing to a close the final chapter of unionist rule.

The first demonstration took place along a stretch of the north coast near the newly opened detention centre at Magilligan Prison in County Derry. This demonstration ended in violent clashes between participants and troops guarding access to the prison. Nevertheless, it did not deter the Civil Rights Association from announcing that it would continue defying the ban on marches by holding another demonstration in Derry the following Sunday. It was in the course of this second demonstration that the events which came to be known as 'Bloody Sunday' took place. Thirteen people were shot dead by British troops as the Derry demonstration approached the centre of the city. The troops alleged that they had been fired on, but during the subsequent British government inquiry no evidence was produced to suggest that anyone had in fact fired a weapon at the army.[34] The reaction from the nationalist community was utter outrage as a wave of anti-British sentiment swept the country. Ending the 'injustice of partition' seemed to more and more Nationalists the only way out of what they saw as a terrible nightmare. In Dublin, a demonstration outside the British Embassy resulted in the building being set on fire and completely gutted, while diplomatic relations between Dublin and London were strained, and the Irish ambassador, Donal O'Sullivan, was recalled.

As nationalist anger simmered and boiled, so too did the anger of Loyalists. Drawing on the membership of the Loyalist Workers' Association, Bill Craig took the initiative in mobilizing a tough and defiant loyalist response by setting up, on semi-military lines, the Vanguard Movement to defend Ulster's British heritage.[35] Across Northern Ireland, Vanguard mounted several large public demonstrations of men marshalled in military rank, holding their arms aloft in Nazi-style salutes. One such demonstration in Belfast involved over 50,000 participants. Politically, Craig had no solution to offer other than to suggest that Northern Ireland should cede to the Republic those parts of its territory close to the border. These areas, he argued, were overwhelmingly nationalist and were the location for much of the recent unrest. As for any broadening of the government's base to give Nationalists a more meaningful role in their governance, Craig declared himself and his movement totally opposed, saying 'it was a recipe for civil war'.[36]

Within the British cabinet the conviction had firmly taken hold that only the direct involvement of nationalist politicians in the government of Northern Ireland stood a chance of breaking the stalemate. To encourage Unionists to accept this prospect it was suggested that a referendum to test local opinion on Northern Ireland's constitutional status should be held at regular intervals. This was not a new idea. Harold Wilson had included it in his step-by-step proposals for Irish unity published the previous autumn. More significantly, it was also clear, as Faulkner himself acknowledges in his autobiography, that the complete transfer of all law and order powers from the government of Northern Ireland to the British authorities was, following 'Bloody Sunday', being contemplated.[37]

February, 1972 was a month full of political rumour about an imminent British political initiative, and heightened IRA activity – with bombs exploding at a rate of almost four a day – and of increasing unrest in loyalist circles, as evident in Vanguard's demonstrations. Sensing that time was at last running out for his government, Faulkner made one last set of proposals to the British cabinet.[38] While he remained opposed to a place in government by right for nationalist representatives, he again proposed that Nationalists share certain senior parliamentary offices such as Speaker of the House. More interesting and innovative was his willingness to consider the establishment of an Inter-Governmental Council between North and South, to promote consultation on matters of joint concern. He also accepted the idea of a referendum on the constitutional status of Northern Ireland and agreed that much greater representation should be given to the nationalist community in appointments to public bodies.

Just as Faulkner was proposing the most radical reforms ever to have been considered by Unionists, London was considering a major initiative that included some of Faulkner's own proposals but also went much further. In addition to the idea of a regular referendum, London proposed that government in Northern Ireland be established on a proportional basis, thereby giving Nationalists a place by right at the cabinet table; internment would end, and all security powers would be transferred to British control to be administered by a Secretary of State for Northern Ireland. In effect, London was proposing a government for Northern Ireland without the authority to ensure that its mandate would be upheld in its own jurisdiction. Such a proposal would effectively undermine the basis of Protestant rule in Northern Ireland, undoing in one act the major tenets of settlement and covenantal politics.

Stunned by the proposal to remove security powers from his government and filled with a sense of betrayal, Faulkner felt he had no option but to recommend to his cabinet colleagues that these terms were unacceptable. He did so and offered his resignation on March 28, effectively bringing to an end fifty-one years of unbroken unionist government in Northern Ireland.[39] The Vanguard movement called a two-day general strike in protest, and Northern Ireland awaited the arrival of its new political masters.

FOUR

COMMUNITIES AT RISK:
FROM DIRECT RULE TO POWER-SHARING

According to Marc Ross, 'The standard explanation of persistent conflict in Northern Ireland is a structural one which emphasizes constitutional anomalies and weak cross-cutting ties between Protestants and Catholics. Consequently, each community is presented as having unique constitutional interests to defend, while severe communal distrust and fear are explained in terms of economic inequality, differential access to resources, such as housing or jobs, and political inequalities. Viewed in such terms Northern Ireland is a classic structurally divided society in which other sources of division, economic, social and political, are superimposed on the religious cleavage.'[1]

These structural explanations focus on the interests which members of each community define as real. For most Catholics this has meant an end to discrimination in housing, economic opportunities, political involvement and, for many within that community, a resolution of the 'national' or constitutional question which would at least open the way to a united Ireland. For Protestants, real interests include fears of being made subject to an all-Ireland state which would deny their Britishness and threaten their Protestantism, fears of losing control in Northern Ireland itself, and threats to their persons and property from militant nationalism.[2]

Not surprisingly, structural analyses, which were those most favoured in the 1970s, produced structurally based remedies to address these fears. So, the immediate goal of the British administration which took responsibility for Northern Ireland in 1972 was to encourage broad agreement on new political structures. The agreements, in 1973, to create a 'power-sharing' executive and a Council of Ireland marked the culmination of these initial efforts. The first of these agreements formally included representatives of the nationalist community in a coalition type administration and established a legislative assembly based on proportional representation to deal with the region's internal affairs. The second, commonly referred to as the Sunningdale Agreement,[3] was intended to lead to the establishment of a north-south body, the Council of Ireland. Both agreements met with approval from constitutional nationalists and from a section of unionist opinion. It was, however, short-lived, ending after only five months when challenged by the general strike called by militant unionist workers and supported by many unionist politicians.

This chapter examines developments which led to the short-lived 1974 experiment, its demise, and the barren political landscape which lasted virtually without interruption until 1985 when the Irish and British governments signed a new accord, the Anglo-Irish Agreement, and succeeded in inducing a new dynamic into the situation. This discussion is followed, in Chapter 5, by a detailed critique of the basis upon which these initiatives were made.

A FORMIDABLE PRO-CONSUL

With the abolition of the Northern Ireland government and parliament, the British were in a position where, constitutionally speaking, they could almost return to a blank drawing board. Within the limits of UK membership they were at liberty to attempt almost any experiment which might address the problems of the region's deeply divided society. The task of starting from scratch was entrusted to William Whitelaw MP who took up the office of Secretary of State for Northern Ireland.[4]

At first sight Whitelaw appeared an avuncular, amiable gentleman in the traditional mould of British conservatism. Exuding charm and goodwill wherever he went, he must have seemed to many the very antithesis of the kind of person needed to deal with the critical situation gripping Northern Ireland. But, as the first person to exercise direct responsibility in Ireland on behalf of the British government since 1921, he was to display, beneath all his outward joviality, a keen and incisive grasp of realities and of what was needed to address them.

With terrorism reaching new levels of intensity and the local political parties placing strict pre-conditions for the resumption of dialogue Whitelaw was faced with a very bleak situation. The IRA was exercising a degree of control over so-called 'no-go' areas in some nationalist areas of Derry and Belfast. These areas were very small in extent, but the form of control exercised over them by young paramilitaries who patrolled their streets demonstrated a considerable degree of popular local support for the IRA, as well as the latter's capacity to deny access to these areas to the RUC and the British Army. As such they had a significance far beyond their size. In loyalist areas, especially in Belfast, the recently founded Ulster Defence Association was flaunting its support and its determination to defend their areas by mounting large public parades of uniformed men and women. Overall, it was a highly volatile situation containing most of the ingredients for widespread inter-communal violence.

Whitelaw's period in office consisted of a short initial phase in which he seems to have believed that a direct approach to the IRA might hold out the prospects of ameliorating the situation. When this failed, he turned to the so-called constitutional politicians and began engaging them in discussions about a new way forward.

CONTACTS WITH SINN FEIN-IRA

The initial phase lasted from Whitelaw's arrival in April until late July 1972. During these months the IRA's campaign was dramatically intensified. On one day alone, 14 April, thirty bombs exploded all over Northern Ireland while the death toll in May became the highest since the outbreak of violence in 1969. In response, loyalist paramilitaries also intensified their violence with random assassinations in predominantly Catholic and nationalist areas.[5] Within the nationalist community the new levels of IRA violence created their own tensions leading to pressure on IRA leaders to call a ceasefire. The SDLP publicly appealed to the IRA to end its campaign saying: 'We ask those engaged in the campaign of violence to cease immediately, to enable us to bring internment to a speedy end and make a positive response to the British Government's proposals'.[6] The IRA's response to such pressure was, initially, defiant. Martin McGuinness, a leading Derry republican, declared that the IRA was intent on 'fighting until we get a united Ireland'.[7] Nonetheless, Whitelaw seems to have believed that the IRA might be persuaded to abandon its campaign of violence in return for an opportunity to participate directly in the political process.

He was not the first leading British politician to have had such thoughts at this time. Just before Stormont had been prorogued, Harold Wilson, then leader of the opposition, and a number of his colleagues agreed to meet leading figures of the IRA while on a visit to Dublin.[8] The meeting followed approaches from the IRA who were said to have been impressed by views expressed by Wilson regarding the possibility of a ceasefire if detainees were released. While no progress was made on the broad political issues, this meeting, together with the pressure on the

IRA from within the nationalist community, probably contributed to Whitelaw's decision to release large numbers of detainees and to grant 'special category' status to others who had been interned.[9] In this way the ground was prepared for an IRA ceasefire at the end of June and for his own contacts with the Provisionals in early July.

Whitelaw's contacts with the IRA were to prove totally unproductive. A meeting took place in London involving several leading members of Sinn Fein and the IRA from North and South.[10] At the meeting they demanded that the British government should publicly state its support for a referendum on Irish unity in the whole of Ireland and to an amnesty for those convicted of terrorist crimes. These demands were totally unacceptable to the British government not least because they came from an organization with no clear political mandate. More significantly, however, acceptance of the referendum demand would have implied unilateral abandonment of British sovereignty over Northern Ireland. Both demands were rejected out of hand and the IRA ended its ceasefire.

Harold Wilson then made his second and final attempt at this time to persuade the IRA to re-establish the ceasefire and to recognize that the political realities of the situation were such that they were in no position to dictate terms.[11] His second meeting met with no tangible success and three days later, on 21 July, the IRA attempted to prove its strength with some of the worst bombing atrocities which Northern Ireland had yet experienced. On a day that has become known ever since as 'Bloody Friday', twenty-two bombs exploded in Belfast killing eleven people, injuring scores of others and destroying property worth millions of pounds.

The government's reaction was swift. Within days large numbers of troops were moved into Northern Ireland and on 31 July in a huge display of its armoured might the British Army entered the so-called 'no-go' areas and the barricades were dismantled. Talking with the terrorists was over, at least for the time being, and a new phase in Whitelaw's strategy was to begin, involving the 'constitutional' politicians.[12]

A NEW POLITICAL INITIATIVE

Having dented the paramilitaries' pride with the ease with which the 'no-go' areas were breached and now, in his own view, much more able to influence the direction of events, Whitelaw initiated a round of consultations with the main political parties. The process was to be complex because, despite the region's small size, there were several parties to be consulted.

The Ulster Unionist Party was still the largest party but its supremacy was no longer as clear as in the past. From without, the establishment of Ian Paisley's Democratic Unionist Party (DUP) had given the more stridently religious element in unionism an organized political base. Already the DUP was beginning to attract membership and supporters from those within the unionist community who viewed the Ulster Unionist Party as too conciliatory and too willing to make concessions to those whom they regarded as Northern Ireland's 'traditional enemies'. From within the Ulster Unionist Party itself, William Craig's Vanguard Movement was a significant pressure group also opposed to what it regarded as a concessionary approach. Craig would soon translate this pressure into the separate, short-lived Vanguard Unionist Party.[13]

Sharing what many commentators described as the 'centre' ground because they drew support from both the Protestant and Roman Catholic sections of the community were the Liberal Party, the Northern Ireland Labour Party and the recently established Alliance Party. However, the term 'centre' cannot be used for these parties without a degree of qualification. If it was simply a case of a religious divide the term 'centre' would be non-problematic, but since all three parties fully accepted the region's constitutional position as part of the UK, they were not neutral on the main issue which divided Unionists and Nationalists. These parties must, therefore, also be seen as unionist, albeit with a small 'u'. While such parties drew degrees of support from both denominational communities, they were competing on the same very narrow electoral ground and it was no surprise that only one, the new and more dynamic Alliance Party, was to survive the traumas of the next few years as a significant political force.

For most Unionists, direct rule was, at least initially, the worst possible situation and their immediate aim was to seek the return of regional government, more or less on the same basis as previously. The political, communal, and ideological foundations of unionism were threatened by the new political situation. The historic fears about encroachment and abandonment were now no longer threats but virtual realities. Direct rule was seen as one further link in the chain of Catholic advances which stretched back to the previous century, including emancipation, land reform, the establishment of the independent Irish state and, more recently, concessions to the civil rights movement. Beyond Catholic encroachment, there was the ultimate fear of complete abandonment by Britain whose commitment had, in any case, always been seen as conditional. For Unionists who feared the worst if Britain reneged on its pledge to protect their constitutional status, they would be released from their bond of loyalty to the Crown and would be left to fend for themselves in whatever seemed the most effective way. But whatever happened, unity with the rest of Ireland would be resisted to the last.

The debate which emerged within unionism in the wake of direct rule was between those who favoured an independent state, the return of devolved government under unionist control, or full integration into Britain. Most Unionists recognised that Northern Ireland did not have the capacity to attain or sustain independence and so, the option remained a marginal one at best. The only significant effort to advance the case for independence was to come in the late seventies from within the UDA, some members of which invested considerable effort in lobbying widely for independence using the argument that it could become the catalyst for a more united Northern Ireland.[14] For Nationalists, independence held few attractions and for most Unionists it remained the fall-back position for a doomsday situation, i.e. in the event of Britain totally abandoning its sovereignty over Northern Ireland.

While the desire for the return of devolved, unionist, controlled government, was to remain strong, many Unionists slowly began to realize that the British would not endorse such a return. Some began, therefore, to consider what had previously been ruled out, a form of government in which power could be shared with the nationalist community albeit with some account for majoritarian principles.[15] However, they were a minority and their influence was weak throughout the seventies and early eighties. For other Unionists, not withstanding the fact that Britain had never shown any interest in re-integrating any part of Ireland back into the UK, 'integration' did emerge as the preferred constitutional option following direct rule. Devolution, they asserted, had been foisted on the region by Britain as a prelude to a united Ireland and had not been the solution which all Unionists prior to 1920 had sought; by definition it weakened rather than strengthened links with the rest of the UK. According to Paul Arthur, 'There is some historic merit in this argument but it ignores the fact that by the mid-1920s, when virtually free of Westminster's interference, they (most Unionists) became enthusiastic devolutionists. The views of both devolutionists and integrationists are summed up in a 1926 report of the Ulster Unionist Council: "Northern Ireland without a Parliament of her own would be a standing temptation to certain British Politicians to make another bid for a final settlement with the Irish Republic".'[16] This fear is the common ground of unionist resistance.

Nationalists, on the other hand, regardless of their place on the ideological continuum, greeted the declaration of direct rule with great satisfaction that the despised unionist regime was gone. Denied any meaningful participation in the governance of the North, there was a conviction among moderate Nationalists that they might finally have the opportunity to re-define constitutional relationships and, at least, participate in the government of the region. For the more extreme Nationalists, direct rule, more than simply ridding Northern Ireland of unionist government, revealed the fundamental issue that had always driven the conflict, namely British control over, or 'occupation of', as they preferred to term it, part of Ireland.[17] Emerging from a period when it had been served by a relatively weak political organization, into one in which a more vibrant and coherent voice, that of the SDLP, was speaking on behalf of the majority of its population the nationalist community began to appear politically stronger. However, the SDLP was not the sole voice of that community. Sinn Fein, although not as yet playing any directly representative role in the region's politics, was still in existence with support estimated at approximately thirty per cent of the nationalist electorate. Also, despite being virtually moribund as organisations, two other parties retained residual representation on behalf of small sections of the nationalist community, the old Nationalist Party itself and the Belfast based Republican Labour Party. Their declining base would soon leave the SDLP and Sinn Fein as the sole parties representing that community.[18]

WHITELAW CONSULTS

Whitelaw's consultations with political parties began with an invitation to attend a three-day conference at Darlington in England to be held at the end of September. Invitations were extended to all of the 'constitutional political parties', a designation which excluded Sinn Fein. Whitelaw wanted to be as inclusive as possible of political opinion and in all seven parties were invited: the Ulster Unionist Party, the Alliance Party, the Northern Ireland Labour Party, the Ulster Democratic Unionist Party, the SDLP, the Nationalist Party and the Republican Labour Party. However, the responses from the parties invited to Darlington did not suggest that Whitelaw was likely to meet with any greater success in dialogue with elected politicians than he had had from the paramilitaries. Only the first three parties agreed to attend, leaving the conference

without any nationalist presence, and without any representation from
Paisley's DUP.

The reasons for refusal from the nationalist parties were most clearly
signalled in the SDLP's demand that internment would have to end
before it could become involved in political dialogue.[19] The SDLP also
complained that the Dublin government had not been invited, a failure
which implied that only an internal, exclusively Northern Ireland
context for a settlement was being sought.[20] The two smaller nationalist
parties took a similar line and Sinn Fein was not invited because of its
close association with the IRA and, since none of its members had been
elected to public office, it could not be argued that it was entitled to an
invitation by virtue of an electoral mandate. Paisley's DUP declined on
the grounds that the government had refused an official enquiry into the
shooting by British troops of civilians in a unionist area of Belfast.
Paisley's excuse seems to have been motivated more by a desire to avoid
a negotiating situation in which he might be compromised, than by a real
concern for the enquiry he had demanded.

In an immediate sense, the Darlington conference achieved nothing.[21]
What it did reveal, however, was that Faulkner and his party were still
not prepared to envisage a role for nationalist politicians beyond parliamentary committee level. Still wedded to the Westminster concept of
adversarial parliamentary politics, Faulkner could not envisage cabinet
government in which Unionists and Nationalists would be seated around
the same table. Unionists and Nationalists, in Faulkner's view, were so
fundamentally divided on the constitutional question, that the Unionist
Party was not prepared to admit to cabinet members of a party which it
viewed as potentially subversive of the region's constitutional status. He
was prepared to acknowledge that nationalist representatives had a role
which could be enhanced beyond that of mere opposition, but not
elevated to one of equality as would be implied by their being involved
in cabinet. On the wider question of North-South relations in Ireland, the
Unionist Party was prepared to be more radical, indicating that it would
consider a formal institution of an inter-governmental kind.[22]

On the question of the government of Northern Ireland itself, it
became clear at Darlington that the British government was much more
interested in an administration in which representatives from both the
nationalist and unionist communities could share executive responsibility. The line of questioning which its delegation pursued with the
Unionist Party made this objective evident.[23] In this, the government
was supported by the Alliance Party's delegation who argued in favour
of a community style administration operated through a series of execu-

tive committees established on the basis of party strengths in a new assembly. The Alliance party was, like the Unionist Party, favourably disposed to the idea of North-South political institutions.[24]

Although it did not attend the Darlington conference, the SDLP did publish its proposals for a political settlement in a pamphlet entitled *Towards a New Ireland*.[25] These proposals were radical since they posed a challenge to Northern Ireland's constitutional status by suggesting that the region become the joint responsibility of both the British and Irish governments. Coming from the main nationalist party this proposal amounted, in effect, to saying that the status of Northern Ireland as an exclusively British responsibility could not be made acceptable to the nationalist community. In its view, Northern Ireland had to become a shared responsibility of the two governments. In contrast to the Sinn Fein-IRA policy of 'Brits Out', the SDLP's approach could be represented more as an 'Irish In' policy. In practical terms, the SDLP proposed that both the British and the Irish governments should each appoint a commissioner to take joint, overall charge of the government of Northern Ireland, though leaving the day-to-day control of the region to an executive elected from an assembly of eighty-four members; the executive, according to these proposals, would have to reflect party strengths within the assembly which, itself would be elected on a PR system. The SDLP document further argued that these proposals should only be seen as providing for the 'interim government' of Northern Ireland pending the creation of a 'new system of Government in Ireland, democratically agreed by all sections of the people of Ireland, North and South'.[26]

Such proposals were not only radical in terms of the government of Northern Ireland itself, but they clearly signalled that the SDLP wished to see constitutional as well as institutional change. The joint responsibility proposal lay essentially in the constitutional realm and would have required the support of a majority in Northern Ireland if it was to meet the long established British government test for change of such a nature. The SDLP's proposals for internal government were also radical, given that they were based on a concept of political partnership which would confer equality of status and esteem on both the nationalist and unionist communities.

Quite obviously there was a wide gap between the major parties. The Unionist Party was still addressing the problem from a very traditional approach rooted in a firm determination to ensure that the constitutional status would be upheld and did so within familiar British concepts of governmental institutions. The SDLP was equally indicating a commitment to the nationalist goal of Irish unity and could only see Northern Ireland as a temporary phenomenom for which highly unusual constitutional and institutional arrangements would have to be made. Only in so far as it based its proposals for the ultimate destiny of the region on the democratic consent of 'all sections of the people of Ireland, North and South',[27] could it be said that the SDLP was indicating a move away from more hardline and traditional nationalist thinking about Irish unity. Consent lay at the heart of the British government's terms for constitutional change also, likewise for the Unionist Party. Set against the range of quite radical constitutional and institutional measures which the SDLP was proposing, the party's explicit acceptance of this consent may have appeared a rather insignificant change. Nonetheless, acceptance of this principle was to prove the basis on which political progress of a kind was to be achieved over the next twelve months. More immediately significant in terms of public perception of its stand, the SDLP was being urged by its own Deputy Leader to 'come out and say frankly that we are prepared to talk to anyone and to talk now'.[28]

So, despite the apparent failure of Whitelaw's first attempt to promote debate between Northern Ireland's constitutional parties, the basis for a political dialogue of sorts was gradually being laid down.

WHITELAW PROPOSES

Following Darlington, Whitelaw published a discussion document entitled *The Future of Northern Ireland*.[29] This document is of seminal importance for any understanding of the approach which was to characterize British policy towards Northern Ireland over the next two decades. As merely a discussion document it contained no firm proposals, but, for the first time since 1921, it did recognise the political complexities which had to be addressed and it clearly implied the parameters within which a British government would set about addressing them.

The contentious question of sovereignty over the region was the first substantive issue to be addressed. Whitelaw made it quite clear that while the British government would be prepared to consider a change in its constitutional status whereby the region could become part of an all-Ireland state, it would only do so on the understanding that such a change was sought by a majority of the people living there. However, in firmly signalling this basic stand, the discussion document did not rule out the possibility of 'some form of joint machinery, either at inter-parliamentary or at inter-governmental level' with the Republic of Ireland. Indeed, the discussion document admitted that 'There is now much common ground between a number of the Northern Ireland parties on the need for some form of joint Council'.[30]

With respect to the administration and government of the region, the document clearly indicated the British government's disposition towards some form of cross-community involvement. The point is made that 'the British democratic system only works where a regular alternation of parties is possible; that the real test of a democratic system is its ability to provide peaceful and orderly government, and that by that standard the existing system has failed in Northern Ireland; that other countries with divided communities have made special constitutional provision to ensure participation by all'.[31]

The last two sections of the document attempted to set down some key guidelines and principles for a new political settlement. On the constitutional issue it began by ruling out as unrealistic 'any proposal which considered Northern Ireland in isolation', i.e. the creation of an independent state outside the UK and the Repubic of Ireland.[32] It would appear that this was done, not because any political party was seriously arguing such a solution, but in order to emphasize that for as long as the region remained part of the UK, the authority of the UK government 'must be a necessary condition of the financial, economic and military assistance from which Northern Ireland benefits'.[33] It was, in effect, a warning against defying the ultimate wishes of that government and was clearly directed at those unionist politicians who seemed opposed to reform of the kind now being supported by the British government. The right of a majority to determine the future constitutional status could, if narrowly interpreted, exclude 'legitimate rights of other parties'.[34]

Significantly the document then discussed the interests of the Irish government and makes explicit the need to recognize that 'any new arrangements for Northern Ireland should, whilst meeting the wishes of Northern Ireland and Great Britain, be so far as is possible acceptable to and accepted by the Republic of Ireland . . . Such measures would seek . . . to make possible effective consultation and co-operation in Ireland for the benefit of North and South alike.'[35] From the heading and contents of this part of the document the phrase 'the Irish dimension' passed into common currency to denote North-South relationships and their inherent place in the search for a settlement.

The British document concluded by setting out the criteria which the UK government believed had to be met if that search was to be successful. Their importance warrants the reproduction in full of these criteria:

In accordance with the specific pledges given by successive UK Governments, Northern Ireland must and will remain part of the UK for as long as that is the wish of a majority of its people; but that status does not preclude the necessary taking into account of what has been described in this Paper as the 'Irish Dimension';

As long as Northern Ireland remains part of the UK the sovereignty of the UK Parliament must be acknowledged, and due provision made for the UK Government to have effective and continuing voice in Northern Ireland's affairs, commensurate with the commitment of financial, economic and military resources in the Province;

Any division of powers and responsibilities between the national and the regional authorities must be logical, open and clearly understood. Ambiguity in the relationship is a prescription for confusion and misunderstanding. Any necessary checks, balances for controls must be apparent on the face of a new constitutional scheme.

The primary purpose of any new institutions must be first to achieve a much wider consensus than has hitherto existed; and second to be such as will work efficiently and will be capable of providing the concrete results of good government: peace and order, physical development, social and economic progress. This is fundamental because Northern Ireland's problems flow not just from a clash of national aspirations or from friction between the communities, but also from the social and economic conditions such as inadequate housing and unemployment.

Any new institutions must be of a simple and business-like character, appropriate to the powers and functions of a regional authority.

A Northern Ireland assembly or authority must be capable of involving all its members constructively in ways which satisfy them and those they represent that the whole community has a part to play in the government of the Province. As a minimum this would involve insuring minority groups of an effective voice and a real influence; but there are strong arguments that the objective of real participation should be achieved by giving minority interests a share in executive power if this can be achieved by means which are not unduly complex or artificial, and which do not represent an obstacle to effective government.

There must be an assurance, built into any new structures, that there will be absolute fairness and equality of opportunity for all. The future administration of Northern Ireland must be seen to be completely even-handed both in law and in fact.

It is of great importance that future arrangements for security and public order in Northern Ireland must command public confidence, both in Northern Ireland itself, and in the UK as a whole. If they are to do so they must be seen in practice to be as impartial and effective as possible in restoring and maintaining peace and public order. In any situation such as that which obtains at present, where the Army and the civilian police force are both involved in maintaining law and order and combating terrorism, it is essential that there should be a single source of direct responsibility. Since Westminster alone can control the Armed Forces of the Crown this unified control must mean Westminster control. For the future any arrangements must ensure that the UK Government has an effective and a determining voice in relation to any circumstances which involve, or may involve in the future, the commitment of the Armed Forces, the use of emergency powers, or repercussions at international level.[36]

The government's preferences for new political structures emerged quite clearly from the above set of principles. In particular, the government was indicating that any new structures should involve representatives of both communities at all levels of decision making. For Faulkner's Unionist Party this was a preference which ran counter to a principle central to its proposals, namely that there could be no place in any cabinet for those representatives who ultimately wanted an end to Northern Ireland's separate existence. The government's discussion document, obviously anticipating the difficulties which could arise in this respect, also indicated that an early plebiscite would be held to ascertain 'The wishes of the people of Northern Ireland on their relationship to the UK and to the Republic'.[37] In other words the government was to invite the people of the region to indicate whether they wished to remain in the UK, or become part of an all-Ireland state separate from the UK. Since the outcome to such a poll was a foregone conclusion, it could only serve to underline Northern Ireland's continued membership of the UK and make it impossible for any representatives of the nationalist community to do other than accept that fact given their declared position on consent for constitutional change. Unionists, it was apparently hoped, could then be persuaded to accept Nationalists alongside them in cabinet.

A second matter of importance to the Unionist Party was also likely to be problematic on the basis of these criteria, Brian Faulkner's declared position that a regional government should control policing. The government's discussion document made it clear that control of the security forces, i.e. police and army, had to be unified, a condition that could only be met through Westminster control.[38] This was an absolute position and one which it was clear Unionists would have to accept if they wished to participate in new political structures.

The explicit recognition of the 'Irish Dimension' as part of the very first of the above set of criteria was of critical importance, especially to the nationalist community for whom it opened up the prospect of North-South political institutions. The absence of any mention of a direct involvement by the Republic's government in any new internal structures indicated that the British government was highly unlikely to accept innovations along the lines of the SDLP's joint authority proposal. It seemed, therefore, that on the basis of the government's criteria the Irish Dimension would have to be sought purely in terms of North-South structures.

The commitment to fairness and equality of opportunity as one of the criteria indicated that the reforms sought and won by the civil rights movement would have to be upheld and that, if necessary, further measures could be taken to reinforce and strengthen provisions for human rights. The document then concluded by indicating that it was the government's intention to engage in wide-ranging consultations within Northern Ireland prior to formulating proposals on new political structures for submission to parliament. There was to be, therefore, no face to face negotiations between the political parties themselves. Whatever new proposals would emerge would be the government's, though informed by the consultations which it was proposing to have with the political parties and a range of other interests.

CREATING NEW STRUCTURES

The publication of the government's discussion paper did not result in immediate acceptance of the above principles as the basis for the way forward. The political parties took time to consider the government's outline and it was not until the early spring of 1973 that serious consultations between them and the government commenced. Meantime, paramilitary violence continued to escalate. 467 persons were killed in 1972, the highest annual figure to be recorded over the twenty-seven years from 1969-96; the figures for 1973, although lower, were to suggest no let-up in the use of violence by either loyalist or republican paramilitaries. On its own this violence was to exercise its own pressure on politicians anxious to achieve a new beginning.[39]

The political pace began to quicken from March when a number of important events took place: a general election in the Republic of Ireland brought an end to a long period of uninterrupted government by Fianna Fail replacing that party with a coalition of the Fine Gael and Labour parties with Liam Cosgrave of Fine Gael as Taoiseach. Secondly, the border poll was conducted and it produced a 98 per cent vote in favour of Northern Ireland remaining part of the UK. Because of the obvious nature of the outcome and to avoid the acrimony that a campaign on the issue would entail, the SDLP and other nationalist groups had recommended that their supporters not vote, thus ensuring the very high margin in favour of the constitutional *status quo*.[40] Thirdly, the British government published a white paper containing its plans for new political structures.[41]

The significance of the new government in Dublin was that it represented in some of its leading ministers, most notably in Garret FitzGerald and Conor Cruise O'Brien, a new set of attitudes to the North.[42] Both men had frequently visited the North, had family connections there and had written extensively about its problems. Neither of them shared the more hardline attitudes which had been evident amongst sections of Fianna Fail; instead they shared an openness and a willingness to understand the concerns of Unionists as well as Nationalists, and were to bring these sympathies to bear on their government's policies towards Northern Ireland.

The border poll demonstrated unequivocal majority support for membership of the UK and, as such, could have been expected to have reassured Unionists that their constitutional status would be under no threat within any new institutional framework for the region. That it was not to have this effect would reveal a great deal about the pyschology of a political community which continued to see itself under threat no matter what the nature of reassurance about its position

WHITE PAPER

An intense debate on Whitelaw's proposals began within all political parties. In essence these amounted to a totally new concept of coalition government. Elections would be held on a proportional representation basis to a seventy-eight member assembly from which would be formed an executive of a cross-community, or 'power-sharing' kind to take responsibility for those functions of government which would be devolved to it.[43] It was not envisaged amongst these proposals that control over law-and-order would be devolved, at least not to begin with. In addition, the proposals included provision for a North-South Council which would promote co-operation between both parts of Ireland.[44] The white paper also contained a commitment to continuing the process of civil rights reform.[45]

Despite their differences, reactions from unionist leaders were uniformly negative, varying only in the degree of hostility displayed. Not unexpectedly, Unionists like Craig and Paisley were bitterly hostile to what they regarded as a 'sell-out' that, in their view, could only end in the ultimate subversion of Northern Ireland's place within the UK. They denounced the proposals and, by doing so in quite absolute terms, posed a serious challenge to any Unionist who might be tempted to see merit in them. Faulkner, as the unionist leader most likely to find himself in such a position, began by expressing his unhappiness with the white paper taking care, however, to allow himself room to manoeuvre by saying that 'we neither reject it totally nor do we accept it totally'.[46] Only the SDLP and Alliance, amongst the major parties, offered any words of welcome.

A BRAVE EXPERIMENT

The government's intention was to proceed with elections to the assembly and to leave negotiations on the formation of the executive to those elected to it. These elections were held in June and the new assembly met for the first time soon afterwards. The election results did not bode well for Whitelaw's plans. Of the seventy-eight seats, Unionists who were totally opposed to any sharing of executive power with Nationalists won twenty-six seats.[47] Those Unionists who supported Faulkner and appeared more likely to negotiate along the lines set down by Whitelaw won only twenty-four. The Alliance Party gained eight seats and the Northern Ireland Labour Party only one, while the SDLP won nineteen. Unionism was ominously divided, though with support from Alliance and Labour it seemed that an administration involving the SDLP and the Faulknerite Unionists might stand a reasonable chance of success. It was on this prospect that Whitelaw was to pin his hopes for a cross-community form of government over the coming months.

Following a summer recess, negotiations on the formation of an executive between the Faulknerite Unionists, the SDLP and the Alliance Party commenced in earnest in the autumn. They were protracted but, skilfully chaired by Whitelaw, the negotiations inched towards agreement. Finally, on the 21 November Whitelaw announced that a formula had been agreed in principle which enabled him to nominate a prospective 'power-sharing' executive.[48] The executive would consist of six Unionists, one Alliance and four SDLP ministers with Brian Faulkner as Chief Executive and the SDLP Leader, Gerry Fitt, his Deputy. Final agreement to bring the executive into operation had to await the outcome of negotiations on the North-South Council scheduled to take place some weeks later.

Reaction to Whitelaw's announcement was predictable. Anti-Faulknerite Unionists and their Paisleyite allies denounced it as 'the greatest betrayal since Lundy' and 'the worst possible news for those who want to keep Northern Ireland in the UK' while the IRA described the SDLP as 'arch-collaborators' and declared that it would 'destroy' the executive.[49] Paisley, Craig and their supporters immediately set about disrupting assembly meetings, but, initially, found no other means of venting their frustration.[50] Not until the next stage of the political process was completed did the opportunity for more concerted unionist opposition to the new political framework present itself. The IRA was not so constrained, and during the weeks that followed it intensified the bombing of civilian targets in Britain, as well as in Northern Ireland.

From many sections of the population at large, however, there was a warm welcome for the prospect of a cross-community administration, holding out as it did the hope that the communities themselves would soon emulate the example being set by a majority of their political leaders. As John Hume of the SDLP stated, the executive would represent the first occasion on which 'Protestant, Catholic and Dissenter' would be seen working together for the benefit of all sections of the community.[51] Just how difficult it would be to achieve this two-hundred year-old dream of the father of Irish republicanism, Wolfe Tone, the next six months would dramatically illustrate.

COUNCIL OF IRELAND

Although each of the three parties that had agreed the power-sharing executive, had also proposed the establishment of a North-South Council, wide areas of disagreement existed between them as to the form and functions of such a Council. The SDLP was very anxious to achieve a council which would have considerable power and influence.[52] The SDLP argued, firstly, that the political crisis in the North was not merely one affecting relationships between the unionist and nationalist communities living there, but that central to it were relationships between Unionists and the nationalist people of the whole of Ireland. In evidence, the SDLP quoted the main reason offered by Unionists themselves for being opposed to the SDLP's participation in the government of Northern Ireland, namely that because Irish unity was the SDLP's ultimate aim, its members could not be trusted to make the welfare of the North a top priority. This being so, the SDLP argued that Unionists' fears of Nationalists could only be allayed by a new and meaningful arrangement with the whole of nationalist Ireland whereby Unionists would be guaranteed that no attempt would be made to coerce them into any form of Irish unity. Secondly, the SDLP argued that in order to win the allegiance of the nationalist community for new regional institutions and, in particular, nationalist support for policing, a significant North-South, or all-Irish element, would have to be achieved; only then would it be possible to encourage Nationalists to play a full role in supporting and participating in such institutions. A council which would merely focus on practical forms of cooperation and be devoid of what the SDLP regarded as a politically significant role would not achieve these ends.

Unionists, on the other hand, had two concerns as far as North-South relationships were concerned. The first was a pragmatic desire to promote security, economic and social co-operation between both parts of the island. The second and more complicating concern was to achieve 'acceptance by the South of the right of the people of the North to self-determination'.[53] While the first was essentially non-controversial, the second concern presented severe difficulties given the historic refusal of Nationalists, North and South, to formally recognise as a 'right' unionist demands to separate not only themselves, but half a million Nationalists along with them from the rest of the Irish body politic. To Nationalists, accepting self-determination for 'the people of the North' would mean, in effect, self-determination for only one section of the northern population and, furthermore, would be seen as abandoning the South's claim on the North as expressed in Articles 2 and 3 of the Irish Constitution. Given nationalist opinion in the North as well as the feelings which could be aroused in the South, this was not a step which any Irish government felt itself free to take. However, without firm guarantees on this issue from the South, Unionists believed a North-South political institution would be represented as merely the first step on the road towards a united Ireland and that any unionist politician who agreed to such institutions would not survive. By and large this view was also shared by the Alliance Party.[54]

The Irish government's position was almost identical to that of the SDLP; it too believed in the necessity of a Council with significant functions, one which could address security and judicial matters on an all-island basis, as well as laying the basis for integrating aspects of the two economies.[55] The British government did not have a fixed view as to what shape a Council of Ireland should take, preferring to leave the details to the Irish to work out for themselves.

Negotiations on the shape and functions of a North-South institution took place at Sunningdale in England and involved the British and Irish governments as well as leading members of the North's prospective power-sharing administration;[56] representatives of the unionist groupings opposed to the power-sharing executive had been invited to the opening session, but not to the substantive sessions and so declined to attend at all. The outcome was the Sunningdale Agreement which proposed the establishment of a two-tier Council of Ireland, one an executive tier composed of government ministers from Belfast and Dublin and, the second, a parliamentary tier to be composed of members of the northern assembly and the Irish parliament.[57] To address unionist fears regarding the alleged territorial claims in the Irish Constitution, a declaration by the Irish government was included in the agreement which stated that it 'fully accepts and solemnly declares that there would be no change in the status of Northern Ireland until a majority of the people desired a change in that status'.[58] In terms of the powers and functions of the agreement it was proposed that these would lie in the areas of practical cooperation on social and economic matters, but through consultation with police authorities in both parts of the island would also deal with policing and security cooperation. Final ratification of the agreement was left to the northern assembly and to the Irish parliament.

In terms of what the various parties to the negotiations had been seeking, it certainly seemed as if the proposed Council of Ireland was much closer to realising the aims of the SDLP and the Dublin government, than it was to those of Brian Faulkner's Unionists and the Alliance Party. The council promised to have a substantial role in integrating aspects of the economies of both parts of Ireland, of harmonizing initiatives in border areas, as well as addressing security and policing issues on an all-island basis. Reassurance for Faulkner and his followers lay in two features of the agreement, the 'unanimity' rule for decision making and the Irish government's declaration on the status of the North, in particular the latter.[59] The unanimity rule would, Faulkner hoped, ensure that no decision could be taken which did not enjoy support in the North, while the latter could be represented as providing the kind of constitutional guarantees long sought by Unionists from the South.

Generally, except for the Sinn Fein-IRA element, who denounced it as a means of reinforcing partition,[60] the agreement was warmly welcomed by the nationalist community. However, to those Unionists who had not been invited to Sunningdale the Council of Ireland marked the final step in the betrayal of fundamental unionist interests.[61] In their view, the proposed Council of Ireland pointed to an alternative source of political authority to which they would be subject and, in the final analysis, one over which they believed they could exercise no control. They immediately set about its destruction and with it the destruction of the power-sharing executive. Within three weeks of the Sunningdale Agreement being signed, it was formally repudiated by the supreme policy making body of the Unionist Party, the Ulster Unionist Council.[62] As a result, Faulkner was forced to resign as leader of the Ulster Unionist Party to be replaced by Harry West.[63] Thus, just as he was assuming office as Chief Executive he was being deprived of the support of his own party. In effect, all that now remained to Faulkner by way of a political mandate was the support he had from his nineteen unionist assembly colleagues who had committed themselves to the power-sharing arrangement and who had also accepted the Sunningdale Agreement.

Worse was to come for Faulkner and the power-sharing executive when, in February 1974, Prime Minister Heath decided to call a UK general election. This provided opponents of the agreement with an immediate opportunity to rally and measure their support, objectives they were to achieve with considerable success. Of the twelve Northern Irish MPs elected in February eleven were Unionists opposed to the agreement, the twelfth was the SDLP's lone voice at Westminster, Gerry Fitt.[64] The elections had turned out to be effectively a referendum on the power-sharing and Council of Ireland package, with those opposing it victorious. The elections also resulted in the return to power of a Labour government under Harold Wilson and the appointment of Merlyn Rees as Secretary of State for Northern Ireland.

EXECUTIVE UNDER SIEGE

From the moment it took office on 1 January 1974, the power-sharing executive was clearly under siege, most particularly on its unionist flank. Consequently, despite the very commendable efforts and commitment of its members over the next four months to work the new arrangements, it faced a struggle far beyond its resources to overcome. Unionist pressure was unremitting, reaching new levels of disruption within the assembly following the February elections.[65] For a while this pressure proved somewhat ineffectual because whatever disruption might be caused, the power-sharing executive continued to enjoy support from a majority of the assembly members.

Outside the assembly opposition was hardening within the unionist community, especially amongst workers in a number of key utilities and industries in Belfast representatives of whom had formed the Ulster Workers Council (UWC).[66] The council began urging direct action in the form of an all-out strike, a tactic that was, initially, rejected by unionist politicians who preferred to confine their protests to the assembly chamber. However, within the assembly opposition to the power-sharing arrangement and to the Council of Ireland was winning no new converts and, given the arithmetic, a motion condemning the Sunningdale Agreement faced inevitable defeat. It was at this point that the UWC moved to take the initiative by declaring that an all-out strike would commence once the vote on the motion had been taken. The democratic justifiction was that following the February elections, unionist repesentation in the assembly no longer was a true reflection of the unionist community at large. Strike action commenced on 15 May, the day after the motion was defeated.

Despite their earlier opposition to strike action, Paisley, West and

Craig agreed to be co-opted on to the UWC, but it was the workers themselves, rather than the politicians who were to dictate the terms under which the strike was conducted.[67] After a very hesitant start the strike quickly gained support and within a week had achieved all-out status in most unionist areas. Intimidation by gangs of youths called out by the UDA ensured a response from reluctant businesses in many places, but, despite widespread reports of such intimidation, as the days passed there was no doubting that support for the strike was real and deeply felt. As electricity generation was reduced and the situation became critical in hospitals, on farms, in factories and in homes, the authorities seemed more and more powerless to deal with the crisis. The British Army refused to move into power plants and appeared reluctant to confront those who erected barricades to prevent traffic circulating. Slowly normal life ground to a virtual stand-still. Faced with such a massive display of opposition from his own community, Faulkner and his unionist colleagues resigned from the executive on 27 May bringing to an end Northern Ireland's first experiment in cross-community government. Unionists led by Craig and Paisley were triumphant and tens of thousands marched that afternoon to Stormont in a huge victory demonstration.

Ironically, the Council of Ireland which had infuriated so many Unionists and had helped win support for the strike never met. A legal challenge in Dublin by a former Fianna Fail minister, Kevin Boland, to the constitutionality of the Sunningdale Agreement had delayed its ratification by the Irish parliament,[68] while the collapse of the executive in Belfast sealed its fate.

PICKING UP THE PIECES

The collapse of the power-sharing executive was a major setback for the two governments as well as for the parties which had participated in the experiment. If the 'moderate' political forces in both communities could not win support for a joint undertaking in government, what hope was there for Northern Ireland? There was no easy answer and the outlook seemed very bleak indeed. The establishment of the executive had not brought peace any nearer, nor had it brought a reduction in the scale of the violence; the IRA and loyalist paramilitaries had continued their campaigns of bombing and killing at a high level throughout the first half of 1974.[69]

British policy in the aftermath of the executive's demise was to gradually focus political attention almost exclusively on the region's internal relationships apparently on the premise that the 'Irish dimension' was the fatal distraction that had undermined the power-sharing experiment. Also, instead of the British government taking the lead, it was decided that virtually full responsibility for negotiating a new political framework would be devolved to local politicians meeting in a constitutional convention. The convention would be elected on the same basis as the assembly had been, but apart from the requirement that any new arrangements would have to have 'cross-community support', the British government decided to leave the nature and details of that framework to its members. The intention to establish the convention was announced in June 1974, but elections to it did not take place until the following May.[70]

Meantime, another aspect of British policy had revealed itself, namely that a further attempt should be made to deal directly with the IRA. A concerted effort by churchmen and government ministers was made to encourage the IRA to announce a ceasefire in order to allow negotiations to get underway with Secretary of State Merlyn Rees stating that the government would not be found wanting if 'a genuine and sustained cessation of violence occurred'.[71] Eventually, after a number of false starts, the IRA did announce a ceasefire in February 1975 and there followed the first and only period of sustained contact between the British government and the IRA until the 1990s.[72]

Formally the ceasefire lasted until the end of 1975, but in effect, as any examination of the evidence reveals, it would be difficult to conclude that any cessation of violence had occurred at all – in fact more people were killed in 1975 than in 1974.[73] Nonetheless, throughout this period a form of contact between both government officials and the IRA existed through what were called 'incident centres' established to monitor the ceasefire. Whatever expectations the IRA had of the ceasefire and of their contacts with officials, and it would appear that some in the leadership believed that a British withdrawal was a real prospect, they were disillusioned. Rees and his officials were not at the point of conceding IRA demands for withdrawal. What they had meant by responding to a cessation of violence had more to do with the release of detainees than with the IRA's political aims. As a result, nothing positive was achieved by the ceasefire.

The Northern Ireland Constitutional Convention commenced its meetings in May 1975, but despite a number of hopeful signs, it failed to achieve the goal set for it by the British government.[74] In terms of its unionist membership the overwhelming majority opposed any form of power-sharing, or coalition with the SDLP while the latter would not agree any basis for government which did not provide its representatives with a place at the highest level.[75] The British government then dissolved the convention in the spring of 1976 and set about governing Northern Ireland directly while attempting to defeat terrorism primarily by a combination of military and economic means.[76]

For the next ten years, until the need for an Irish dimension had impressed itself on their minds to the point where *that* dimension became the priority, British ministers and their officials struggled to contain a crisis that increasingly proved to be beyond their resources. As for the local parties, a perceptible hardening of attitudes took place with the result that, as indicated at the beginning of this chapter, their respective external referents became more important than their relationships with each other: a majority of Unionists adopted a policy position which aimed at fully 'integrating' Northern Ireland into the UK, while the SDLP came close to adopting a policy of 'Brits Out' similar to that of Sinn Fein and the IRA,[77] before stressing the need for a joint initiative by both the British and Irish governments as a prelude to any fresh internal approach involving local parties.[78]

FIVE

SOURCES OF STRUCTURAL FAILURE

As we pointed out at the beginning of Chapter 4 most explanations of the conflict in Northern Ireland have emphasized its structural features and have proposed solutions based on alternative structures. Not only were the 1973 agreements essentially structural but so were all of the other attempts at a settlement which had preceded them and likewise those which followed until 1985. All were aimed at resolving the conflict by devising new political structures and eliminating interest-based differences. Indeed, the same is true of most efforts to bring peace to the island going back to the Act of Union in 1800. It is an impressive record of futility.

In divided societies, such as Northern Ireland, structural solutions require, as a critical prerequisite, the existence of strong cross-cutting. Given the glaring absence of such ties and the weakness of those that do exist, the reliance on structural approaches in Northern Ireland is surprising. The weakness of overlapping ties between the communities which could limit the outbreak and escalation of conflict has been noted by many observers.[1] As Ross, in particular, argues:

Cross-cutting ties theory emphasizes how the strength and configuration of economic, social, political and affective ties among members of a society affect the expansion of conflicts and make their peaceful resolution more likely. Consider two different patterns: one in which an individual's multiple identities and affiliations reinforce each other, and a second in which the same identities and affiliations can compete with each other at different times. In the situation of reinforcing ties, a person's kin group, residence, age group, ritual group, and political affiliations all place the person with a core group of people who share those same identities. In contrast, in the cross-cutting ties situation, there is variation in the people with whom any individual shares different identities.[2]

The significance of this from our point of view is that the management of conflict in societies with cross-cutting ties is very different from that in societies, like Northern Ireland, whose separate communities possess exclusive, reinforcing intra-community ties. As Ross also points out:

> In societies with a reinforcing social structure, conflict is expansive and difficult to resolve because the mobilization of others in one's core group is relatively easy, because there are fewer people directly interested in resolving disputes, and because conflict may persist unless a common external foe appears to push disputants to resolve their differences.[3]

Although there is some disagreement about the magnitude of the problem in specific areas, there is no doubt that the pattern in Northern Ireland conforms to the reinforcing cleavage pattern, i.e. an absence of significant cross-cutting ties. On its own, the pattern of reinforcing cleavages tends to exacerbate the conflict by polarizing the parties, enabling extensive mobilization based on group and communal solidarity, intensifying competition, and hardening hostile stereotypes. As a result parties become isolated from each other, with a consequence that only magnifies each of these tendencies.[4] Proposals for a settlement which receive little or no support in one community have, therefore, in the absence of cross-cutting ties, almost no chance of being effectively implemented, short of being simply imposed by one party on the other. The one-sided origins of proposals such as complete integration into the UK, unification with the Republic, or an independent Northern Ireland have effectively placed them out-of-court. Indeed, as we have seen in the previous chapter, even power-sharing, which appeared the most attractive basis for a settlement in the early 1970s, had so little support within the unionist community, precisely because it seemed only to advantage Nationalists, that it too lacked sufficient support to be successfully implemented. Each proposal betrayed the absence of relationships that would mitigate the conflict sufficiently to allow implementation. Beyond this, there was significant dispute even within the originating communities about the merits of their own proposals.[5]

Despite serious efforts to create opportunities for cross-cutting relationships, for example by the adoption of a preferential proportional representation system for local and regional elections and by the creation of a political centre drawing support from both communities, the results were not encouraging. The new voting system produced little or no strategic voting and the few electoral shifts that have occurred have been for the sake of intra-communal loyalty. The Alliance Party, the one-time hope of the centrists, achieved a high water mark of about thirteen per cent of the vote in the mid 1970s, but that had declined to between seven to nine per cent by the mid 1990s.

As we have seen, between 1964 and 1974, two major structural efforts for dealing with the conflict were attempted. The first began by extending civil rights to the nationalist community and by promoting economic modernization. We lump civil rights and modernization together because they were based on the same assumptions and were promoted by the same parties. The second was through the power-sharing and the Sunningdale agreements promoted by the British government after direct rule in 1972. Following a brief review of the civil rights-modernization efforts, this chapter will devote itself to the power sharing-Sunningdale approach.

CIVIL RIGHTS AND MODERNIZATION

The parallel civil rights and modernization efforts of Terence O'Neill were discussed in Chapters 2 and 3. While neither was grounded in a coherent or systematic approach to conflict resolution, serious efforts were made to implement substantive aspects of both. The closest we get to a theoretical justification is to be found in certain speeches made by O'Neill, but even then his comments are slim and undeveloped.

The civil rights and modernization efforts reinforced each other in two crucial ways consistent with what we know about the dynamics of social and political change. Rather than appease the disadvantaged, both efforts fuelled grievances, intensified demands, and promoted reaction. Expectations and anxiety simultaneously increased. In a variety of ways, the old patterns of isolation and togetherness were intensified. Eventually intimidation of one community by the other led to greater internal migration than had been seen in Western Europe since the end of World War II,[6] and intra-communal surveillance and control by local paramilitaries increased. Most importantly, the rate of social mobilization in the two communities increased dramatically. More than in the past, these events produced, especially in ghetto areas, much greater public participation in political forms of mobilization. The majority of the nationalist community, which had previously elected to remain distant from active political involvement, came to demand a productive and representative role in the government of Northern Ireland. The more militant Nationalists, supporters of Sinn Fein and the IRA, prepared to renew the war to free Ireland of British rule. Unionists, particularly those who described themselves as Loyalists, as always, alert to even minor threats, began to organize against the perceived Catholic threat as early as 1966, most notably under the leadership of Ian Paisley. By the late 1960s, Protestant paramilitaries and unionist factions of all stripes were marching in large numbers against any concessions to what they claimed was a nationalist agenda.[7]

When most of the civil rights agenda had been satisfactorily dealt with, the expectation among moderate Unionists was that Catholic demands would begin to subside. Yet, the conflict persisted. Horowitz explains how the political and social mobilization encouraged by both the civil rights movement and O'Neill's modernization efforts, actually contributed to the momentum of the conflict. 'Social mobilization, it is argued, fosters ethnic competition especially in the competitive modern sector, for 'it is the competitor within the modern sphere who feels the insecurities of change most strongly and who seeks the communal shelter of "tribalism", even as he seeks the many new rewards brought by modernization'.[8] O'Neill and others in his camp seemed to be unaware of these possibilities. The ethnic mobilization encouraged by civil rights and modernization efforts was intensified by the massive ethnic migration that occurred in several places, most notably in Belfast, after the 1969 riots.[9]

The modernizing wing of the Unionist Party did not appreciate that such would be the effects of the kind of social mobilization witnessed in Northern Ireland in the mid to late 1960s. O'Neill assumed that sameness of social status produced satisfaction rather than competition, as predicted by social mobilization theorists. Indeed, O'Neill's failing was fundamental in that he could not see that ethnic conflict is an integral part of the modernization process in ethnically divided societies.[10] It was as though Unionists and certain elements of the civil rights movement believed that the unsettled historical issues did not require resolution.

The social mobilization literature is persuasive in its argument that the changes brought about by reforms and modernization would be likely, in the Northern Ireland situation, to lead to intensified conflict. Yet, naively, both civil rights advocates and O'Neill believed that their efforts might lead to a pacification of Northern Ireland. They assumed either that cross-cutting ties existed or they would be created. The extremists on both sides suffered no such illusions.

POWER-SHARING

The power-sharing agreements were the most far-reaching effort prior to 1985 to resolve the Northern Ireland conflict. The proposals appeared to deal with most of the major grievances of the nationalist community while maintaining the pledge to Unionists that the constitutional status of the North within the UK would be protected. The SDLP's acceptance of these agreements gave a number of its leading members, as representatives of the nationalist community, a substantial share in the governance of the North. Secondly, the Irish Dimension to the conflict, a key plank in the SDLP's programmme, was formally recognized through the Council of Ireland proposal. The council provisions were extremely important because they offered the nationalist community in the North a measure of protection provided by the southern government. Republicans, those affiliated with either Sinn Fein or the IRA, however, rejected the agreements immediately, arguing that they effectively frustrated the Irish people's right to self-determination by retaining the link with Britain and in doing so, had recruited Nationalists to uphold that link.[11]

The Alliance Party welcomed the agreements because they democratized the Northern Ireland system and yet maintained the link with Great Britain. Alliance had insisted that a government composed of representatives of both major communities would resolve a dispute fundamentally based on mutual misconceptions. A substantial number of Unionists were also prepared to accept the proposals because they maintained the link to Great Britain with a return to a devolved form of government. Many others, as we have seen, opposed the admission of the disloyal minority into the government, and they would not accept even a consultative role for Dublin in the formal affairs of the North. In their minds, there was no doubt that this was a move toward unification.

Unionist resistance to the power-sharing agreements was consistent with the majoritarian norms associated with fifty years of devolved government in which the British Parliament had allowed the Northern Ireland government a free hand. Many Unionists argued that there appeared no justifiable reason why any minority party should be admitted to government in the contrived manner advanced by the power-sharing agreement, especially when that party was committed to the abolition of the very institutions in which it was being asked to participate.

Most importantly, unionist opposition to the power-sharing and Council of Ireland agreements was consistent with previous, and successful, experiences of resistance to British policy – the most famous instance in the period from 1912 to 1914 when Home Rule was being negotiated. Resistance was so great at that time that it nearly precipitated a constitutional crisis in Britain.[12] Unionist compliance with British policy, then as in 1974, was clearly conditional, as it had been for almost 300 years, on Britain's support for the unionist view of government.

The Ulster Workers' Council strike pulled together the main forces of strident unionism, both political and paramilitary, in a concerted and ultimately successful attempt to bring down the power-sharing executive. As George Dangerfield points out:

This extra-parliamentary action was supported by the leading anti-powersharing politicians, such as Ian Paisley and the former Unionist cabinet minister, William Craig, but the real strength of the strike lay with Protestant paramilitary organizations; the Ulster Defence Association (UDA), the Ulster Volunteer Force, the Ulster Special Constabulary Association and the Orange Volunteers.[13]

When white-collar workers and the British Army failed to challenge the UWC's control of electricity generating facilities, it was clear that the challenge to powersharing had prevailed. The unionist members of the executive were forced to resign and the executive collapsed. The loyalist coalition relied on the historic unwillingness of the British to intervene in direct confrontation with Protestant unionism. While British officials and politicians criticized and condemned the strike, there was nevertheless no sustained effort to force an end to it. In 1912-14 and again this time, the British decided against a collision with unionism.

INTRA-ETHNIC RIVALRIES

While the movement against power-sharing underscored the absence of cross-cutting ties and the appeal of basic interests peculiar to one community or the other, it also revealed the manner in which intra-community, or intra-ethnic forces and rivalries compete and colaesce. This was most evident at the time of the power-sharing crisis within the unionist community, but it would soon also become evident within the nationalist communty. Unionists, despite the existence of deep fissures in their political ranks, had shown themselves, by and large, able to contain and control rivalries within their own community and prevent them from overriding the greater need for solidarity against the threat posed by power-sharing and the Council of Ireland. Once the threat receded the rivalries and fissures they had produced quickly surfaced again. However, as in 1974, future events would reveal that any threat to their basic position would quickly be met by the restoration of that solidarity. Understanding the nature of these fissures is, nonetheless, very important to our discussion of developments in the decades that followed 1974 and the next section is devoted to a consideration of their effects following the collapse of the power-sharing agreements.

The party most vulnerable to the effects of any threat to unionism has been the Ulster Unionist Party (the UUP as it became most commonly known from the 1970s). For the most part, the party expresses what Jennifer Todd calls the Ulster-British ideology, an amalgam of affection for Britain, insistence on individual liberty, and commitment to economic progress.[14] The party does not flinch in its opposition to the unification of Ireland and, once Stormont fell and the immediate threat of power-sharing had been removed, it proposed the full integration of Northern Ireland into Great Britain. Only when there was little indication of any British interest in such integration, did the party grudgingly move towards an acceptance of the need for a form of what it would term as responsibility sharing with the SDLP, though all the time opposed to close ties with the Irish Republic.[15]

Its long period in government had given the UUP a sense of invincibility that was not seriously challenged until the civil rights movement launched its campaign. While the North remained more or less at peace with itself, the covenantal tradition within unionism had remained a marginal political force. However, once the turmoil of the civil rights period produced dissent within and without the ranks of the UUP, the covenantal tradition emerged as a potent element. As we saw in Chapter 3, this gave rise to the formation of the Democratic Unionist Party founded by Ian Paisley.

The DUP is committed to the preservation of a Protestant state for a Protestant people, indeed the very existence of a Protestant people requires the preservation of the state.[16] A united Ireland, heavily influenced if not dominated by the Catholic Church is a major motivating factor for many members of the DUP which always favoured a return to a devolved government for Northern Ireland within the United Kingdom but with no more than normal inter-state, functional links with the South.[17] Power-sharing, from the DUP perspective compromised the majoritarian principle that alone ensured the survival of a Protestant state. With regard to Britain, the DUP was bound to the severest form of the covenantal tradition, one in which an 'individual . . . supports a particular definition of the existing regime so strongly that he is willing to break laws, or even take up arms, to recall it to its "true" way'.[18] It was essentially this tradition that had threatened mutiny against the Crown during the Home Rule crisis of 1912-1914.

A second dimension to the DUP's motivation has been a visceral anti-Catholicism, to a considerable extent personified in the dominant figure of Ian Paisley and the other clerical figures in the party. As we pointed out in Chapter 1 this very Calvinist tradition holds that Catholics cannot be trusted on religious grounds, and so neither can they be trusted on political grounds. Historically those holding such views at first abstained from trying to convert the presumably damned Catholics. Allowing Catholics to convert, as later happened, did not, however, result in reconciliation between Catholics and Protestants. According to Miller:

Now, however, Catholics were being treated as individuals. Not surprisingly, few were converted, and the refusal of the vast majority left them individually responsible for their contumacy. Though no theologian would have put it this way, in effect Catholics were offered the opportunity to demonstrate their election, and, virtually to a man, they turned it down. The . . . evidence provided for the first time 'empirical' verification that the Catholics were not among the elect.[19]

It is in this light that Paisley and his religious following understand the peculiarly Catholic nationalist threat.

Finally, there is the working class element of the DUP, the segment that was so influential in the success of the anti-power-sharing strike and that figures so large in the collective memory of the loyalist paramilitary movement. While much attention has been given to the economic discrimination against Catholics throughout Northern Ireland's history, it is important to note that Protestant workers have also suffered, from time to time, from prolonged recession, economic disadvantage, and high rates of unemployment. In the Belfast shipyards, in particular, employment was always vulnerable to the unstable conditions of the market.

From its beginnings, the DUP also had a certain political advantage since it had not been in government, nor even in existence during the time of the early civil rights agitation, and thus could not be held responsible for the civil rights debacle. Nor had it spawned the 'traitor' O'Neill and his, from the DUP's perspective, weak-kneed successors. Indeed one of the striking differences between the two parties was in the nature and security of the leadership. The Ulster Unionist Party had, from its inception, been a 'bottom up' party – that is, its leaders had to keep in close touch with grassroots opinion. After all it was the Orange Order with its fraternal instincts that had launched and sustained the party; and it was devolution and a highly decentralized local government structure which added to the sense of importance of the individual activist. The DUP, on the other hand, was very much the property of its leader, Ian Paisley. His unquestioned rhetorical and organizational gifts gave him total command over the rank and file. When he spoke, the party spoke.[20]

There were, of course, divisions within the nationalist ranks as well, divisions that had their origins in the mid-nineteenth century but which solidified in the period following the height of the civil rights movement. The major distinction most often cited involves the commitment to use violence to achieve the unification of Ireland made by Sinn Fein-IRA and rejected by the nationalist SDLP. In the 1970s Sinn Fein remained outside the northern political system. It did not engage in elections and played only a minor support role for the IRA. Nonetheless, it was clear that Sinn Fein's support was greatest in predominantly nationalist working class urban and rural areas. Amongst the middle-classes and in more mixed areas, the SDLP held sway. Beginning with the prison protests by IRA prisoners in the late seventies and the ensuing hunger strikes, this would change and Sinn Fein would emerge as a strong rival to the SDLP for electoral support within the nationalist community.

POLITICAL COMPETITION

These divisions established the essential framework within which the structural efforts to resolve the conflict were pursued. Horowitz analyzes the nature of political competition in non-ethnic and ethnic two-party systems, such as that in Northern Ireland. His observations on ethnic two-party systems will not only help us to understand why an exclusively structural strategy in a divided setting, like power-sharing, will likely fail, but it will help in fundamental ways to expose the forces that contribute to the intensity and persistence of the conflict. The pattern described by Horowitz, we will argue, has had a continuing and important influence on the course of the conflict.

Horowitz describes the dynamics of this model by saying that 'the two ethnically based parties are not in the same competitive system. Since the parties are ascriptively defined, no significant number of floating voters is located between them. Competition, if it comes, will be located on the flanks in the form of new parties appealing for support within each ethnic group. Voters who may shift party allegiances are located at the extremes. The threat of such competition drives both parties to protect their flanks, thus pushing their positions apart.'[21] It is a truism in Northern Ireland that there is no cross-over voting of any substance. It is a rare event when a seat at any level, European, Westminster, or local assembly, changes from one community to another. The voting data in Table 5.1 show clearly the constancy in share of the vote at the different electoral levels.[22]

Horowitz offers three major explanations as to why this competitive configuration exacerbates the conflict. 'First, there is one principal issue axis – the ethnic conflict axis – which pre-empts others. All parties are positioned on it.'[23] This is precisely the point we made above in reference to the existence of reinforcing ties and the absence of cross-cutting ties. The divisive issues are not only aligned unilaterally, they reinforce one another. Inter-ethnic group politics is pre-empted. This means that there is little relief from the ethnic character of politics. The one exception is the Alliance party whose share of the vote has, however, rarely been above ten per cent.

TABLE 5.1   Political party competition in Northern Ireland

	SINN FEIN	SDLP	UUP	DUP	APNI
1982 (N.I. Assembly)	10.1	18.8	29.7	23.0	9.3
1983 (Westminster)	13.4	17.9	34.0	20.0	8.0
1987 (Westminster)	11.4	21.1	37.8	11.7	10.0
1992 (Westminster)	10.0	23.5	34.5	13.1	8.7
1996 (N.I. Forum)	15.6	21.5	24.5	17.4	7.0
1997 (Westminster)	16.0	24.1	32.7	13.6	8.0

'Second, there is party competition, or the possibility of it, within ethnic groups. The possibility of intragroup party competition creates strong incentives for parties to be diligent in asserting ethnic demands, the more so when they consider the life-or-death implications of that competition for the party's fortunes. Outbidding for ethnic support is a constant possibility.'[24] By 1980, the DUP had become a major rival of the UUP, and Ian Paisley had become the single largest vote getter among Unionists. It was well understood in unionist circles that Paisley could control the unionist agenda by moving further to the right as circumstances demanded. A similar phenomenon affected the SDLP when a more explicitly nationalist agenda began to overtake the reform agenda from the mid 1970s on. After the hunger strikes were concluded, Sinn Fein decided to pursue an electoral strategy and in 1983, won nearly forty per cent of the nationalist vote in local assembly elections. This prompted an SDLP reassessment of its electoral strategy and an eventual re-evaluation of the entire situation by both the Irish and British governments.

'Third, because ethnicity is a largely ascriptive affiliation, the boundaries of party support stop at the boundaries of ethnic groups.'[25] There are many working-class conservatives in Britain, but there are very few

Catholic Unionists in Northern Ireland. In an ascriptive system, it is far more important to take effective steps to reassure ethnic supporters than to pursue will-o'-the-wisps by courting imaginary voters across ethnic lines. The near impossibility of party competition for clientele across ethnic lines means an absence of countervailing electoral incentives encouraging party moderation on ethnic issues.[26] Statistics on potential party support show just how minimal the possibility of cross-over voting is in Northern Ireland. For example, in one survey, when questioned as to which political party Catholic and Protestant respondents felt closest, there was no significant crossing of the religious divide by either group.[27] In other words, hardly any Protestants claimed to be close to nationalist parties and hardly any Catholics claimed to be close to unionist parties. The one exception was the Alliance Party which attracted support from ten per cent of the Protestants questioned and from fourteen per cent of the Catholics.

We wish to add a fourth reason which reinforces and strengthens the tendency of each of the above to polarize the Northern Ireland system. While the necessity to end the violence was agreed to by almost everyone, even the paramilitaries using this language, there has been relatively little analysis of the political impact of chronic violence. In his study of democracies, Powell argues that elite attitudes toward political violence are a major factor affecting the success or failure of democratic government.[28] In Northern Ireland, as we pointed out in Chapter 4, elites have consistently demonstrated substantial ambivalence towards the use of violence for political objectives. In many ways, Protestants and Catholic communities parallel each other in this respect. This view of violence helps us to understand the Horowitz model by demonstrating that intra-group tensions not only push the ethnic groups apart, they also allow the more extremist groups to pull the moderate parties towards the poles. Time and again, this pattern seems to have been repeated in both communities.

As Powell argues, 'the accumulated grievances and hatred caused by so many deaths and attacks made development of cooperative democratic action that much more difficult. Moreover, as long as fundamental change in the political community was demanded, violently, by one side, and violently opposed by the other, there was simply no room for democratic compromise.'[29] The magnitude of the violence from the early 1970s to the early 1980s should not be underestimated. The combination of killings, injuries, bombings and the omnipresent threat of violence meant that few people completely managed to escape the violence in some form or other. It was very easy, therefore, to personalize the violence.

In this context, Powell makes his argument that 'it is hard to escape the conclusion that the reactions of the democratic parties are at least as important as the terrorist strategies or military sympathies'.[30] In the early 1970s, major segments of the Unionist Party were still either condoning or ignoring extremist violence against the nationalist community. Meantime, neither unionist group was willing to propose measures designed to secure the SDLP's endorsement of the regime. Unionists were not in error when they charged that the IRA and the SDLP shared the same general objective of a united Ireland. The alleged difference in means was, for them, of little consequence and thus all Catholics were, at least, potential conspirators.[31]

Within the nationalist community, unionist attitudes towards the RUC's and the British Army's aggressive counter-terrorist tactics were sufficient to persuade most Nationalists that unionist leaders were prepared to see the violence against their neighbourhoods continue. At the outset of the conflict, especially in the period 1969-71, many constitutional nationalist politicians found it difficult to condemn violence which appeared to be committed in defence of their own community.[32] Nationalists had come to recognize that it was the Northern Ireland system and not the regime that needed to be changed. In both cases, democratically elected leaders exhibited varying degrees of ambivalence about the violence committed by the extremists within their respective communities.

Sinn Fein's post-hunger strikes strategy of 'The ballot paper in one hand and the Armalite in the other', represented the most explicit expression of this ambivalence. The theme recalled a tradition of ambivalence toward violence that had played an important role in the history of the conflict. Almost one hundred years previously, Parnell often appeared to threaten the British with the possibility of losing control over Irish politics to the violent insurrectionists associated with the Land League.[33] 'Deal with me now', Parnell appeared to say to Prime Minister Gladstone, 'because I can't be sure just how long the agrarian radicals can be held in check'. While the SDLP strongly rejected temptations to be drawn into such an ambivalent approach, the hunger strikes of 1981 did place the party in an extremely difficult position as demands on communal loyalty intensified. The SDLP's decisions to stand down its candidates for the two Fermanagh-South Tyrone by-elections in 1981, the first which led to the election of Bobby Sands, the second when Sands died two months later, revealed the depth of the party's discomfort. The SDLP's discomfort allowed Unionists to make the accusation that there were no substantial differences between Nationalists and Republicans.

On the unionist side, the conditionality of allegiance contained within the covenantal tradition, allowed for the emergence of a paramilitary tradition at odds with the well-known law-abiding propensity of the Protestant community. Such paramilitarism was not new; the creation of the Ulster Volunteer Force during the Home Rule crisis of 1912-14 was an earlier example of a phenomenon which built on the Orange Order and its precursors. The Orange Order has traditionally promoted participation in the defence of Northern Ireland across class lines. The parades, for which the Order is so well-known, are seen as provocative and triumphal by the nationalist community and have routinely been associated with violence. Yet, it would be unthinkable for most unionist politicians to abstain from participation in some type of parade during the 'marching season'. The paramilitary forces which emerged in the early 1970s did so as control of the police, upon which Unionists had depended for their first line of defence since Northern Ireland had been established, moved to Westminster. Unionist and Protestant Ulster was once again taking steps to defend itself. The relationship between certain unionist factions and leaders and the paramilitaries has never been satisfactorily examined, but it is clear, for example, that during the general strike of 1974, there was a close working relationship between paramilitary and political leaderships.

Nor is this ambivalence confined to Nationalists and Unionists. The British government itself has engaged in behaviour reminiscent of the outrages of the English colonial administration described by Richard Lebow.[34] False arrests and imprisonment, over 300,000 house searches since 1969, torture, the alleged shoot-to-kill policy, ambushes, and a pattern of harassment and intimidation are all part of the British record in Northern Ireland. The Diplock Courts, in which a defendant is tried by a single judge without benefit of jury, continue to be sustained despite its obvious inconsistency with British judicial norms.[35]

In the South a degree of ambivalence was also evident amongst political elites. There, leading members of the Fianna Fail government were dismissed from office and subsequently tried having been suspected of involvement in attempts to import arms for use in Northern Ireland to defend Catholic areas following the violence of 1969.[36] Fianna Fail, which also styles itself the Republican Party, has, since its foundation in 1926, been the most outspoken anti-partitionist party in the South. While eschewing violence to remove partition Fianna Fail, rhetorically, maintained a position which seemed to allow a degree of ambivalence towards violence to be tolerated, provided that ambivalence did not endanger its own position, or the security of the southern state.

Within the two communities attitudes towards violence were revealed in several surveys. In his 1968 'Loyalty Survey', Richard Rose asked Catholics and Protestants if they thought it would be right to use 'all means necessary' to achieve a united Ireland or to maintain the union with Britain respectively.[37] The responses were as follows:

TABLE 5.2   'Using all means necessary'

	Protestants	Catholics
yes	52	13
no	45	83
don't know	3	4

Obtained almost on the eve of the present conflict, this evidence suggests that while there was a degree of tolerance for 'all means necessary' (including violence) in both communities it was four times greater in the Protestant community than amongst Catholics. Yet it was from the latter that the greater violence was to come when conflict did break out two years later.

In Mulvihill's own doctoral research conducted in Derry in 1973, related questions were asked concerning support for violence as a means of social control and, secondly, as a means to achieve social change.[38] Support was measured with respect to high and low levels of violence. The results are in Table 5.3:

TABLE 5.3

	Support for Social Control		Support for Social Change	
	Violence High	Violence Low	Violence High	Violence Low
Catholics	6.0	94.0	30.0	70.0
Protestants	69.4	30.6	8.0	92.0

The most striking thing about this data is that it again suggests that Protestants are much more likely to condone the use of violence for political ends than are Catholics. These results are consistent with the general finding that the advantaged are more likely to support violence for social control than are the disadvantaged to support violence for social change. The data, not contradicted since, seem to confirm the view of Unionists as a highly threatened population attempting to hold on to the residues of power. Equally important, however, is the fact that a substantial proportion of the Catholic community supports violence for social change. Simultaneously, however, both communities overwhelmingly condemn the violence associated with the other community, whatever the motivation.

A Catholic priest once described to one of the authors how he had to gather his thoughts about the use of violence when he was called upon to preside over the funeral of an IRA man killed by British troops during an attack on a police station. He talked approvingly about the church's position that membership in the IRA caused immediate excommunication, and he talked passionately about how his church and his service would not be used to provoke the IRA. Before the conversation ended, however, he spoke very quietly about how sometimes he lay awake, tormenting himself with the thought that the Catholic population would still be on its knees were it not for the IRA's violent campaign. Indeed, Catholics frequently insist they will never again go down on their political knees.[39] The metaphor mirrors directly unionist claims that they (Unionists) will 'never surrender'.

CONSEQUENCES

The competitive political system outlined above produced two structural patterns that substantially contributed to the persistence and the intensity of the conflict. Each consequence tended to distort the relationships between the major parties. First, the major parties were far less interested in between-group than within-group politics. Electoral strategies focused on within-group prospects and only very rarely took into consideration between-group politics. The proportional representation system that was intended, mistakenly as it turned out, to usher in a moderate centre actually contributed to this polarization by ensuring little more than the certification of the census results. The Alliance Party, once thought to be the beneficiary of this move to the centre actually diminished its political support over the period of the 'troubles'.

Second, the parties and their leaders from the two ethnic groups were increasingly unable to negotiate with each other and were, as the conflict escalated, almost totally incapable of empathizing with each other. Indeed, apart from the brief but aborted efforts in 1980 during the Secretary of State's Conference, fifteen years, 1976-1991, elapsed between all-party talks being held. There were almost no significant contacts between nationalist and unionist politicians throughout this entire period, a stunning indicator of political isolation given how small is the geographic territory involved.

In some ways, as Volkan points out, long-term involvement in conflict renders parties increasingly inept at dealing with each other and thus with the conflict.[40] It was too costly for politicians to interact since, in doing so, they risked the alienation of crucial supporters. In a filmed interview, Gregory Campbell, a DUP representative from Derry, was asked if he would talk with Martin McGuinness, a leading Sinn Fein representative, if it could be arranged. Campbell replied by asking what his supporters would say if he sat down to talk with the men who killed their brothers and husbands and fathers. According to Campbell his supporters would say that there was only one way to deal with men like McGuinness, and that was to 'kill them'.[41] Men who in 1974 were prepared to join together in a power-sharing government, now mirrored the population in having little to do with one another. Many Unionists saw little distinction between the SDLP's John Hume and Sinn Fein's Gerry Adams, making discussions even with Hume a controversial undertaking. Meantime, Nationalists appeared to be much more interested in talking to their fellow Nationalists in the Republic or to politicians in Britain than in negotiating with representatives of the unionist community at home.

STRUCTURAL FAILURE

Not only did the structural efforts of the 1970s fail, but they contributed to the polarization of the conflict. While the structural account is not an inaccurate reading of this conflict, it is far from complete and cannot answer several important questions we will attempt to address in the remainder of this book. As Mulvihill and Ross point out: 'Structural explanations of the Northern Ireland conflict seem not so much wrong as incomplete, for they never address directly the question of the persistence of intense conflict.'[42]

An alternative view suggests that civil rights and power-sharing might have developed cross-cutting ties and multiple loyalties where they did not previously exist. This may have been one of the major incentives behind the nationalist SDLP's enthusiastic support of power-sharing. We have already mentioned that the civil rights-modernization theories had been expected to produce cross-cutting ties in the short-term, and they did not. Power-sharing suggested the possibility of governmental and electoral coalitions that would have created necessary cross-cutting ties.

Although the theory was never tested in Northern Ireland, owing to the workers' strike of 1974, many Nationalists came to suspect that power-sharing merely formalized their minority status. For Unionists, however, the powersharing experiment set in motion very divisive forces which challenged the very existence of an autonomous and Protestant Northern Ireland.

Even though our major reservation about structural approaches to peacemaking in Northern Ireland has to do with the absence of cross-cutting ties, we want to draw attention to three further criticisms of structural approaches that have special relevance in the Northern Ireland situation. First, even if cross-cutting ties were present, they would almost certainly have not been sufficient to provide a basis for resolving the Northern Ireland conflict. In short, the conflict was too polarized for cross-cutting ties to produce the anticipated results. Nordlinger argues that cross-cutting ties will only create the kinds of cross-pressures that will lead to moderation when the sources of division are equally salient. This is surely not the case in Northern Ireland where religious and national identities are more important than other sources of division.

Second, structural explanations, as Ross argues, don't identify which interests each side sees as vital.[43] We have already pointed out that intra-communal divisions within each community make it difficult to determine which interests are vital. An example will help illustrate this dynamic. The city of Derry was nearly destroyed in the early 1970s by a relentless IRA bombing campaign. Bombed-out buildings and homes were everywhere, thousands of security forces, including as many as 7,000 British soldiers, patrolled the streets in this city of 80,000. The IRA attempted to make the city ungovernable. In the late 1970s, a well-known local figure, Paddy Doherty, began an ambitious and very successful effort to re-build the city. In 1987, Doherty took one of the authors on a tour of 'his' city and pointed out all the evidence of reconstruction and vitality, including the many new jobs that were being provided to the Catholic community. However, the benefits of economic reconstruction to the economically depressed Catholic community were lost on the Sinn Fein leadership of Derry. Later that afternoon, when a leading Sinn Fein activist was asked to comment on Doherty's efforts, his response was quick and to the point, 'We tried to bomb the city into submission, and he re-built it. What do you think we think of him?' It was plainly difficult for a working-class Catholic to know what to do in such a fractured environment. Disagreement about interests was endemic and critical.

In this regard, for example, one might hear it said many times that the major objectives of the civil rights campaign were attained and yet the conflict expanded. Combined with the reforms of the O'Neill period, it was clear that material interests alone did not fuel the conflict. Nordlinger and Horowitz point out that groups and individuals often subordinate interests to other claims, for example, issues of identity, dominance, or status.[44] It is noteworthy that many analysts define the conflict in structural terms as a zero-sum game in which the motives of actors can be simply inferred from the matrix of possible payoffs. But Deborah Larson argues convincingly that such a view oversimplifies the role of motives and ignores what she calls the 'relative gains orientation', in which actors prefer relative to absolute gain in intensely competitive situations. Payoffs, then, are not nearly as predictive as the structuralists would have it. Indicative of this is the well-known observation that Catholics in the North are and would most likely continue to be economically better off in the North than in the South, and yet they continue to desire unification.

Where fears of extinction are at work, as they are in both communities, even minor losses, such as those concerning parade routes, flags and emblems, sites for talks, etc., are seen as critical – the proverbial slippery slope. During the 1980s, several Catholic priests argued that a programme to arrange the gradual release of prisoners arrested for non-capital crimes, especially in the wake of the disastrous policies involving special status, dirty protest, and hunger strikes, might have significantly disarmed the republican movement's supporters and removed the stimulus to revenge. Loyalists, clearly determined to end IRA violence, nevertheless rejected proposals for gradual release, despite the fact that such a programme would also have benefited their own imprisoned volunteers. In a polarized ethnic system, such as described above by Horowitz, this rigidity is likely to characterize responses by both sides to any new initiatives.

The third criticism of structural approaches, also provided by Ross, maintains that the intensity of emotions and hostile feelings cannot be explained by the differences in interests, sometimes rather minor, between the parties to a conflict. Horowitz notes that 'the passions invoked by ethnic conflict far exceed what might be expected to flow from any fair reckoning of the conflicts of interest'.[45] By any standard, Catholics in the North were discriminated against by the unionist regime, and they continued to suffer from employment discrimination under Direct Rule. However, most Catholics in Northern Ireland, and the overwhelming majority of Catholics in the Republic, have consistently rejected the view that the discrimination justified the armed IRA insurrection. 'Most opinion polls indicate that only a minority, typically less than ten per cent of respondents in each community, are prepared to express any support for the use of paramilitary violence.'[46] Still, the intensity of the conflict increased as Catholic interests, generally consistent with prevailing British norms, were satisfied. This distinction uncovers a fiction about the conflict that went unchecked for years, namely that the conflict was simply between Irish republicans and the British state. In fact, moderates on both sides were also bitterly divided, committed as they had been since Northern Ireland's establishment to mutually exclusive positions, Irish unity on the one hand and the maintenance of the union with Britain on the other.

In summary, then, the structural approach is likely to produce intra-communal fragmentation in intensely divided societies. Equally important, this approach does not account for the intensity and persistence of the Northern Ireland conflict. To cope with the persistence and intensity of the dispute, we need to turn to a body of theory that considers the accumulated grievances experienced by all the involved communities. The sheer passion expended in pursuing ethnic conflict calls out for an explanation that does justice to the realm of the feelings. It is necessary to account, not merely for ambition, but for antipathy. 'A bloody phenomenon cannot be explained by a bloodless theory.'[47] To understand how two communities so much alike have managed to sustain their emnities we will turn in the next chapter to a consideration of the role played by social identity theory in sustaining the deeply emotional character of the conflict.

SIX

PSYCHOCULTURAL THEORIES OF CONFLICT

In 1987, a Protestant member of the RUC was visiting his parents' home across the border in Donegal. While working on some repairs to the foundations of their home, the IRA murdered him with a shot to the back of the head. The killing was bitterly condemned in both communities and on both sides of the border. When asked about the killing, a Sinn Fein official in Derry commented to one of the authors that 'He wore a uniform'. In the midst of exhorting his young son to put his shirt on, the official went on to say that it was a 'soft kill', referring to the fact that the IRA's operatives were in no danger on this particular mission. There was no expression of compassion for the victim or his family.

At about the same time, a leader of the UDA graciously welcomed the same author into his office and talked vigorously about the constructive role being played by the UDA in the formulation of political alternatives for the governance of Northern Ireland. His assistant popped in, mid-interview, and informed him that the young Catholic worker shot to death the previous evening by loyalist paramilitaries after leaving work in East Belfast, had died. 'He'd been warned', commented the UDA leader, and then asked if there was anything that could be done to get the State Department in Washington to lift the ban on members of the UDA entering the United States!

We already know that there are good structural reasons for the existence of communal separation but structural factors alone do not explain the persistence and intensity of the antagonistic relationships that produced the above two atrocities, and many more. To understand these dimensions of the conflict, we will consider what Ross calls the psychocultural elements of conflict. In particular, we look at one set of psychocultural factors, which together relate to what is termed 'social identity' theory,[1] and examine the relevance of this theory to the nature of the conflict and to its persistence. We emphasize social identity theory

103

because of its theoretical relevance and because the parties themselves have in recent years begun to attach more importance to it on the assumption that it represented a path to the resolution of the conflict. At the conclusion of this chapter, we evaluate this assumption.

As our earlier discussions have indicated, the stress under which both communities in Northern Ireland have lived forced them not only to separate from one another, but to become emotionally confined to their respective communities. 'Under political stress a group will adhere more stubbornly than ever to its sense of nationality or ethnicity, which becomes increasingly grandiose',[2] and this is precisely what happened in Ireland and later in Northern Ireland as the two communities responded to the inflated demands of communal togetherness and isolation. Demands for a united Ireland and for a Protestant-Unionist state were advanced as though the other party simply did not exist.

As the incompleteness of the structural approach has become evident, emphasis has shifted to what Ross calls psycho-cultural approaches. According to Ross, 'Deeply held dispositions are significant elements in determining how participants interpret conflict and how these interpretations affect the actions they take'.[3] In addition to disagreements over interests, this approach suggests that the Northern Ireland conflict is also about 'deeply rooted psycho-cultural interpretations of the conflict which evoke past grievances, threats to identity, and primordial fears of extinction'.[4] These interpretations, which link particular events to culturally shared threats to self-esteem and identity carry, according to Ross, the emotions of earlier confrontations from one generation to another.

Psycho-cultural dispositions shape how groups and individuals process events and the emotions, perceptions, and cognitions the events evoke. A psycho-cultural approach will help us to understand why disputes which would provoke little conflict in other settings are so disturbing in the Northern Ireland context. Comparative analysis . shows that similar provocative actions can evoke very different patterns of cultural response. This distinction means that objective situations alone do not cause conflict; interpretations of such situations also play a central role.[5] Psycho-cultural approaches to the study of conflict in Northern Ireland were until the late 1980s few and far between. Indeed, the nationalist definition of the issue had been widely accepted not only by the parties to the conflict but by many of those who studied it even from outside of Northern Ireland. Either it was England's Irish problem or it was Ireland's English problem. Most of the work was strictly historical and narrative in character. The few social science efforts that were made focused largely on the psychological effects of the violence on the young. It was not until around the period of the Anglo-Irish Agreement in 1985 that organizations like the Centre for the study of Conflict at the University of Ulster and the Community Relations Council came into being and began producing psycho-cultural, especially ethnographic, studies of the conflict, many of which focused on identity-related questions.

In Northern Ireland threats to social identity are particularly important for two reasons. The first has to do with the exclusivist demands of the two communities, demands which threaten each other with extinction. It can be argued that the exclusive demands of Protestants from the start and from Catholics later set in motion parallel and accumulative fears of extinction. The fear of extinction, Horowitz argues, must be seen against the exclusivist demands of the group entertaining such fears.[6] In Ireland before partition and in Northern Ireland since partition, Loyalists and Republicans both made demands which engendered and reinforced such fears. A 'Protestant state for a Protestant people' was proclaimed by many Unionists throughout Northern Ireland in a manner which could only have instilled a fear of extinction in Catholics. Within the Protestant community fear of extinction is the key to unionist success, especially as it is experienced by Ian Paisley, in whom unionism's darkest impulses are incorporated. Moloney and Pollak write that this fear of being an embattled religious minority in Ireland is rooted in Protestantism's history in Ireland which, they argue,

takes its puritanism from the rigid beliefs of the seventeenth century Scottish planters; its separatism and elitism from their feeling that they were a small band of civilized Christians surrounded by barbarian hordes; its hatred of Catholicism from fears going back to the 1641 massacre of the Protestant settlers by the Catholic Irish they had dispossessed; its religious enthusiasm from the 'Great Revival' of 1859.[7]

All these elements conspired to keep the unionist community alone and insecure.

Extreme Nationalists have been equally exclusive. The very name, Sinn Fein (We Ourselves), suggests an exclusivist vision. Sinn Fein has long dismissed the legitimacy of Protestant fears and concerns, arguing, first, that their quarrel is with the British and not with Protestants, and second, that Protestant concerns would, of course, be accommodated in a new, united Ireland. However, the very essence of Protestant fears is reinforced in Sinn Fein's intended reassurance. 'Protestants are', says the republican movement, 'Irish, like the rest of us'. The record is not so reassuring, though. Some of the most horrific IRA attacks have been against essentially Protestant targets, the La Mon House Hotel attack in 1978 and the Enniskillen 'war memorial' massacre in 1987. Promised

accommodation has not prevented the decline of the Protestant population in the Republic and, more immediately on the west bank of the
Foyle in Derry City. Perceived exclusion from civic life led some Derry
Protestants to support a demand for two separate councils in the city, one
for the population on the west bank of the river, a second serving the
population on the east bank.[8] Controversies over Orange Order parades
through or even adjacent to nationalist areas are seen as further evidence
of the intolerance which Protestants believe they would experience in a
united Ireland.

According to Terrell Northrup, 'it is also likely that this process of
rejection and redefinition will be characterized by a high emotional
charge and a great sense of urgency. If one's core sense of self, the identity, is threatened by the demands, behaviour, or identity of another
person, then psychic or even physical annihilation will seem to be imminent? The response to such a conflict is an immediate and extreme mobilization of resources for the purpose of maintaining the identity.'[9] This is
the fear of extinction to which so many refer. It is the fear that Catholics
felt when Protestants burned the Falls Road and the British Army
interned Catholics with the ferocity of an occupying army.

The second has to do with the idea that social identity in Northern
Ireland is a core construct for most people, i.e. one that has 'great
salience for an individual sense of self and order in the world'.[10] These
concepts help us to maintain a sense of self or identity in the face of a
changing or threatening environment. They are, as one might expect,
highly resistant to change in that they reject threatening or invalidating
incoming information. The implications of a challenge to the core sense
of social identity are explained by Northrup as follows:

When in the course of a relationship between parties, an event occurs that is
perceived as invalidating the core sense of identity, the party or parties perceiving
invalidation experience threat. Invalidation of the group's core constructs is
threatening because it destroys meaning and the ability to predict events. The
intensity of a conflict will be particularly high in the case where identities (or
construct systems) of two (or more) parties invalidate each other . . . . Many
members of both parties believe that their own existence is threatened by the
mere existence of the other. This is especially clear in relation to claims to land.[11]

It has been our argument from the beginning that the covenantal pattern
of dispossession established the relationship of mutual invalidation
which has persisted to this day. At one level, land itself remains the
issue, but the invalidation has extended beyond land and now defines the
entire relationship system between the two communities.

According to social identity theory 'in every society a process called social categorization is at work'.[12] We tend to simplify life, the theory argues, by reducing the complexity of life into a manageable number of categories. 'This has the effect of exaggerating differences between particular categories and also of minimizing differences within categories. In other words, two people who are labelled as belonging to different social categories or groups are seen as rather more different than they actually are while two people from the same group are seen as rather less different than they actually are.'[13] Communal differences in Northern Ireland are, by almost any standard save that of the Northern Ireland communities themselves, minimal, and yet there has been a tendency, especially after the violence of the early 1970s intensified, to assert the importance of cultural differences between Catholics and Protestants. Indeed, a significant and influential movement known as 'cultural traditions developed in order to legitimize the emphasis on cultural differences.[14]

Categorization may seem an innocent enough phenomenon, but as Vincent Crapanzano points out, social categorization especially in polarized societies, gives rise to a phenomenon anthropologists refer to as 'essentialism':

In this view, once an object or being is classified, it is forever that object or being. It has an identity. It partakes of a particular essence. It is subject to certain regularities, which are understood as rules or laws of nature, and has its own place within a particular picture of the universe, rather like a piece in a jigsaw puzzle. [15]

The conflicting parties are reduced by each other to a single, threatening dimension. Consider the seemingly innocuous problem of naming the parties to the conflict in Northern Ireland.[16] Analysts for years have been trying to avoid labelling the parties Catholic and Protestant for fear that this would imply a religious interpretation of the conflict or because it did not sufficiently differentiate the parties to the conflict. In the end, many, even the most detached, return to the Catholic-Protestant distinction because it efficiently conveys a fundamental division in Northern Ireland society. For participants, however, use of these naming conventions makes everyone suspect – all Catholics become Republicans and all Protestants become Loyalists. In highly stressful situations, essentialism contributes significantly to the rigidity of the prejudicial interpretations, images and stereotypes the two communities have of each other, despite the relatively minimal content of their differences. This rigidity has been, as we argue below, a major factor in the conflict's persistence.

It is not at all surprising that strong social identification would occur in the Irish setting. Life in Ireland was, as we know, thoroughly polarized for so long that social identification with one's own community was almost inescapable. Fionnuala O'Connor tells the story of a young Catholic woman from Belfast who grew up in the midst of intercommunal violence and suddenly realized: 'We're Catholics, we're targets for the UVF and they're targets for us. And you started to put two and two together and say, 'Oh Jesus, we're a Catholic area'.[17] Indeed, it seems clear that communal identification increased in the years since Ireland was partitioned. Survival itself was thought to depend on it, especially for Protestants but increasingly for Catholics. Regarding the functions of ethnicity, Volcan argues that 'the sense of ethnicity enhances survival and the cohesion of the group, but on the other hand endangers the group's future by causing it to split off from others and to allocate its own group-dystonic attributes to those from whom it has separated'.[18] For Protestants, this consciousness came early, moved as they were by religious convictions and an awareness of the fragile standing of the setlement and the settlers. Nationalist identity was slower to develop and was not able to generate a coherent political challenge until the end of the eighteenth and the beginning of the nineteenth centuries. Certainly, there were Catholic political movements prior to this, but they were largely anomic in nature. The earlier experiences of dispossession and pogrom coupled with reform, emancipation, and the Home Rule Movement in the 1800s combined to confirm the national and social identity of Catholics.

In Ireland generally and in Northern Ireland in particular, the social categorization effects expected from a dichotomized and polarized society have produced strong attachments to one's social identity. Social identity theory maintains 'that in a highly dichotomized society like Northern Ireland there should first exist a high level of awareness of social identity, defined in terms of the two predominant groups, and second a strong positive emotional investment in this identity.'[19] There is in fact abundant evidence that adults in Northern Ireland are well aware of, and will readily admit to, membership of one or other of the two groups.[20] We know that significant numbers of people from both communities have been able and willing to hate or discriminate against members of the other community. For this to occur, as Tajfel maintains, people must have 'acquired a sense of belonging to groups or social categories which are clearly distinct from and stand in certain relations to those they hate, dislike or discriminate against'.[21] This awareness, a constant feature of the Northern Ireland landscape, was deepened by the communal polarization that developed after the early 1970s.

This sense of belonging is crucial, Isaiah Berlin maintains, because 'the essential human unit in which man's nature is fully realized is not the individual, or a voluntary association which can be dissolved or altered or abandoned at will, but the nation.'[22] It is important, as Volkan points out, to recall that the self becomes attached to the group, the group becoming the source of one's identity. The sense of self, put simply, is the impression one carries of how his emotional, intellectual, and physical components combine in response to the world around him. In ethnically divided societies, an individual's sense of self is closely related to his sense of ethnicity, 'rising and falling with the fortunes of his national group'[23] and, in Northern Ireland, with the threat of extinction. The cardinal sin in such societies is betrayal.[24] This attachment is adhered to more stubbornly as the level of stress in the society rises. In addition, we know from the literature[25] that threat maximizes out-group differences and minimizes in-group differences. In this situation, the 'other', as Todd puts it, is increasingly likely to become the enemy. For Catholics, this sectarianism taps 'deep historical memories of dispossession and pogrom'.[26] For Protestants, the ever-present sense of insecurity was intensified. This is precisely the dynamic that was at work throughout Irish history, and it continued right up until the British imposition of Direct Rule and to the present day. The fragility of the covenantal-settler framework resulted in chronically high levels of stress which could be ignited by even minor disturbances. The relatively high level of vigilante-type organizations from as early as the eighteenth century, in both communities, reveals just how historically rooted is this generalized insecurity.

In Northern Ireland, stress was maintained at relatively high levels throughout the existence of the state as Unionists sought to secure the state against expected rebel assaults. Usually described as the 'siege' mentality, this condition might better be defined as one of hyper-vigilance which psychiatrists describe as 'a state of heightened awareness usually with continual scanning of the environment for signs of danger'.[27] The hypervigilance of fraternal groups such as the B Specials, the Apprentice Boys of Derry, and most importantly the Orange Order ensured a perpetual state of readiness in the Protestant population. Until the nineteenth century, Catholics responded less by organization than by withdrawal and yielding.

Because of the high and constant salience of identity in Northern Ireland, indeed throughout Irish history, social identity is and has been a core construct for each of the two communities. The sense of self is, as we have said, intimately bound up with the social grouping to which one belongs. Theories of ethnocentrism tell us that the invalidation or threatened invalidation of social identity creates a readiness among group members to defend the group. The key hypothesis becomes: 'If the events of one's life in relationship to the world invalidate or threaten to invalidate, the core sense of identity, then the individual or group will respond energetically to attempts to maintain the identity.'[28] This is the crucial mechanism that relates social identity to the evolution of ethnic conflict. The chronic nature of the invalidation and threatened invalidation works its way into the identities of the members of the involved communities. 'It is this dynamic nature of the interface between identity and relationship with the world that is postulated to be a central factor in intractable conflict.'[29] Examination of this connection takes up the next part of this chapter.

THE RELATIONSHIP SYSTEM

From the start, we have argued that the relationship system that evolved over the centuries between Catholics and Protestants is the framework in which the social identities of the two communities have evolved. Catholics and Protestants, then and now, have lived in conditions of high stress, with their core identities invalidated or threatened with invalidation by a relationship grounded in insecurity for both. For Catholics, there was the daily experience of being dominated, of dispossession and humiliation, eventually institutionalized by the penal laws, and later reinforced by Partition and the exclusion from public life wrought by a devolved government in Northern Ireland. As Liam de Paor puts it: 'The thousand petty humiliations of a resentful subservience could be met only with the glib deference and the placating comicality that masked hatred.'[30] Fionnuala O'Connor writes of the 'long years of sullen submission' which preceded forced migration, internment and Bloody Sunday.[31]

For Protestants, the drive for security became a way of life. The physical and moral insecurity of the Ulster plantation and the threat of a meaningless existence in a united Ireland forged a relatively simple and dichotomous, or binary, view of their world. Terence Brown describes the situation of the contemporary Protestant: 'That his history seems impoverished by comparison with nationalist historical awareness is because that history has had to perform fewer functions and is necessarily simpler. By its nature, it is bound to comprehend imaginatively much less of the human condition.'[32] Always in the Protestant mind was the anxiety that Catholics would try to undo the settlement. It was a world in which 'Protestant survival depended on Catholic suppression'.[33] Protestants were required to be hypervigilant with respect to the traitors in their midst. This constant sense of threat gave rise to the 'self-defence' tradition of banding in which small groups of Protestants organized for protection in the face of weak central government and later, by the end of the eighteenth century, to subdue or eliminate potential Catholic challenges. The legendary Orange Order, founded in the tradition of banding in the 1790s, continues to this day to organize Protestant determination to resist the Catholic threat.[34]

CORE SOCIAL IDENTITIES

We have identified three dimensions of the nationalist-unionist relationship which help to define the core social identities of Protestants and Catholics: dominance, mourning and rigidification. The chronic invalidation of core identities we have discussed involves these three dimensions. These, we argue, are the mechanisms by which the covenantal tendencies toward isolation and togetherness are reinforced. They are, therefore, very important in any effort to understand the intensity and persistence of the conflict. It is important to recall that these dimensions emerge out of the totality of the relationships involved in Northern Ireland and are not unique or independent characterological traits. Nor are they experienced symmetrically by the two communities. Taken together these aspects of social identity, each a function of invalidation, will help in our understanding of the persistence and intensity of the conflict in Northern Ireland. In effect, these factors shape the manner in which communities understand themselves and their relationships to one another.

DOMINANCE

'Ulster loyalism is dominance', Jennifer Todd tells us,[35] and most would agree, but it is not as uncomplicated as that assertion sounds. Protestants enjoyed a power advantage in Northern Ireland, but, as their acute fears remind us, they were never really in control of the region. 'To be dominant in a system is not to dominate the system. Both the dominant and the dominated are equally caught in it. One has the advantage; the other does not.'[36] This is the sense of dominance that Todd has in mind when she says that the core assumption of Ulster loyalism 'is that the only alternative to Ulster loyalist dominance is Ulster loyalist defeat and humiliation'.[37] The Protestant-loyalist position in Ireland, and in Northern Ireland was and is threatened by two major factors, Catholic 'encroachment' and British 'abandonment'. Indeed, it is these fears of encroachment and abandonment, that testify to the failure of the Protestant people to dominate the country in any stable fashion. Protestant fear reveals the profound insecurity, both real and imagined, of their position. The centrality of this fear, as it affected both communities, is noted by Marianne Elliott. 'That Ireland became such an intensely Catholic nation was due to Protestant fears'.[38] The hypervigilant mind that saw all Catholics as traitors or potential traitors, that saw 'life as a recurrent struggle between good and evil with its own existence continually threatened by evil forces',[39] drove Catholics into communal enclaves while Protestants organized themselves in the Orange Order and later the B Specials, to defend themselves against an enemy that was largely of their own making. In effect, Protestant-Loyalists can be said to have largely created the enemy they needed to remain intact.

Butterfield uses the term 'security dilemma' to describe the situation in which attempts by one state to provide for its own security often only deepen its own insecurity because of the response triggered in the other group.[40] This aptly describes the situation of Protestants in relation to Catholics, not only in Ireland historically, but in Northern Ireland since partition as well. Protestants could not provide for themselves that for which they most yearned, a high degree of security for a Protestant Ulster. 'The drive for security will also produce aggressive actions if the state either requires a very high degree of security or feels menaced by the very presence of other strong ties.'[41] Thus, Protestants expected the RUC and the British Army to provide for their security, almost exclusively. These were the conditions imposed on Protestants by the settler-covenantal framework. And yet these anti-Catholic practices and politics only deepened the enduring threat posed by a dispossessed Catholic population. Despite the futility of this search for security, Protestants persisted because domination was seen as the only alternative to humiliation.

From the penal laws to the Special Powers Act, Catholics, of course, had been the object of this dominance. Dispossession, humiliation and exclusion were, as we indicated earlier, routine. The Catholic response to dispossession and humiliation was a nationalism grounded in their 'common sorrow', a sorrow which led to the long years of sullen submission noted earlier. But as we have pointed out, neither British conquest nor Protestant dominance was complete. At first organized in locally recruited volunteer bands of their own, Catholics began to organize effective political resistance on a national scale only toward the end of the eighteenth century. From that point on, however, Catholics experienced continuous and substantial political success. Each success, of course, further stimulated the Protestant insistence on domination.

Protestants, much like South African whites, were in a 'waiting' posture. How to characterize the fear that infused their waiting is very difficult, but perhaps what Crapanzano says of South African whites will inform our understanding of Northern Ireland's 'whites'. 'Nor is it the fear of change: the loss of power, status, and wealth, the good life, as many South Africans put it. It is, I believe, a much more primordial fear that comes from the absence of any possibility of a vital relationship with most of the people around one.'[42] Despite decades of co-existence within Northern Ireland, and despite substantial similarities in culture and religion, large numbers in both communities simply did not talk to each other. The emphasis on 'talking' should not be underestimated since, as Barber points out, talking 'engenders empathy, nourishes affection, and engages imagination', qualities all of which are sorely lacking in the Northern Ireland system.[43] This perspective helps us to understand the unionist preoccupation with the past. 'The past gives us security when we are waiting.'[44] Only in a triumphal, even if exaggerated, past could a chronically anxious unionist community find any reassurance.

MOURNING

Observers of Northern Ireland are wont to point out, always somewhat critically, that the people of Northern Ireland seem to live hopelessly in the past. For the waiting Unionists, the past provides security, while for the anxious Nationalist, the past deepens discontent. Indeed, many argue that the 'past is present' in the Northern Ireland case. Seldom, however, are the mechanisms by which groups invoke the past addressed. Instead, a nostalgic or disoriented recollection is implied. Why this is so, or of what relevance the past is, or even how it is experienced, is scarcely addressed.

Volkan argues that groups and individuals often relate to the past through what he calls a 'chosen trauma' or a 'chosen glory'. A chosen trauma 'is an event that induces in the members of one group intense feelings of having been humiliated and victimized by members of another group'.[45] A 'chosen glory' is an event that induces in members of one group intense feelings of having been successful or of having triumphed over members of another. It tends to bolster a group's self-esteem and gives rise to exaggerated and triumphal claims. Both are vehicles through which emotions are sustained over generations, a major point we will discuss in the next chapter. The idea of a chosen trauma or glory is entirely consistent with J.E. Mack's emphasis on the collective experience of wounds and hurts as the major source of national or ethnic identity.[46] The significant difference is, of course, that the chosen trauma or glory concept treats these experiences as condensed in one major evolutionary symbol that evokes all the emotions of communal struggle. Stories of defeat and glory, highly condensed, are passed from one generation to the next and help to amplify the experiences of loss or triumph experienced in contemporary situations.

Mack uses the term 'egoism of victimization' to refer to how people connect the historical suffering of others to their own experience of pain.[47] Characteristic of this egoistic victimization is the inability of the victim to empathize with the other. Mack argues that 'The rhetoric of 'the extremists' in both communities emphasizes a we-they thinking in which the other side is the incarnation of evil and one's own side can do no wrong'.[48] There is little humanization of the opponent and hence little opportunity to develop empathy which can be vital in helping to understand why an enemy has adopted a certain position even while not necessarily accepting that position as correct. Missing is any identification of mutual needs, or nuanced images of one's own community and the other side. Tempting as it is to think this characteristic only of the extremists, there is abundant anecdotal evidence to indicate that this inability to empathize is widespread throughout Northern Ireland. Ulster loyalism drew no distinctions between Nationalists who reject the use of violence and republican supporters of Sinn Fein and the IRA who condone violence in the service of unification. There was no difference between SDLP's leader, John Hume and the leader of Provisional Sinn Fein, Gerry Adams. For many Catholics, there was scant regard for the Catholic-Protestant relationship and nearly exclusive attention given to the British connection. Blaming is far more prevalent than empathizing. Chosen traumas and glories are, in effect, stories or myths, long removed from their origins, which express this egoistic victimization and perpetuate the view of the other as the enemy.

An event may evolve into a chosen trauma as group members are unable successfully to mourn the changes or losses they have experienced. 'When the inability to mourn is chronic, grievances remain active and are passed from one generation to another. The original trauma becomes mythological infusing present relationships and perceptions.'[49] In this way the emotion of an event may be re-captured without the actual experience of that event. The casual visitor is often stunned by the fierceness of historical recollection in Northern Ireland. Defeats and triumphs in the distant past are treated as personally meaningful events.[50] What is most important about this, of course, is its implication for political change. 'Man cannot accept change without mourning for what is lost to the past.'[51] In a society, such as Northern Ireland, where the emotions, triumphal and tragic, can be quickly resuscitated, cultural change will be very difficult.

There is a variety of reasons for the inability of Catholics or Protestants to complete the work of mourning. Most important is the continuation of the relationship that maintains the conditions of loss and threatened loss. In political analysis and discussion, words like loss tend to be ignored or trivialized. In ethnic conflicts, loss or threatened loss is often at the heart of the matter. O'Malley concisely summarizes the significance of loss as it relates to both communities in Northern Ireland. Loss in the Northern Ireland context means that

The sense of belonging is severed: the focus of meaningful interpersonal relationships is destroyed; the sense of spatial identity – that sum of experiences that are grounded in spatial memories, spatial imagery, and the spatial framework of social activities which is fundamental to human functioning – is traumatized; the sense of group identity, of communality with other people, of shared human qualities is undermined.[52]

The chronic conditions of threat and dispossession combine with the circumstances of fear and siege to prevent successful mourning from occurring for either Catholics or Protestants. Northern Ireland institutionalized the relationships that frustrated communal mourning. Up until 1985, in short, the fundamental relationship connecting Catholics and Protestants had not changed. As implied in the victimizing mentality, there may be no outside or public acknowledgment[53] of the hurt and humiliation of the affected groups, and this may contribute to the persistence of anger. A victimizing group, the antagonist, may 'refuse to mourn its own guilt because of shared unwillingness to accept responsibility or to identify with bad ancestors'.[54] Both of the stories at the beginning of this chapter illustrate the ways in which elements on both sides 'airbrush violence' that is inconsistent with their respective self-images. Thus, the antagonist persists in behaviour certain to deepen the wounds and humiliation of the dominated group. Hurt and humiliation are transmitted, through song and stories and parades, across generations, enhanced by the pain of everyday exclusion and the threat of extinction. The accumulated experiences of Catholics and Protestants created inter-generational reservoirs of emotions that preserve the hurts and wounds which allow conflict to continue long beyond its original rationalizations. Only recently have political and church leaders, for example, begun to commiserate with members of the other community over the violent deaths of one of their own.

The 1689 Siege of Derry and King William's victory at the Battle of the Boyne a year later, combined to form a 'chosen trauma-glory' mythology that continues to infuse the lives of Ulster Loyalists to this day. The combination provides justification for the Protestant insistence on refusing to change. 'Not an inch,' is the popular expression. The preservationist impulse of Protestants is supported by the dual nature of their commemoration. When the Anglo-Irish Agreement was initialled in 1985, the huge banner spanning the front of Belfast City Hall simply proclaimed, 'Belfast Says No', just as was said in 1690, 1912, and 1974. The Siege of Derry and the victory at the Boyne River are replayed in covenantal form on a continuing basis in the lives of thousands of Protestants. Certainly, the most obvious re-enactments are the triumphal and defiant marches of unionist and loyalist Protestants throughout the long 'marching season'. Todd has described the significance of these marches in terms that complement the mourning idea:

The Twelfth marches ritually commemorate the ternal battle faced by Protestants and their winning of that battle in 1690. They provide a motivation and rationale for the continuing battle and they imaginatively resolve the existing contradictions faced by Northern Protestants by having them win the battle. They destroy all ambiguities which might disrupt the binary opposition of good and evil in Orange ideology by clarifying and completing the proper social boundaries. Further, the celebratory aspects of the day – preparations, paraphernalia, noise, picnics with the women and children – reaffirm for Orangemen the benefits of their Protestant identity by having their rigid creed culminate in festival.[55]

To appreciate the full significance of these marches, one would have to go back to the early period of civil unrest, 1968-71, when the year-round marches and counter-marches so polarized the two communities that the British Army was called in to separate them. Marching was not simply a re-enactment, however, but a political instrument. Each march reconstitutes the struggle, recalling old and new challenges to Protestant supremacy.

We have already noted that Catholic grievances did not give rise to a coherent nationalist movement until the nineteenth century. Emancipation, land reform and home rule dominated the agenda of the increasingly self-conscious nationalist movement. But it was not until the execution of the 1916 Easter Rising's leaders and the partition of Ireland in 1920 that the collective experiences of Irish Catholics coalesced in identifiable and coherent 'chosen traumas'. The execution of the Rising's leaders seemed a gratuitous insult to a people who, up until then, had suffered their injustice with equanimity and quiescence. As Elliott says, 'on every level, martyrolatry had taken over'.[56] O'Malley highlights the effects which the Rising was intended to produce:

'The Easter Rising of 1916 was mythic. Planned in secret by a small cabal in the IRB (Irish Republican Brotherhood) itself a small cabal in the Sinn Fein Volunteers, it was designed to fail, to be a blood sacrifice that would redeem the Irish nation and rouse it to action.'[57]

At a time when IRA fortunes appeared to be slipping, the hunger strikers of 1980-81 succeeded in connecting themselves to the mythic sacrifices of the martyred 1916 leaders. Indeed, Bobby Sands wrote prison poems in images remarkably reminiscent of the sacrificial and redemptive poetry of writer-rebel and a leader of the rising, Patrick Pearse. The hunger strikers, too, had no hope of success, but rather 'an intense consciousness of failure',[58] and yet they also galvanized nationalist insistence. The fortunes of the republican movement rose with each death, threatening to undo the nationalist majority previously conceded to the SDLP.

Partition, of course, was the great humiliation for Nationalists. It further divided not just Protestant from Catholic, it divided the historic Irish nation – at least that nation as it had come to be defined by Nationalists. Furthermore, it appeared to legitimize the oppression of the Catholic community by maintaining it, even solidifying it, in the North. British consent to devolved government in the North seemed to sanction the result. Foster reminds us of the words of William O'Brien who, four years before partition, wrote in terms which the hunger strikers and the whole republican campaign saw themselves required to implement:

If once Ireland were, by the votes of its own representatives, to accept dismemberment, that act could never be undone except by a bloody revolution . . . The work, I am afraid, will have to be left to other men and other times.[59]

RIGIDIFICATION

As might be expected, groups experiencing significant invalidation of core aspects of their identity tend to develop increasingly rigid interpretations of their divided world. Rigidification is, therefore, another aspect of social identity that evolved in Northern Ireland and which contributed to the intensity and persistence of the conflict. Northrup writes that

Rigidification, then, is a process of crystallizing and hardening what is construed as self and not-self. It serves the purpose of separating the 'invalidated' party from the 'invalidating' party, putting distance between the self and the threat. It is significant that not only the behaviours or demands of the other party are construed as threatening, but also the beliefs, or even characteristics of the other which are not related to the original threat, may over time become interpreted as threatening.[60]

The icy co-existence in which Catholics and Protestants had been living for fifty years clearly reflected such rigidification. Indeed, the patterns of communal isolation and togetherness hardened as within-group differences were minimized and differences between the groups were maximized. 'Instinctively the Protestants drew closer together and adopted hard-shell defensive postures, for the assaults by the nationalists confirmed everything they had always known about the Canaanites who still were abroad in the land.'[61] Demands on both sides for group loyalty increased. Many Catholics came to rely on the IRA and other self-help measures, further confirming the worst fears of Unionists. Catholics showed scant regard for their relationship with Protestants and republicans insisted that the conflict was the sole responsibility of the British government.[62] While Protestants were deeply concerned with the nationalist community, they, too, were inclined to blame the British for failure to deal more effectively with the IRA and militant nationalism generally.

Catholics and Protestants separated themselves from each other in Belfast, Derry and other urban areas after the violence and internal migration of 1969. The historic walls of Derry were recreated physically and psychologically as the two communities went about enclosing themselves. Concrete 'peace lines', so-called, constructed in many parts of Belfast, exclusive communal taxi services, an intense and exclusive focus on one's local community, all reinforced separateness. Hadden and Boyle provide data which show that after 1971 there was a tendency

for members of both major communities to congregate in areas where they feel safer and less exposed . . . in the majority of wards in the area, the population was highly segregated in the sense that fewer than ten per cent declared themselves as members of the 'other community, whether Protestant or Catholic . . . In many wards in communally exclusive parts of the city (Belfast) it is not unreasonable to assume that the population has been almost completely 'purified' by a mixture of actual or feared intimidation and the desire of most households to live in an area where they feel safe.[63]

As Northrup points out 'In effect, rigidification involves increasing efforts to secure the boundaries of the self'[64] and when the self is defined in social identity terms, as it was in Northern Ireland, boundary setting is precisely what is to be expected. The result, according to Ross, is that 'To an outside observer, perhaps the most disturbing and disquieting aspect of the current situation in Northern Ireland is the paradoxical side-by-side existence of overt violence with an icy politeness between Catholics and Protestants in their everyday interactions'.[65] In response to the destruction of commercial sections of Belfast, Derry and other towns, the British devised a security system which allowed shoppers to use the services of downtown areas without fear. At the end of the day, however, the two communities exited for homes on opposite sides of the 'peace wall' that divided them. In this context, there simply was no possibility for a vital relationship to develop between the communities. This stalemated and rigidified behaviour suggests 'severe boundary problems in which people who are trying desperately to maintain separate identities must yet come together for a variety of group functions and interpersonal transactions'.[66]

The most important consequence of this rigidified behaviour was the unwillingness and inability of the involved parties to negotiate or to devise creative solutions to their problems. If anything, the politicians avoided each other more than did the two communities. When it came to dealing with differences, the parties were in effect disabled.

CONCLUSION

Psycho-cultural conflict theory argues that these polarized mutually hostile images rooted in both historical experiences and cultural institutions and practices are powerful barriers preventing the parties from addressing their substantive interest differences. A final transformation of the conflict requires that the parties alter their polarized images of each other. Sometimes this can occur through a single dramatic gesture, such as Egyptian President Anwar Sadat's trip to Israel in 1977. More often, such shifts are slower and grow out of changed relationships among the parties.

There is little doubt that a long term transformation of the Northern Ireland conflict would require changed identities in both communities. The distinction between self and not-self is simply too overwhelming. The development of a mututal identity which overcomes this division imposed by centuries of covenental intractability is required. But, as we have tried to show, these changes in identity are not only extremly difficult to obtain, they are very slow to develop. In Northern Ireland such change was not likely to come quickly not least because the parties had found themselves unable to cooperate. Instead, a significant shift in the network of relationships between them is what is often required in order to make movement towards a resolution possible. This is what would be achieved by the next major development, the Anglo-Irish Agreement of 1985.

SEVEN

FORGING NEW RELATIONSHIPS:
THE ANGLO-IRISH AGREEMENT

The 1980s opened with a series of crises and failed political initiatives. Secretary of State Humphrey Atkins' conference in 1980 was attended by only three of the major parties, SDLP, DUP and Alliance, the UUP effectively boycotting the conference.[1] This failure together with the upheavals surrounding the hunger strikes of 1980 and 1981 and the failure of the local parties to achieve agreement on the plans for devolved government devised by Atkins' successor, James Prior, in 1982 led to one of the most dramatic political developments in the whole history of the search for a settlement, the Anglo-Irish Agreement of 1985.[2] This agreement established a new basis to relationships between the two governments with respect to Northern Ireland and, eventually, with respect to other aspects of Anglo-Irish affairs.

While not directly involved in making the agreement, the Northern Irish political parties were dramatically affected by its terms. The agreement was novel and perhaps unique in that it virtually reformulated the Northern Ireland question and while the governments never intended that the agreement itself would resolve the conflict, they did expect it to provide a more stable framework than had previously existed for addressing all of the relevant relationships necessary to a settlement. In effect the agreement was to initiate a process undermining the emotional dynamics of the relationships that had sustained the conflict since 1921

In the agreement, Britain's neutrality with regard to a final constitutional outcome and the Irish government's new role and status, conceded without any consultation with the Unionists, appeared to challenge the very foundations of the settler-covenant compact. In so doing it provoked instant and profound hostility in the entire Unionist community. The fear of extinction was substantiated in British concessions to Irish influence in Northern Ireland and the demonstrated willingness of the British to concede a united Ireland in the future. It was hardly surprising that unionist reaction was, initially, profoundly hostile.

Within the nationalist-republican community, the SDLP enthusiastically endorsed the new arrangements. The SDLP believed that the agreement would ultimately force Unionists to negotiate the 'totality of relationships', a critical dimension of nationalist strategy. The fact that the agreement acknowledged the so-called Irish Dimension by creating the Intergovernmental Conference for close co-operation between both governments on Northern Ireland, was to be critical in persuading Unionists to negotiate, if only in an effort to undermine the entire agreement. Sinn Fein and the IRA rejected the agreement because they believed it sustained the unionist veto over the constitutional status of the region. Nonetheless, the new status and role afforded the Irish government was difficult to regard as other than an advance for Nationalists.

In short, Northern Ireland's political agenda was to be rearranged by an agreement that seemed deliberately open-ended about the most important issues. Early criticism of the agreement tended to focus on its incompleteness, the apparent lack of structure, and the provocative fact that Unionists were not directly consulted while it was being negotiated. This exclusion seemed to violate a basic tenet of peacemaking strategy, namely, that the critical actors have to be involved in attempts at resolving the conflict.[3] Missing in most early analyses on the agreement was commentary on the ways in which it had altered key relationships.

CONFLICT TRANSFORMATION

In his discussion of the role of social identity in intractable conflicts, Northrup identifies three levels, peripheral, identity, and relationship, at which fundamental change in a conflict may occur.[4] 'Levels' indicate the proximity of the change to core identity constructs. The first two levels correspond to the structural and psycho-cultural approaches we discussed in Chapters 4 and 5 respectively. In this chapter, we briefly examine these two levels and then proceed to an examination of the emergence of the third, a relationship approach to conflict transformation. Our analysis of the third level focuses on the failed effort of the British government to force an identity change on the republican movement in Northern Ireland.

The first level is what Northrup calls 'peripheral changes, such as changes in a specific condition external to the parties or a specific behaviour of one or both (or all) of the parties'.[5] Such changes in the late 1960s did lead to the settlement of some outstanding issues, indeed many substantial reforms were accomplished in the areas of housing, voting, and police practices, all affecting everyday realities for both communities. But they did not lead to the transformation of this intractable conflict. Satisfaction of interest-based grievances not only did not transform the conflict, it didn't even lower its intensity. Instead, the level of violence increased in the wake of peripheral change. As Northrup puts it, 'Peripheral changes tend to have minimal impact on future relations and future disputes if the parties are involved in an intractable conflict'.[6] This is the argument we made in Chapter 5 with regard to structural interpretations of the conflict.

The second level involves changes in the identity or identities of one or more players. The expectation is that long-term resolution of the conflict would result from resolution of identity-based differences. As we indicated in Chapter 6, however, this kind of change is very difficult, and long-term, especially since it rarely comes from within. Change in identity involves a loss of self and so is most often bitterly resisted. When identity change does happen, it is usually, as we have argued, the result of a very long-term process.

In a very perceptive analysis, Jennifer Todd analyses the capacity for identity change present in the two major unionist communities, the 'Ulster-British' and the 'Ulster Loyalist'. She says that the Ulster-British community is open to change 'either by the Ulster British following the implications of their liberal ideals, or by structural changes in the British state and its relations with Northern Ireland disrupting the sense of a Greater British community'.[7] It is this last which the Anglo-Irish Agreement makes possible. The situation is very different when it comes to the 'Loyalist' community.

Ulster loyalist ideology approximates a self-contained, closed system. The binary structure of thought, purity vs. corruption, domination vs. humiliation, does not allow for any gradual move towards compromise with or understanding of political opponents. No new evidence or argument can prove that humiliation won't follow from loyalists' letting down their guard. It follows that there can be no gradual change in loyalism towards a more moderate or tolerant stance. There will be no slow 'modernization' of Ulster loyalist ideology. Change in Ulster loyalist ideology can only be radical change in the basic structuring binaries of thought. But there is little within Ulster loyalist ideology that could internally generate such a change. It appears that radical change can only be externally produced, when Ulster loyalists face what they have perceived as defeat and humiliation and if they find the experience different from what they had anticipated.[8]

Political developments within Ulster loyalism support this analysis. Despite the abolition of Stormont, the destruction of Unionist Party hegemony, the proliferation of loyalist groupings and the increased class consciousness among working class Loyalists,[9] Ulster loyalism did not radically redefine its imagined community in class rather than sectarian terms. Direct rule and loyalist conflicts with the British state have weakened the sense of British loyalty among some Loyalists but the 'primary imagined community of Northern Protestants remains Britain'.[10]

For Unionists of both types, it is precisely this linkage that the Anglo-Irish Agreement appeared to threaten. So, it was to undo the agreement and restore covenantal relationships that Unionists eventually agreed to join the Brooke talks in 1991. Ian Paisley insisted for his party, at least, they were not entering 'peace talks', but rather that they had come to overturn and replace that agreement. Any near-term hope of a change in identity among Loyalists leading to changed relationships with the other major players is consequently not well-grounded.

The third level 'involves change in the dynamics of the relationship between the parties'. It is at this level that Northrup argues that significant change in the conflict system is most likely to occur precisely because social 'core identities', though certainly involved, are not directly challenged, thus allowing parties to behave in a non-reactive manner.[11] The preservationist resistance associated with identity change does not set in because there is no effort at forced or willed change of any of the protagonists. Instead, the focus of change is the relationships between them. Bowen's natural systems theory provides a framework especially well-suited to the analysis of changed relationships and their impact on the behaviour of the participating parties.

WILLING THE IRA

Prior to the signing of the Anglo-Irish Agreement, the British had tried to 'will' or impose change on Northern Ireland by concentrating all their energies throughout the late 1970s on the military defeat of the IRA. The 'willing' was evidence of the fact that Britain was as much an actor in the emotional system that sustained the conflict as were the Nationalists and Unionists. In the context of family systems theory, willing is a recipe for failure in the promotion of peaceful change and an indication of Britain's emotional overcommitment to the unionist community. Most of the British effort was directed at the IRA but its effects were felt by the entire nationalist community. From internment on, the British army's activities appeared to accuse the entire nationalist population. When the structural remedies, including power-sharing, failed to promote resolution, an intense military effort to coerce the republican movement into abandoning its violent campaign was launched by the British government. Thousands of house searches (329,049 from 1969 to 1984), ubiquitous military patrols, criminalization, and Diplock courts pointed to a campaign of coercion conducted by the British. There was, (see Table 7.1), it seemed, an army of occupation at work in the most involved areas of Belfast, Derry and Armagh. In Derry in 1973, about 7,000 British soldiers and another 4-6,000 local police and security forces were on duty, one security force member for every five people. In the early 1990s, there were still about 31,000 security forces, nearly 18,000 of them heavily-armed British soldiers patrolling on foot or in armoured vehicles, in cities and towns, often down narrow streets, throughout Northern Ireland. All this among people previously noted for their law-abiding behaviour.[12]

TABLE 7.1 Numbers in the British Army, the UDR and the RUC, 1972-92

	British Army	UDR	RUC	Total
1972	17,000	8,500	5,500	31,000
1982	10,500	7,000	12,500	30,000
1992	12,000	5,500	14,000	31,500

Willed change threatens individuals or groups with loss of identity, thus reinforcing the very aspects of identity one may be trying to change. We have already referred to the resistance brought about by efforts to deny identity. Friedman writes that 'All willing of others immediately creates an emotional triangle . . . since it puts the willer between the willed one and that person's own will or habit. That is enough reason to understand its ineffectiveness. But willing others is also generally a reactive phenomenon.'[13] Willing others to change, unless accompanied by overwhelming force, rarely works because it usually provokes the escalatory processes that inhibit reconciliation and resolution. In this case, the British and the IRA tried to coerce one another despite the fact that the professed aim of the IRA was not, under certain circumstances, unacceptable to Britain, i.e. Irish unity. But military coercion had the effect of increasing the demand for communal solidarity in the nationalist community, and IRA resistance was increased, not decreased as the British had hoped. In short, the costs of

compromise to Sinn Fein and the IRA were increased by the British military campaign. Mere infliction of heavy losses on the IRA should not
have been expected to lead to an IRA petition for peace. Indeed, it can be
argued that peace is least likely when a losing party expects, as the IRA
did in the 1970s, to win in the long-run.[14] While the British government
preferred to think of itself as a detached third party outside the emotional
system that contained Northern Ireland, their emotional entanglement
was clear and intense. Nothing could better illustrate the difficulties of
'willing' change and being triangled into an emotional system than the
developments associated with the treatment of IRA prisoners.

THE PRISONERS

In 1976, the British government, as part of its overall policy of defeating
the IRA militarily, had reversed its policy of treating IRA prisoners as
'special category'. Instead, they were declared 'criminals', deprived of
their former status and subjected to all standard prison regulations[15].
Criminalization of the prisoners did not, however, have the anticipated
effects of de-legitimating the IRA in the eyes of its own supporters, nor
of impeding their organizational efforts inside and outside the prisons.
New prisoners refused to participate in the new prison regime, which
included wearing special prison garb. Taking their inspiration from a
nearly one-hundred-year-old 'Fenian' tradition, approximately 450 prisoners went 'on the blanket', in other words went naked except when
moving outside of their cells when they wrapped themselves in their
blankets. Denied permission to use the toilets unless wearing prison
clothing, the prisoners requested buckets into which they could 'slop
out'. The requests were denied, and the famous 'dirty protest'
commenced during which prisoners and wardens drew each other into a
world of 'unrelieved filth'. As O'Malley describes it:

They broke the windows in their cells and threw packages of excrement wrapped
in whatever was at hand out into the yard below; wardens outfitted in special
suits threw it back in. When the windows were blocked, they smeared the faeces
on their cell walls and the ceiling or shoved it under the bottom of the cell doors.
It was disgusting, putrid, and repulsive – and it didn't work.[16]

The British authorities did not budge and neither did the prisoners.
Rather than isolating the terrorists, the British antagonized the nationalist population, provoking communal loyalty and sympathy throughout
the community. SDLP differences with Sinn Fein were minimized in an
effort to change British policy. On the republican side, the incidence of
violence was up, and the prisons were politicized with the result that

sympathy and support for the prisoners grew. Among Nationalists not at all supportive of the IRA's campaign, there was grudging, but real, respect for the sacrifice the prisoners were willing to make.[17] On the unionist side, the protest confirmed the view that the prisoners really were nothing but common criminals willing to create the conditions of their own debasement. While some Unionists thought that the army appeared ready to seek the defeat of the IRA, most sat warily on the sidelines while the British and the IRA punished one another, deepening the already bitter chasms between themselves. The political process was re-defined in the manner described by Horowitz in Chapter 5. Competition was within rather than between ethnic communities, and communal loyalty was the standard of virtue.

Faced with the realization that their sub-human predicament was to continue indefinitely, the prisoners turned, as the means of their redemption, toward the hunger strike, a familiar weapon in the republican tradition. Indeed, it was a hunger strike that secured special status for them in the first place. This time it was to be a tragic failure.[18] The prisoners demanded the right:

- to wear their own clothes
- to refrain from prison work
- to associate freely with one another
- to organize recreational facilities and to have one letter, visit and parcel a week
- to have lost remission time restored.

The British refused to concede.

On 5 May 1981, Bobby Sands died after sixty-six days of fasting, the first of ten hunger-strikers to die that year. All parties to the Northern Ireland conflict were drawn into the emotional storm created by the hunger strikes. For 271 days, Northern Ireland waited, anxious, fearful and angry, while prisoner after prisoner moved toward slow and agonizing death. Martyrs to the nationalist community, the prisoners were seen as willing terrorists by Unionists and the British. Never was the Northern Ireland polity more polarised.

The strikes were called at a time when Sinn Fein and the IRA were being politically marginalized. The popular Peace People's Movement[19] had mobilized opposition to violence, some progress on the political front appeared possible and relentless British security policy continued to threaten the IRA's position. All combined to weaken the republican position. Indeed, before the hunger strikes political support for republicanism in the North was not growing, and Sinn Fein was hardly a factor in southern politics. The republican movement was once again in danger of being kept to the margins of political life when the hunger strikes provided it with a new dynamic.

While it is clear that the strikers may have been motivated to free themselves from the terrible conditions of their confinement, the strike as a whole was an attempt to invoke the mythical and sacrificial elements of the Republican tradition, from the 1798 Revolution to the Easter Rising of 1916. It was a claim the IRA had had difficulty establishing since 1968. They had after all been scorned in the early days of the civil rights movement, had no measureable electoral support in the North, had scant support from the people of the Republic of Ireland, and were condemned by the Catholic Church.

For the 1916 national martyrs, it had been more important to suffer and to endure than it was to triumph. Faced as they were with certain defeat, it was imperative only that they sustain the national ideal. Similarly for Sands and his comrades, this was the latest but surely not the last chapter in what they perceived to be a centuries old struggle for Ireland's freedom. Popular versions of Irish history had long recounted the tales of heroic blood sacrifice and had sanctified these efforts by identifying them with the sacrifice of Christ Himself. In was in this tradition that the hunger strikers of 1980-1 wished to cast themselves.

It was not quite so glorious. After Sands' death, there was more resignation than planning among the fasting prisoners. They were entrapped, as was their society, now more bitterly divided as a result of the strikes. Yet, however marginal they may have been before the strike, the ten men significantly influenced the political agenda of Northern Ireland. Feelings of shame, guilt and outrage silenced moderation and defeated discourse everywhere. Nationalists who failed to honour the sacrificial heroes were seen by many to have betrayed their community's cause. People who only a short time before were marching for peace were now banging trash can lids upon the announcement of each new death. The moral advantage seemed to be passing to the hunger striker.[20]

The republican tradition for which the men died had only one story to tell: the source of Ireland's problems was and is Britain. The conflict as seen by Sinn Fein and the IRA remained strictly an anti-imperialist one, they scarcely noted the descendants of the settlers in their midst. The strikes, and Margaret Thatcher's uncomprehending, 'What do they want?' (the question she put to the Catholic primate, Cardinal O'Fiach, when he made representations to her about the prisoners' conditions),[21] invoked myths and images of past struggles against British imperialism. Not a word was spoken concerning relations between Catholics and Protestants. All that would have to await the resolution of the colonial struggle.

As had happened in the wake of the British executions of the 1916 leaders, the political fortunes of the IRA and Sinn Fein rose dramatically, threatening to give Sinn Fein majority status in the nationalist community. In the wake of the electoral support recorded for Sands, entered as a candidate in a parliamentary by-election shortly after he went on hunger strike and the subsequent success of Owen Carron, the candidate chosen to replace Sands when he died, Sinn Fein decided to re-engage in electoral politics. Five of their candidates were elected to the Northern Ireland Assembly in 1982 and nearly forty per cent of Nationalists voted for Sinn Fein in the 1983 elections to the Westminster Parliament.[22] 'An Armalite in one hand and a ballot paper in the other', had become Sinn Fein's calling card. Momentum as well as moral advantage seemed to be on the republican side.

STALEMATE

Before movement towards conflict transformation can occur, the escalatory processes of a conflict have to cease. Pruitt and Rubin in their *Social Conflict: Escalation, Stalemate and Settlement* argue that at some point all conflicts reach a stage of stalemate. The existence of a stalemate means that maximum conflict intensity has been reached, and the outlooks of the antagonists begin to change with the growing realization that the opposition cannot be subdued.

People in an escalated conflict can do only so much damage to each other, and for only so long. Eventually, after each has heaped on the other's head all the nastiness, manipulativeness, and abuse that he or she can muster, there comes at last a time of stalemate . . . At the point of stalemate, neither party can or will escalate the conflict further, though neither is yet able or willing to take the actions that will eventually generate an agreement.[23]

The point is not that the violence will cease, it doesn't, but only that it will not escalate in a sustained manner. A stalemate condition of this type began to develop around 1982, when the British and Irish governments, as well as the IRA, came to accept that victory in a strictly military sense was not possible either for the IRA or for the British. After the hunger strikes the violence tended to level off, never reaching a hundred deaths again, and averaging about seventy-eight deaths a year. This, generally speaking, was the situation that prevailed when the Anglo-Irish Agreement was ratified. Following the agreement, however fitfully and slowly, the political climate began to improve adding further to the 'military' stalemate. Using the framework developed by Pruitt and Rubin, three reasons can be suggested for the development of the stalemate.[24]

The first refers to the failure of the contentious tactics employed by the respective players. By contentious, we mean tactics used in an effort to get your own way at another's expense. Both the British army and the IRA acknowledged, in the early 1980s, that a military victory by either side was not possible. The much vaunted, post hunger strike 'ballot paper in one hand and Armalite in the other' campaign of Sinn Fein-IRA faltered when Sinn Fein's electoral prospects dimmed, North and South, after 1982, and little prospect of significant new electoral support for Sinn Fein emerged. On the other hand, while security policies were becoming more effective, more professional, and more coordinated between North and South, they remained unable to defeat the IRA. Significantly, unionist defiance did not, unlike in 1912 and 1974, recruit Britain to the unionist side. The 'Ulster Says No' campaign which followed the Anglo-Irish Agreement was more nostalgic than productive.

Second, the human and financial costs were becoming unacceptably high. While low when compared with other conflict situations, human losses were substantial in Irish terms (see Table 7.2), and increasingly meaningless once it began to be acknowledged that a military victory was not possible. While data clearly indicate a significant reduction in the levels of violence in the period between the end of the hunger strikes and the signing of the Anglo-Irish Agreement, violence persisted. In particular, it is important to note that though British army deaths decline, RUC fatalities fluctuate and, overall, remain high (see Table 7.2).[25] Such fatalities impact considerably on the unionist community and inhibit any willingness towards an accommodation.

TABLE 7.2   Deaths 1982–85

	Army	UDR	RUC	Civil	Total
1982	21	7	12	57	97
1983	5	10	18	44	77
1984	9	10	9	36	64
1985	2	4	23	25	54

In financial terms Britain was spending over 200 million pounds a year on the military mission, while the subventions to Northern Ireland amounted to over three billion pounds a year. The British subvention provided 'twenty-five to thirty per cent of the Northern Ireland population's disposable income',[26] a subvention that the British government

was unhappy to allow to continue indefinitely. Inward and local investment was also being frustrated, thus exacerbating an already costly
unemployment problem (see Table 7.3).[27] The result was that the
economy became even more dependent on British subventions.

TABLE 7.3 Unemployment Rates

	Protestants (%)		Catholics (%)	
	Male	Female	Male	Female
1971	7	4	17	7
1981	12	10	30	17
1991	14	9	36	15

Third was the question of electoral support. Sinn Fein's entry into
electoral politics did not result in majority nationalist support for an
escalation of the armed struggle. Despite achieving the degree of electoral support over the period 1981-83 noted earlier, Sinn Fein's share of
the nationalist vote indicated no overwhelming desire for an escalation
of the conflict. The SDLP remained firmly at the head of nationalist
opinion and firmly committed to its non-violent, constitutional approach.
Within the unionist community the same election results also indicated
no growth in support for the more extremist DUP, nor were loyalist paramilitaries ever able to mount an electoral strategy of any significance
during this period. At the same time, the language of nationalist
proposals became much more inclusive with regard to Unionists.
Statements from the SDLP, for example, respecting the legitimate aspirations of Unionists were much more likely than before. In particular, the
Forum for a New Ireland of 1983-4 indicated a nationalist willingness,
North and South, to consider, in addition to its own preferred proposals,
'any alternative' that might be proposed, a clear invitation to Unionists
to enter negotiations.[28]

As John Darby has argued, Northern Ireland about this time achieved a
manageable level of violence, one which allowed the normal life of the
country to continue, even if it were occasionally punctuated by violent
episodes.[29] Boyle and Hadden point out that the 'level of deaths and
serious injuries' attributable to the violence in Northern Ireland is about
half that due to traffic accidents. Moreover, a 'holiday in Northern Ireland
for a Frenchman or an American is a good deal less risk than staying at
home. And most people in Northern Ireland have less direct contact with
death or injury from the conflict than from ordinary accidents.'[30]

At best, therefore, a dangerous form of stalemate had been reached which, if allowed to persist, could degenerate into something worse but, either way, entailed an unacceptable level of costs. Breaking the stalemate would require an initiative from a participant, or participants with considerable freedom of movement, i.e. either the British or Irish government, or both. Of the two, it was the British government which had the greatest freedom of movement, given its historic willingness to accept a form of Irish unity and its actual distance from the conflict.

NEUTRALITY

The British government began to understand, after seeing Sinn Fein's electoral success in the early 1980s, that a thorough policy reversal was required if they were to avoid turning the nationalist population, North and South, over to the republican movement. Old myths persisted, and old wounds had deepened after a decade of political and military struggle. In the aftermath of the hunger strikes and in the years before the signing of the 1985 agreement, the British concluded their effort at willed change had failed.

According to Bowen's natural systems theory, the principal way in which emotionally charged relationships can be substantially changed is through the adoption of a posture of emotional neutrality by one of the key actors.[31] Neutrality locates the cause of conflict in the emotional processes of a system, not in the dispositions of a particular person, group or the characteristics of a particular event. Natural systems theory argues that the relationships that comprise the system can be altered if one of the parties within the emotional triangle adopts a neutral or differentiated position within the emotional triangle. That is, the neutral actor remains connected to the other parties, but is not entrapped by them. Instead, there is now a balanced approach in which the actor refuses to be driven by the emotional demands of one or the other. Entrapment itself may be a condition of escalation of conflict, and thus its central place in Bowen theory.[32]

The emotionally neutral actor is less concerned with willing either structural or psycho-cultural change in the other actors, than with defining his own position in relation to the conflict. The neutral is able to be in the 'presence of disharmony without taking sides'.[33] Such an actor is not without commitments or position, but establishes these for himself, or herself. Nor does the neutral actor withdraw.

Indeed, the actor remains connected and involved with both parties but continues to be independent of their attempts to will its own behaviour. Neutral third parties thus avoid the blaming and side-taking manoeuvres that either recruited them to one side or opposed them to another because they incite the very emotions – defensiveness and resistance – which tend to prolong conflict. This actor remains in the system as an enabler, i.e. one who promotes responsibility in the other actors.

DE-TRIANGLING

While the idea of an emotionally driven triangle reveals how and why conflicts expand, the alteration of the triangle in certain ways will also reveal how conflicts can be transformed. When the neutrality of one key actor induces or elicits greater responsibility in one or more of the other actors in the emotional system, Bowen says that de-triangulation has occurred.[34] The major strategic contention of Bowen theory is that the emotional neutrality of one in the system will produce higher neutrality or differentiation in the other members of the triangle, though not necessarily simultaneously. De-triangling becomes the single most important peacemaking mechanism in the natural systems framework.

How does neutrality produce this de-triangulation effect? The argument is that the greater differentiation of one actor will cause greater differentiation in others, i.e., there will be a reduction in the level of the other's emotional reactivity. Neutrality works in this fashion because it reduces significantly the degree of emotional dependence on the now neutral actor. A basic tenet of family systems therapy is that the tension in a two-person relationship will resolve automatically when contained within a system of three persons, one of whom is emotionally detached. In other words, despite togetherness urges to the contrary, a problem between two people can be resolved with the well-intentioned efforts of a third person to 'fix' it. A resolution requires only that the third person be in adequate emotional contact with the other two and able to remain emotionally separate from them. The process of being in contact and emotionally separate is referred to as de-triangling.[35]

Previously, Unionists who always feared for their own extinction, were able to rely on the British to sustain them against real or imagined threats. The Anglo-Irish Agreement effectively undermined this covenantal relationship. In the next section, we first examine the substance of the Anglo-Irish Agreement and then study how it produced the de-triangling effect with regard to the major actors.

THE ANGLO-IRISH AGREEMENT

The Anglo-Irish Agreement is itself the most important example of a British effort at neutrality or de-triangling. A formula for addressing the Northern Ireland conflict already existed, one propounded in the 1980 summit meeting between Taoiseach Charles Haughey of the Republic and Britain's Prime Minister Thatcher, emphasizing that the 'totality of relationships' had to be considered if a political solution were ultimately to be achieved. A similar realization had already occurred to the SDLP and it, too, advanced, in the New Ireland Forum (1983-84), the search for new relationships. In general, this approach identified three major sets of relationships: first, those between the two main communities within Northern Ireland; second, the relationships between Northern Ireland and the Republic of Ireland, and third, those between Ireland and Britain.[36] It was the specific emphasis on relationships rather than on sovereignty and territorial claims which was the distinguishing characteristic of this approach. While the New Ireland Forum proposed three specific, structural remedies (a united Ireland, a North-South confederation, and joint responsibility), it 'also declared that its members would be prepared to consider any other proposal that might win widespread support and be likely to achieve peace and reconciliation'.[37] Prime Minister Thatcher rejected the first three with her famous 'out, out, out' utterance[38] and, initially, refused to take up the suggestion that alternative proposals be considered. Nonetheless, following an intense diplomatic initiative, only a year later, at the urging of Garrett FitzGerald, the two governments, worried at the growing acceptance of Sinn Fein in the nationalist community, were to seize upon the open-endedness of the Forum's approach and sign the Anglo-Irish Agreement.[39]

The Anglo-Irish Agreement was unique in that it was not a conventional plan for peace in either a structural or a psycho-cultural sense. It did not promote an interest-based resolution nor did it deal with the seemingly irreconcilable identity-related psycho-cultural differences between the two groups. Instead, the agreement focused on creating new relationships within the Northern Ireland system and transformed the conflict to one defined by an array of forces within Northern Ireland and between those forces and their immediate external referents, the Republic of Ireland and Britain.

Two particular articles of the agreement precipitated this transformation. The first was Article 1 which stated:

The two Governments
a) affirm that any change in the status of Northern Ireland would only come
   about with the consent of a majority of the people of Northern Ireland;
b) recognize that the present wish of a majority of the people of Northern
   Ireland is for no change in the status of Northern Ireland;
c) declare that, if in the future a majority of the people of Northern Ireland
   clearly wish for and formally consent to the establishment of a united Ireland,
   they will introduce and support in the respective Parliaments legislation to
   give effect to that wish.

In this first article, Britain moved toward a more neutral position by
acknowledging its acceptance of the principle that a majority in the
North would determine the constitutional status of the province, thus
allowing for either the *status quo,* or a united Ireland at some point in
the future. In the strictest sense, this article ended Britain's entrapment
and affirmed its status as an independent actor.

The affirmations contained in this first article are significant for a
number of reasons. First, they restate the British government's repeated
commitment to the unionist community that no change in the status of
Northern Ireland would ever be agreed to by Britain against the wishes
of a majority of the people of Northern Ireland. At least in part, then, the
covenantal arrangement is maintained. A second reason is that for the
first time in a formal agreement with a British government, an Irish
government also committed itself to the constitutional status supported
by the majority in Northern Ireland. While Unionists wanted the
Republic to go further and rescind Articles 2 and 3 of the constitution,
this affirmation signalled to Unionists that a united Ireland would not be
imposed on them. Finally, the British government formally, and for the
first time, committed itself to facilitating the achievement of a united
Ireland should a majority in Northern Ireland consent to the same goal.
It was this commitment more than any other that finally established
Britain's emotional neutrality with regard to the constitutional outcome
in Northern Ireland.

On previous occasions, Britain had backed away from reforms or
changes in its relationship with Ireland and later Northern Ireland. This
time, however, the commitment to accept any agreed outcome was actually deepened over time. In 1990, Peter Brooke, the British Secretary of
State for Northern Ireland, declared that Britain had no selfish strategic
or economic interest in Ireland.[40] He stressed that Britain was not
opposed to political unity in Ireland and went further in saying that if a
majority of people in Northern Ireland expressed a wish for a united

Ireland, then Britain would make the necessary political provision to facilitate that eventuality.[41]

The second article provided that the Irish government would have a role to play in the governance of Northern Ireland.

Article Two of the agreement established a formal means whereby both governments would consult over Northern Irish affairs. An Anglo-Irish Intergovernmental Conference was established and given wide powers of consultation on political matters, security matters, and legal issues including the administration of justice, as well as on the general promotion of cross-border cooperation. As set out in Article Three, the conference would have a permanent secretariat to assist in its work and its meetings could be attended by various officials from both governments.[42]

Informally, the Conference provided members of both governments numerous opportunities to discuss the elements of a workable solution to the crisis in the North. In other words, it established a permanent negotiating table for both governments. Furthermore, the establishment of the Conference gave the Irish government a formal role in the affairs of Northern Ireland that it had never previously enjoyed. Ministers from the Irish government were now in a position to make their views known on a regular and formal basis to their counterparts in Northern Ireland and, as Article Two stated, 'determined efforts shall be made through the Council to resolve any differences'. This latter commitment was intended to demonstrate that the consultative process was to be a very serious one as far as both governments were concerned.[43] Indeed, Article Two was crucial to the nationalist community because, through the Irish government, it gave their representatives a channel of influence on decision-making much more powerful than anything they could muster on their own at that time. In contrast, given Britain's implied neutrality, Unionists were to resent this role of the Irish government more than any other feature of the agreement, not just for its own sake but because it seemed to signal starkly how much on their own they now were and how much more influence nationalist representatives could acquire.

CONCLUSION

Interestingly, the major variable affecting the outcome seems to be the adroitness and persistence of the differentiating partner, not the degree of reactivity of any member wanting to de-differentiate the relationship. This is why Britain's decision to sign the Anglo-Irish Agreement and asssume a neutral, de-triangled position was so important. Britain went from 'out out out' to the signing of an agreement in which it acknowledged its neutrality about the constitutional outcome.

The depth of the change was buttressed by the changes that the British made in security policy. Not only did the British back away from various policies that offended against human rights, but the number of deaths attributed to security forces declined and stayed low. In the ten years following Sinn Fein's electoral success in 1982, the security forces were responsible for an average of 6.9 deaths per year. In the ten years preceding that successs, they had been responsible for 21.3 deaths per year.[44]

The Anglo-Irish Agreement had several very important effects on the unionist-loyalist elements of the population, most notably with respect to the historic settler-covenantal relationship to which we have assigned so much importance. First, unionist dependency on, and collusive behaviour with, Britain was diminished greatly. We started this chapter by referring to Britain's significance for communities in order to maintain themselves and their identities. The history of unionism is replete with settler and covenantal themes of dependence derived from the inability of the Protestant settlers to provide for their own security. Unionists frequently called on Lord Randolph Churchill's famous 'Orange Card' in order to avoid abandonment. Since the imposition of Direct Rule, that dependency had deepened. Northern Ireland was, by the mid-1980s, without a locally elected government of its own for nearly a quarter of its existence. Richard Sennet warns that dependency almost always results in a paradoxical form of negation (revealed in the fear of extinction) where the dependent party maintains the appearance of independence by criticizing the authoritative actor.[45] Dependence is thereby disguised. This helps us to understand the vitriolic criticisms of British governments and policies launched by many Unionists from the late 1800s to the present, even as these arguments seek to maintain the link with Britain.

Once the British government's resolve to remain committed to the agreement was apparent, Unionists began to recognize that, with the dependency relationship substantially compromised, they had to become increasingly responsible for themselves. They understood that Britain would not again be triangled into the conflict on the unionist side and that they would be unable to persuade Britain to resume the covenantal role. Feelings of threat would no longer suffice to have Britain pull unionist and much less Protestant chestnuts out of the fire. Nonetheless, Unionists were not completely abandoned and although slow to accept, they had gained a significant and this time a joint constitutional guarantee. Both governments were now formally agreed that there could be no change unless and until a majority in the North agreed to such a change. Beyond that, however, Unionists were to be left to determine the nature of their relationships with Nationalists within the North, with the rest of Ireland and indeed with the political order in Britain itself.

A second major effect of Britain's neutrality was that Unionists were no longer able to rely on the past. The mythologies of the past, while they suggest communal togetherness, were of little use in defining a future constrained by the Anglo-Irish Agreement. The past, with all its metaphors of resistance, not an inch, and no surrender, counted for less in a new world where compromise was necessary in order to maintain self. Unionists now realized that there was no hope they could overcome the Anglo-Irish Agreement unless they first joined the kind of comprehensive political talks they had previously disdained. Unionists were learning that they could not determine their fate by themselves.

EIGHT

DIFFICULT RELATIONSHIPS: FROM HILLSBOROUGH TO STORMONT

The immediate aftermath of the Anglo-Irish Agreement was not the benign scenario suggested in the agreement's preamble. Despite a continuing decline in the overall number of fatalities, IRA violence continued unabated and with a viciousness previously not evident, the Enniskillen massacre on Remembrance Sunday in 1987 being the most horrendous. More ominous was the growing threat of loyalist violence once again accompanied by a form of constitutional rebellion by the unionist political parties. In view of long held suspicions towards the Republic of Ireland, the Anglo-Irish Agreement was, not surprisingly, greeted with considerable opposition in unionist circles.[1] Guarantees on Northern Ireland's status, the stress on respect for identity and the agreement's commitment to reconciliation all paled into insignificance set against the formal involvement in the affairs of Northern Ireland afforded to Irish governments. A flood of anger burst from most sections of the unionist community. In particular, Unionists claimed that they had been betrayed by the British government whose Prime Minister had, only twelve months previously, so firmly and dismissively rejected the main proposals of the New Ireland Forum. Their sense of betrayal was succinctly expressed by Peter Robinson, Deputy Leader of the DUP, who talked about the Anglo-Irish Agreement having pushed Unionists onto the 'window ledge of Union'.

Public protests were held throughout the North, culminating in a giant rally in Belfast at which all leading unionist politicians came together on a common platform of resistance to its implementation. Outrage at what they described as an act of betrayal by the British government was profound. The betrayal was seen as two-fold: first, the unionist leadership claimed it had been deceived by the British into believing that no such agreement was in preparation and that any new arrangements with the government of the Irish Republic would not pose constitutional problems; second, the nature of the agreement itself with its consultative role for the Irish government was a development which no unionist had seriously contemplated would have been conceded, least of all by a Conservative government which, only twelve months previously, had so strongly rejected the main recommendations of the New Ireland Forum.[2]

Unionist opposition translated into several forms: attempts at disrupting the operation of local government by adjourning meetings where the unionist parties were in a majority; a boycott of contacts with government ministers by unionist politicians; the resignation of unionist members of parliament in order to force a series of by-elections which would provide a measure of popular support for this opposition. The first of these forms of protest was the most acrimonious and the most persistent and in several local councils business was seriously impeded for long periods The most dramatic protest was the resignation of fifteen unionist members of parliament, necessitating by-elections in all but two of Northern Ireland's seventeen constituencies. The results were, however, not as positive for the unionist parties as they had expected. In several constituencies there was hardly any contest since the SDLP and the other major parties did not field candidates, while in one of the constituencies in which there was a contest the seat was lost to an SDLP candidate.

MOST NATIONALISTS SAY 'YES'

Within the nationalist community, the SDLP and its supporters welcomed the Anglo-Irish Agreement while stressing that it was not a solution to the political crisis, but rather a framework within which a solution could be found. Sinn Fein, however, found itself in considerable difficulty over the agreement. At first, the party denounced the agreement arguing that Article 1 formally acknowledged the British presence in Northern Ireland and conceded a veto to Unionists on progress towards Irish unity. However, the general welcome which the agreement received within the nationalist community made it difficult for Sinn Fein to denounce it too stridently. Indeed with the SDLP arguing quite trenchantly that the agreement effectively confirmed Britain's neutrality on the constitutional future of Northern Ireland,[3] and that it was now a matter for those who believed in Irish unity to convince those who did not share this conviction of their case, a basis for a dialogue with Sinn Fein was being carefully laid. That dialogue was to be one of the first positive political products of the agreement within Northern Ireland itself.

SDLP-SINN FEIN DIALOGUE

In the mid-1980s, the Sinn Fein strategy was still 'the Armalite and the ballot box', i.e. combining popular support gained in the ballot box with the pressure of the IRA's terrorist campaign. However, when it became clear that there was a limit to the success which Sinn Fein could achieve through its electoral strategy, a reassment was required. After the Anglo-Irish Agreement support for Sinn Fein stabilized at around ten to twelve per cent, a little more than half of the support that the SDLP was receiving.[4] Furthermore, the Anglo-Irish Agreement was beginning to demonstrate that the constitutional approach could win concessions from the British. Placed alongside this evidence, the 'long war', or 'Armalite' strategy was not paying any dividends and did not appear likely to do so within the foreseeable future.

It was against this background that approaches were made to the SDLP suggesting that exploratory talks between it and Sinn Fein might be worthwhile. These began with a series of one-to-one contacts between John Hume, leader of the SDLP and Gerry Adams, leader of Sinn Fein and were subsequently expanded to include other members of both parties.[5] For Sinn Fein the talks were essentially aimed at broadening the basis for concerted nationalist pressure, at home and abroad, on the British government to recognize the 'right to self-determination' of the Irish people. However, the SDLP would not seriously consider such a strategy while IRA violence continued. The SDLP's objective was, therefore, to persuade Sinn Fein of the futility of that violence, that it lacked political legitimacy and that IRA violence was counter-productive in terms of Sinn Fein's own declared objectives. Recognition of the right to 'Irish self-determination'[6] had begun to emerge as the central Sinn Fein demand replacing its demand for immediate British withdrawal. It was a demand which Sinn Fein believed had much broader appeal and, so, one upon which it felt it would be more likely to build a nationalist consensus, North and South. The talks between both parties commenced in late 1987 and lasted until the early autumn of 1988 when they ended without any agreement being reached. Nonetheless, in light of developments some years later, it is worth examining some of the main points in the exchanges which took place between them both.

Sinn Fein argued that Britain's continued 'occupation' of Northern Ireland effectively denied the Irish people the exercise of their right to self-determination; secondly, that Unionists had been granted a permanent veto over the exercise of Irish self-determination by means of its 'artificially' created majority in Northern Ireland; thirdly, that a suppressed people, like the Nationalists in the North, had the right to use force to end that suppression. Significantly, however, on this third point Sinn Fein also argued that the use of force was only an option and that it could be set aside if more effective means of achieving an end to suppression could be assured. Hence their case for a broad nationalist coalition in order to achieve that goal by political means. Sinn Fein went on to argue that the only solution to the present political conflict in Ireland was in the ending of partition, a British disengagement from Ireland and the restoration to the Irish people of their right to sovereignty, independence and national self-determination. The 'right to national self-determination' was the basis for the Sinn Fein proposal for 'a broad anti-imperialist campaign' to be led by the Irish government through an international and diplomatic offensive.

There was little that was new in this analysis. What was new, however, was the acknowledgement of a military stalemate and the emergence of a strategy aimed at embracing the major parties within the nationalsit tradition. Sinn Fein alone had not been able to advance its declared aim of forcing a declaration to withdraw from the British. It was politically too weak. So, an alliance of some kind with the other main nationalist parties in Ireland was seen as a more likely means of pressurizing Britain. The New Ireland Forum had demonstrated that a nationalist consensus of a kind was achievable. Secondly, and, particularly to create such a consensus, it was clear that the immediate objective could no longer be a simple declaration from a British government of an intention to withdraw from Ireland. The New Ireland Forum had moved quite a distance from that position with the result that none of the other parties within the nationalist tradition was likely to support such a demand. In was in recognition of these realities that Sinn Fein now began to argue what appeared to be the much more powerful case, that Britain recognize the Irish people's 'right to self-determination'. Thirdly, it was becoming clear that Sinn Fein was very anxious to gain a place within the political process – its talks with the SDLP represented a significant first move towards this end.

The SDLP, in its reply to Sinn Fein, acknowledged the basic point that the Irish people did have the right to self-detemination, but that they, the Irish people, were clearly divided over the manner in which they would wish to express themselves on self-determination.[7] Secondly, and more pragmatically, the SDLP pointed out that Unionists by virtue of their numbers and their concentration in the north-east of the island could frustrate any attempt to impose a constitutional solution to which they objected. The SDLP also argued that violence could not be justified, either constitutionally or practically, as a means of promoting Irish unity. Constitutionally, violence was unjustified because it was being invoked by only a very small minority in defiance of the wishes of the over-whelming majority of the Irish people; practically, it was unjustified because it was not achieving and had no prospect of achieving even its immediate objective of a British declaration of intent to withdraw from Ireland. Furthermore, since violence could not advance Irish unity, the consent of at least a significant section of the existing unionist commu-nity would have to be won if constitutional change in that direction was to ever happen. Seeking that consent meant persuading and negotiating neither of which would happen under the shadow of violent threats.

For Sinn Fein, the case for self-determination was premised on the claim that it was for the people of Ireland *as a whole* to determine their constitutional and political institutions. In other words, the electorate throughout the whole island had a right to vote on such matters, but only as one electorate. Such an approach rejected the case for any special, or separate consideration to be given to the people of Northern Ireland and clearly implied that the wishes of Nationalists in the whole of Ireland should override those of Unionists, a view incompatible with the approach endorsed in the Forum. Sinn Fein's case was not only contrary to the approach adopted by the main nationalist parties in Ireland, it also ignored the manner in which the principle of self-determination had been applied internationally, notwithstanding the fact that it invoked two UN covenants in support of that case: the *International Covenant on Civil and Political Rights*[8] and the *International Covenant on Economic Social and Cultural Rights*. Article 1 of each of these covenants states:

All peoples have the right to self-determination. By virtue of that right they deter-mine their economic, social and cultural development.

Another UN document quoted by Sinn Fein was the *Declaration on Principles of International Law Concerning Friendly Relations and Co-operation Among States in Accordance with the Charter of the United Nations*[9] which states:

All people have the right freely to determine, without external influence, their political status and to pursue their economic, social and cultural development, and every state has the duty to respect this right in accordance with the provisions of the Charter.

Sinn Fein argued that since the population of Ireland as a whole consti-tutes 'a people' in the sense intended by the UN then it follows that by virtue of the country's partition the Irish people were being effectively denied the right to self-determination.

Applications of the principle of self-determination have not been quite so straightforward as Sinn Fein attempted to suggest. Given accepted international practice, it would be contrary to those charters to seek the incorporation of a territory outside a particular jurisdiction simply because an overall majority in both areas, but essentially derived from one, wished to have it so. As Martin Mansergh has pointed out there are several principles involved, notably the consent of the people directly involved in the disputed territory and the resolution of disputes by peaceful means.[10] The first would require in the case of Northern Ireland that the consent of the people living there must be obtained for any change, the position endorsed in Article One of the Anglo-Irish Agreement. The second is the approach adopted by all nationalist parties, Sinn Fein apart, since 1921, i.e. that unity should only be advanced by peaceful means.

While the 1988 series of SDLP-Sinn Fein contacts concluded without any apparent positive outcome, they did mark a significant change in the relationship of Sinn Fein to the overall political process. In signalling a desire by the Sinn Fein leadership to seek a political solution, these contacts had marked the beginning of a development the more positive fruits of which would become obvious in the early nineties. One of the immediate effects of the SDLP's involvement in these talks was to be seen in the strengthened sense of siege within the unionist community. The SDLP and especially its leader, John Hume, came to be regarded as no better than fellow travellers of Sinn Fein, intent upon destroying Northern Ireland and on imposing a form of Irish unity upon the unionist community there.[11] In the latter's eyes, not only had the British government betrayed Unionists with the signing of the Anglo-Irish Agreement but now nationalist Ireland appeared to be moving close to some form of understanding and, eventually, into an alliance which could only be aimed at the final destruction of the unionist people. Violence perpetrated by loyalist paramilitaries gradually intensified in the wake of this perception.

IMPLEMENTING THE AGREEMENT

Notwithstanding the very polarized receptions which the Anglo-Irish Agreement received within Northern Ireland, and unlike the history of previous attempts at major change, its implementation was not frustrated. Indeed its strength was that in terms of many of its practical consequences only a wholesale refusal by the public service to carry out instructions would have had that effect. Moreover, since the main focus of the agreement was at a policy level, identifying what precisely resulted from the intergovernmental consultative mechanisms established was impossible. Those practical matters, especially in the social, economic and cultural spheres, which could be associated with the agreement were usually so obviously beneficial that opposition would have only appeared churlish.

The actual implementation of the Agreement was ensured through regular meetings of the Intergovernmental Conference which received reports and endorsed measures taken on the range of matters mentioned within the Agreement.[12] These meetings, attended as they were by ministers from the Irish government and their British counterparts responsible for Northern Ireland, addressed a wide range of issues relating to security cooperation, political progress within Northern Ireland itself, economic development on an all-Ireland basis, fair employment legislation as well as issues pertaining to health care in border areas North and South, education and cultural matters. However, the issues of most concern to the Conference were political developments within Northern Ireland, security cooperation and economic development.

SECURITY

Security was one of the prime motivating factors for the agreement as far as the British were concerned. The agreement made it possible to strengthen security cooperation between the two countries by providing a formal means whereby those responsible for the implementation of security policies, in particular heads of the police services in both parts of Ireland, could meet and exchange views on relevant aspects of those policies. A considerable degree of satisfaction as to the level of cooperation in this area appeared to have been reached, though the behaviour of British security forces frequently had a counterproductive impact.[13]

Linked to security issues were a number of complex judicial matters, most notably that of the extradition of persons sought in connection with terrorist offences in one or other jurisdiction. Since the outbreak of the conflict extradition had been the cause of considerable tension in Anglo-Irish relations because courts in the Irish Republic tended to uphold what was referred to as 'political exception' in extradition hearings.[14] On the basis of this exception, Irish courts would refuse permission to extradite so-called political prisoners, much to the annoyance of the British government and of unionist politicians. However, with the signing of the agreement the Irish government pledged itself to ratify the European

Convention on the Suppression of Terrorism, a convention which includes a commitment on the part of signatories to the extradition of terrorist suspects. The Irish government finally ratified the Convention in December 1987 and, as a result, extradition virtually ceased to be a matter of serious controversy between both governments.

ECONOMIC DEVELOPMENT

Article 10 of the agreement committed both governments to promoting the economic and social development 'of those parts of Ireland which have suffered most severely from the consequences of the instability of recent years'. To this end the article also states that both governments 'shall consider the possibility of securing international support for this work'. In implementing this commitment assistance was sought from a number of countries with large Irish immigrant populations, most notably the USA, Canada, and to a lesser extent New Zealand. Each agreed to contribute to an 'International Fund for Ireland'.[15] The European Community has also contributed to the Fund, grants from which are administered by an independent board accountable to the Anglo-Irish Conference. Politically the fund was significant because it provided a valuable form of international endorsement for what the agreement represented overall.

NEW REALITIES

As immediate reactions passed and as it became clear that the agreement marked a new reality for Northern Ireland, parties began to reassess their attitudes towards it. The agreement clearly implied that unless they were prepared to participate jointly in the government of Northern Ireland, all parties faced a future in which the region would be governed indefinitely and exclusively by the British in consultation with the Irish government. Only the very limited range of functions which the region's twenty-six district councils controlled would be subject to the decisions of persons directly elected by the people of Northern Ireland.

After considerable hesitation, particularly by the leaderships of the unionist parties, constrained as they were by their non-cooperative stand immediately following agreement, a willingness to explore the prospects for a new accommodation eventually emerged within the four main constitutional parties in the course of 1990. The process of encouraging this willingness was initiated by Peter Brooke, then Secretary of State for Northern Ireland, when he indicated publicly that the British government was anxious to see local politicians take responsibility. To this end he wanted to establish a basis for negotiations which would involve local parties together with the British and Irish governments. There followed a prolonged period of fifteen months consultation during which Brooke negotiated the terms for talks. The outcome was agreement by the four parties to engage in talks which commenced in May 1991.

TERMS FOR TALKING

Critical to the terms under which talks could take place was the unionist demand for a suspension of the Anglo-Irish Agreement as a condition for their parties' participation. Initially it seemed as if the unionist demand was for a total suspension of the agreement, a demand which neither the Irish government nor the SDLP was willing to accept. To do so, they argued, would have conceded a central unionist objective before any talking had taken place at all. The compromise was that there would be a suspension of the workings of the agreement within two specified dates to allow sufficient time for the talks to be completed. Effectively, this meant that meetings of the Anglo-Irish Conference and the operations of the Anglo-Irish Secretariat which supported those meetings would be suspended for a specified period. The time gap thus envisaged was approximately three months, a gap that was very optimistic and, in the event, unrealistic.

According to the terms agreed, the talks were to aim at reaching agreement on political structures for Northern Ireland and, possibly, at replacing the Anglo Irish Agreement with a more comprehensive and more widely acceptable concord. The basis for these talks was set out in a statement made by Peter Brooke, the Secretary of State for Northern Ireland in which he indicated that the talks would 'focus on three main relationships: those within Northern Ireland . . . among the people of the island of Ireland; and between the two Governments'.[16] In other words, the parameters were not merely those of Northern Ireland itself, but included the whole island and British-Irish relationships in general.

The talks were structured to take place in three phases. Phase one was to involve the four constitutional parties in Northern Ireland: Alliance, SDLP, DUP and UUP; the British government would chair this phase of the process. Phase two would involve the two governments along with the four parties, while phase three would be exclusive to the two governments. Each phase, therefore, was intended to focus on one of the three relationships which it had been agreed would form the agenda for the whole talks process.

Sinn Fein was not invited to participate because of that party's association with the IRA. In the past, the absence of an invitation to such talks would not have caused Sinn Fein much concern since its declared position had been that the British government should first announce its intention to 'withdraw' from Ireland. On this occasion, however, Sinn Fein began to stress two points. The first was that as the representatives of approximately ten per cent of the electorate its leaders had a right to participate. The second was its more traditional message that the agenda was essentially a British agenda and, as such, could not succeed in providing answers to problems that could only be addressed by Irish people. The first point was the one to receive greater attention and the one which increasingly became the more difficult to ignore. It will be discussed later in this chapter.

PROCEDURAL DELAYS

When the talks did get underway a long procedural wrangle delayed discussion of substantive issues. The procedural issues related to unionist concerns about the venue and chairing of the second phase. The prospect of their politicians engaging in talks with Irish government ministers in the parliament buildings at Stormont, still the symbol of a separate Northern Irish entity and of unionist rule, was apparently anathema to both unionist parties. Their delegates argued for all phase two sessions to be held in London. The SDLP with the support of the Irish government argued that the involvement of the latter required, diplomatically at least, that some sessions be held in Dublin, a suggestion that many unionists, at first, found totally unacceptable. Eventually it was agreed that phase two would commence in London and, while holding most of its sessions in Belfast at Stormont, would also include sessions in Dublin. The question as to who should chair phase two sessions, provided a further delay until general agreement was reached that Sir Ninian Stephen, a former Governor-General of Australia, would be acceptable.

By the time the procedural disputes had been resolved considerable time had been lost and the talks that took place in 1991 only extended to initial presentations of each party's analysis of the crisis. No proposals had been tabled when it was agreed that the talks should end because the time limit set was about to expire and the next meeting of the Anglo-Irish Conference was scheduled to take place.

ANALYSIS OR PARALYSIS

The exchanges which did take place in 1991 focused on each party's analysis of the problem. These exchanges were intended to provide each participating party with some understanding of how the others saw the situation and, by implication, what would justify each party's proposals. While these analyses offered an intriguing insight into the conceptual gaps between the major protagonists, they also contained some interesting points of convergence.

The DUP analysis of the problem was presented by Ian Paisley who began by referring to the tragic shadow which terrorism, the terrorism of the IRA, was drawing over Northern Ireland. He was quick to assert, however, that the talks which were about to begin were not 'peace talks', because a political agreement alone would not defeat the IRA.[17] Paisley's answer to this latter issue was to demand tougher measures from the British authorities against what he termed 'the Roman Catholic IRA'. He then launched into a lengthy attack on the Anglo-Irish Agreement which he described as 'a great wrong done by the Thatcher administration to the unionist majority in Northern Ireland' and, appropriately for a church minister, as an 'Iscariot scheme'.[18]

When he finally reached the core of the DUP's analysis, he concentrated on the three-fold set of relationships which he preferred to describe as fundamental 'realities' to any new agreement. As might be expected from a unionist leader, the first reality was the constitutional position of Northern Ireland as part of the UK which he declared had to be beyond dispute. He expressed satisfaction with a statement by Peter Brooke in Parliament in which the latter asserted that 'Northern Ireland is part of the UK in National and International law' and that as far as the Republic of Ireland's claim to sovereignty over Northern Ireland was concerned his government 'do not accept or recognize that claim which has no basis in law, or equally important, in International law'.[19] Paisley then proceeded to express more satisfaction with an acknowledgement in the SDLP's submission on the same basic question that

the harsh reality is that whether or not (Unionists) have the academic right to a veto on Irish unity, they have it as a matter of fact based on numbers, geography and history and they have it in the exact same way as Greek or Turkish Cypriots have a factual veto on the exercise of self-determination on the island of Cyprus.[20]

These acknowledgements appeared to offer the DUP leader some hope for success in the process about to be embarked upon.

Paisley then referred to a second 'reality', 'the geographical and historical relationship between Northern Ireland and the Irish Republic'. He argued that while this reality was often seen as one of interest to Nationalists, it should not be seen exclusively as such. While stressing the 'otherness' of the Republic by referring to it as a 'neighbouring country' Paisley stated that 'Unionists wished to create a good neighbourly relationship with the country and people with whom they share this island'. This, he emphasized, would be possible only if the Irish Republic removed 'one of the barriers to improving the relationship between us, namely the claim on our territory contained in Articles Two and Three of the Constitution of the Irish Republic'.[21]

The third reality in the DUP's analysis was the absence of a forum 'in which local politicians can help to find solutions to the problems which face those they represent'. The DUP deplored this absence and said they 'had come looking for a thorough and proper change which will return to the people of Northern Ireland a say in its government'. Interestingly, the DUP document ruled out the possibility of a return 'to the old Stormont', i.e. to any form of simple majority rule, and claimed that 'realistically the Unionist population have had to face up to that fact'.[22] This rejection of the Stormont model was notable in view of the same party's previous majoritarian attitudes.

Paisley appealed to the other participants, in particular, to the SDLP to deal with the problems before them as fellow 'Ulstermen',[23] talking almost as if Ulster was a place apart to which all participants had already given their allegiance, again apparently ignoring the different connotations which those present gave to very name Ulster. While the UUP adopted a more restrained approach in its analysis compared to that of the DUP, certain shared basic concepts emerged. Opposition to the Anglo-Irish Agreement was stressed along with the demand that Articles Two and Three of the Republic's constitution be repealed because both had contributed to the situation where 'there has been ambiguity for twenty years on Ulster's constitutional position'. Central to the UUP's aims for the talks was a plea for an end to this alleged ambiguity and for the achievement, instead, of constitutional stability. The UUP denounced the frequent practice of British government ministers who would state that the constitutional position of Northern Ireland was clear 'in national and international law. It is part of the UK because that is the clear wish of the majority of the people of Northern Ireland', but who would then add the qualification that 'There will be no change . . . unless and until a majority of the people want it'.[24] To the UUP delegation this qualification was unnecessary 'as it merely restates an accepted principle of International Law, namely the right to self-determination'.[25]

In marked contrast to the analysis of the DUP, the UUP studiously avoided any direct reference to the existence of a nationalist community in Northern Ireland with a different set of aspirations and allegiances to those of Unionists. Instead, the analysis dealt with community division simply in terms of religious affiliation, apparently on the assumption that all Protestants are unionist and that very many Roman Catholics are 'unionists with a small "u"'. Roman Catholics who might hold other aspirations were described as being no more than about twenty per cent of their community and their political aspirations obliquely described as wanting to vote 'themselves out of the United Kingdom'. Beyond this, the analysis contained no positive acknowledgement of what the nationalist tradition might represent in the eyes of the main unionist party.

Not surprisingly, once the UUP had 'reduced' the size and therefore the significance of the nationalist community, when its submission addressed the region's political problems it virtually ignored community divisions and concentrated instead on the manner in which Northern Ireland was being governed and administered.[26] In these two respects the UUP argued that the legislative arrangements for Northern Ireland in the British parliament were inadequate while the absence of a parliamentary select committee to question the manner in which the Northern Ireland Office conducted its business meant an absence of administrative accountability.

The essence of the UUP's analysis was, therefore, that whatever problems existed they could be directly attributed not to two conflicting sets of political aspirations, but rather to inadequacies in the manner in which the region was both governed and administered. The thrust of the analysis was to emphasize Northern Ireland's close relationship with the rest of the UK and, in so far as Northern Ireland itself required reform of its government and administration, this should be tied into the general reform of regional government throughout the whole of the UK. In the words of the UUP document itself:

> We are prepared to be used as guinea-pigs in establishing a system of regional administration which could be of use in the interests of good government of the Kingdom as a whole, but at the same time we would be opposed to any distortion of relationships in Northern Ireland which would fuel further instability and violence.[27]

The final clause in this comment could only be interpreted as a coded rejection of a 1974-style power-sharing arrangement which carried with it the implication of an equality of status between the unionist and nationalist communities.[28]

In stressing links with the rest of the UK the UUP analysis did, therefore, acknowledge the need for a regional political institution, but only provided it had a rather limited remit and that its establishment was accompanied by significant changes in the manner in which the region's business would be dealt with at Westminster. The UUP analysis contained one very oblique acknowledgement of nationalist grievances when it stated that 'we are not unmindful of the much smaller number who hold a different view and in our various documents we have recognized that we have a responsibility to redress their grievances – real or perceived – so that they may live in peace and contentment within the UK.' A Bill of Rights and Responsibilities was proposed as the means to that end. Ironically, having all but ignored the nationalist community, the UUP document concluded with an appeal 'for both communities in Northern Ireland to realise that, essentially, their problems will have to be solved in Northern Ireland by their political representatives and that any future prospect for them and their children is best provided for within the Northern Irish context. This will require a mutual recognition of each other's hopes and fears.'[29]

The Alliance Party's analysis stressed several principles which it believed had to be accepted, the first of which dealt with the question of self-determination.[30] On this issue Alliance argued that Northern Ireland 'despite its obvious divisions, is a community, and like any other community, has the right to decide its future, and be fully involved in its own governance'. Perhaps conscious of the charge that its analysis might be seen as stressing too strongly this distinctiveness, Alliance acknowledged the close relationships which exist between Northern Ireland and the rest of Ireland and Britain, and dismissed the claim of 'some people to elaborate notions of a separate racial group, in order to give reason or justification for the establishment of a separate jurisdiction'. Nationalism is seen as a dangerous and divisive political creed by the Alliance Party because the national 'homelands' which its proponents struggle to establish are 'only ever possible at great cost to minorities, and in our case is an injustice to our diverse heritage'.[31]

Nevertheless, throughout the rest of its analysis, the Alliance Party returned again and again to its claim about Northern Ireland's separate and distinct identity, justifying thereby its case for powerful regional institutions of government. The absence of such institutions in which all parties could participate as well as the protection which a Bill of Rights would provide were the implied explanations for the political problems faced by Northern Ireland. The provision of both would, therefore, go a long way towards addressing those problems.

The SDLP cast its analysis in the context of Anglo-Irish relationships arguing that 'The Northern Irish conflict is the last negative legacy of the ancient quarrel between the people of Ireland and Britain'.[32] From that premise followed the party's claim that 'in its contemporary manifestation the Northern Irish problem is in essence a conflict between two identities – or more precisely, the failure to devise political structures which accommodate the differences between, and allow full and mutual expression to those two identities'. The two identities were those of the nationalist and unionist communities both of which transcend the confines of Northern Ireland itself in terms of their core reference points and both of which the SDLP argued were equally valid and, as such, equally deserving of recognition, respect and expression.[33]

The SDLP also stressed a number of 'realities' which it believed had to be accepted in the search for a new political framework. These included (i) acceptance of the political process and the rejection of violence for political ends; (ii) acceptance of the three central relationships, i.e. those between the people of Northern Ireland itself, those between the people of the North and the South, those between the people of Ireland and Britain; (iii) acceptance that the Anglo-Irish Agreement represented an irreversible 'breakthrough in understanding and tackling the underlying causes of Anglo-Irish conflict'. Finally the SDLP stressed what it claimed to be the significance, in its view, of membership of the European Community. As a very pro-European party the SDLP found no difficulty with the diminution of national sovereignty which membership of the Community entailed. In fact it was a point which was very congenial to the SDLP's approach. The party could point to the fact that both Britain and Ireland's membership of the European Community required them to pool aspects of their sovereignty and if this could be done in that context, there was nothing in principle which should prevent both governments doing the same in the Irish situation.

Compared to each other the four analyses revealed the considerable gap that would have to be bridged if agreement was to be reached. Of the two main unionist parties' analyses only that of the DUP offered any significant common ground with that of the SDLP. Like the SDLP, the DUP had stressed the same three relationships as the basis for negotiations and had acknowledged, in positive terms, a willingness to have each expressed in a new agreement. Crucially the DUP had also spoken about the possibility of friendly relationships with the Republic, something which the UUP appeared to ignore completely in its opening analysis. Paisley had also rejected a return to past modes of government for Northern Ireland itself, a point on which the UUP, except by implication, was silent. On these points support was also forthcoming from the Alliance Party.

However, only barely concealed within the DUP's analysis lay a number of major conceptual obstacles which would have to be overcome in reaching an accommodation with the SDLP and the Dublin government. For example, the DUP's use of 'our' to describe the territory of Northern Ireland betrayed a definition of the people of Northern Ireland in exclusivist terms,[34] either as all Unionists, or as predominantly so. Indeed, Unionists frequently referred to the right to self-determination of 'the people' of Northern Ireland, as if there was a 'people of Northern Ireland', singular and undivided. The UUP re-echoed this concept of the people of Northern Ireland in a manner which clearly challenged the SDLP's 'two identities' argument. On this point both unionist parties would appear to have had the support of Alliance with its stress on the distinctiveness of the people of Northern Ireland. In terms of its overall thrust, however, the UUP on the UK context and its references to devolution within other parts of the Kingdom, revealed the continuing influence of that party's 'integrationist' tendencies.

Discussion of these analyses in the sessions which followed merely allowed for clarification of each party's document before the talks broke down. There was neither argument nor negotiation. The breakdown occurred once it had become clear that no further progress could be made within the agreed time gap between meetings of the Anglo-Irish Conference.

A SECOND ROUND

Efforts to restart the talks lasted throughout the closing months of 1991 and into the early weeks of 1992. By then it was clear that a British general election was imminent. While the parties did eventually meet again in February under the chairmanship of Peter Brooke, it was agreed not to recommence until after the elections had taken place. The conditions and terms for the renewal of talks remained the same, but with most of the procedural problems behind them the parties seemed hopeful that greater progress would be made on this occasion.

The elections themselves were not expected to make any significant change to the political complexion of Northern Ireland, in general terms at least. Unionists were expected to hold their thirteen of the seventeen seats which made up the region's representation at Westminster. There were, nonetheless, two features of the campaign which attracted considerable attention: the participation of the British Conservative Party for the first time in general elections in Northern Ireland and the fortunes of the SDLP against Sinn Fein in the key West Belfast constituency which had been held by Gerry Adams since 1983. In the event the SDLP won the West Belfast seat with the help of some tactical voting from the small unionist electorate in the constituency. Indeed the SDLP polled its highest ever vote with over 184,000 votes while Sinn Fein gained only slighly more than 78,000. The Conservatives failed to make a significant impression, gaining only five per cent of the votes cast and, thereafter virtually disappeared as a political organization in Northern Ireland.[35]

The second round of talks was long and intense, lasting as it did from May until early November and necessitating two extensions to the period for which it had been agreed to suspend the Anglo-Irish Agreement. In the course of the talks all three relationships were addressed with negotiations taking place in each of the three strands. Nonetheless, this second round ended without any agreement except a commitment by the participants to resume the process, but *when* was not agreed

PROPOSALS FOR A NEW AGREEMENT

Soon after the second round commenced the local parties tabled their proposals for new political institutions in Northern Ireland and it became clear immediately just how large a gap existed between them. The two unionist parties with the support of the Alliance Party proposed that an assembly of 85-100 members be elected from which a set of standing committees be established to reflect party strengths in that assembly. These committees would then take responsibility for the government departments which would become the responsibility of the new administration. A formula for ensuring that the chairs of each committee would be shared amongst the main parties was also proposed. The three parties argued that such a system of government would be fair and equitable. While not amounting to the kind of proposals adopted in 1973 they argued that the system would be more effective in fostering co-operation because of the involvement of all parties in decisions about each area of government.

The SDLP put forward a very different and radical set of proposals, elements of which are similar to those published in 1972 in the party's very first policy document *Towards a New Ireland*.[36] In essence these proposals were based on that party's view that any new government for Northern Ireland should reflect the dual allegiance of the population. To this end, the SDLP argued that the Irish government should be directly involved with the British government in the administration of the region to an extent that went much further than the consultative role guaranteed by the Anglo-Irish Agreement of 1985. The SDLP proposed that the main instrument of government should be a special commission in which commissioners representing the two governments would share responsibility together with three directly elected commissioners and one other whom it proposed should be appointed by the European Community. The European Commissioner was intended, according to the SDLP's proposals, to reflect the growing importance and influence of European Community membership in Northern Ireland. The SDLP argued that as well as reflecting Northern Ireland's dual British and Irish identity and the allegiances which flowed from that situation, a commission would be less likely to be hostage to an assembly which could at any stage contain a large minority, or even a majority opposed to any form of cross-community co-operation in government. If, as the SDLP also proposed, the Commission was to be obliged to take all its decisions on a consensual basis, there would be a powerful incentive to seek consensus, otherwise the Commission would paralyse itself and, consequently, the operation of government by locally elected politicians. The SDLP also proposed that an assembly be elected, but one which would be restricted mainly to a consultative and interrogative role.

The gap dividing what effectively became two sets of proposals for the government of Northern Ireland was obviously very wide. Further significant gaps became evident when the talks progressed to phase two and began addressing North-South links. Unionist insistence that Articles 2 and 3 of the Republic's constitution would have to be replaced to remove the claim to jurisdiction over Northern Ireland which Unionists argued they contain became a crucial issue, one that could be said to have effectively logjammed the talks. In their demand the unionist parties had the support of the Alliance Party and of the British government. An amendment to the constitution *could* be made, the Irish government argued, after an agreement was reached which commanded the support of all the participants to the talks. The Irish refusal to make any firmer commitment to constitutional change became a major sticking point. Unionists had argued that the Irish delegation should remove any doubt and commit itself to saying that it *would* initiate the process to amend the Constitution.

A second point of disagreement arose out of proposals for the establishment of North-South political institutions which would promote co-operation between both parts of the island. The SDLP and the Irish government argued for the establishment of institutions which would have *executive* functions, whereas the unionist and the Alliance parties appeared to favour institutions which would have no more than consultative powers.

The talks ended in early November without any significant progress on these substantial issues when the two governments insisted on holding a meeting of the Anglo-Irish Ministerial Conference which had not met since April. The unionist parties had made it clear that they would not continue talking if a Conference meeting was held. A contributing factor to the ending of the talks was the withdrawal of the junior partner to the Irish coalition government from the southern administration, a move which precipitated an earlier than expected general election in the South.

SDLP-SINN FEIN CONTACTS RENEWED

Another crucial factor was Sinn Fein's growing demand for a role in the search for a settlement. While Sinn Fein's exclusion from the inter-party talks process still held, there were strong hints of new and more positive emphases within the party, not only in terms of Sinn Fein's own policies and tactics, but also in terms of what the IRA might decide.[37] The reasons for this included several factors. Firstly, acceptance that after twenty years of a sustained campaign, the IRA had not succeeded in obtaining a commitment from the British government to withdraw from Northern Ireland, nor had its political counterpart, Sinn Fein, succeeded in rallying support from more than a small minority of Irish people, ten per cent of the Northern Irish electorate and two per cent in the Irish Republic. Any political advantage which Sinn Fein might have had in the aftermath of the hunger-strikes had slipped away and had been regained by the SDLP, especially as a result of the Anglo-Irish Agreement. As a consequence, both the IRA and Sinn Fein risked being even more politically marginalized, particularly if the basis for a new agreement was to be achieved and widely endorsed in both parts of the island. To exercise any real and positive influence on the political future of Northern Ireland would require major decisions on the part of both organizations. It would be wrong, however, to infer that Sinn Fein's electoral support and its influence were becoming insignificant. The party had retained between eleven and thirteen per cent at the 1992 Westminster elections, and at the district council elections in 1993 won over twelve per cent of the votes placing it more than five percentage points ahead of the Alliance Party and making it the fourth largest party in terms of popular support. It clearly retained significant support in Northern Ireland and a base from which it could still threaten the SDLP.

The prospect of Sinn Fein becoming involved in the political process was enhanced in April 1993 when it was revealed that John Hume had embarked once again on a series of talks with Gerry Adams, this time with the expressed aim of finding a means of ending violence.[38]

In a very significant statement issued after one of their encounters, Hume and Adams declared that what they were engaged in was 'a political dialogue aimed at investigating the possibility of developing an overall political strategy to establish peace and justice in Ireland'.[39] The statement's significance lay essentially in the shift it appeared to signal in Sinn Fein's stand on the kind of consent to constitutional change which the party might accept. Previous Sinn Fein statements on consent usually indicated a very hardline interpretation of the 'right to self-determination' by making no mention, directly or indirectly, of the unionist position. The traditional Sinn Fein stand was that Unionists could enjoy no right to over-ride the will of the majority of the 'Irish people' in expressing their right to self-determination. Notwithstanding its use of the all-embracing phrase 'Irish people' the Hume-Adams statement did, however, imply, without actually saying so, that account would have to be taken of the unionist position in seeking consent for change. Any new political arrangement in Ireland, they argued, would be 'only achievable and viable if it can earn and enjoy the allegiance of the different traditions on this island, by accommodating diversity and providing for national reconciliation'.[40] By accepting that 'the allegiance of the *different traditions*' (authors' italics) was necessary to the viability of any new agreement, Sinn Fein seemed to be accepting, or at least strongly hinting, that they were about to acknowledge the need not just for majority consent to constitutional change in Northern Ireland, but more specifically the need for *unionist* consent. If this was really the case, then a significant change was taking place in Sinn Fein's position.

The revelation that the SDLP was again talking to Sinn Fein evoked a howl of protest. Unionists declared themselves outraged and charged the SDLP with entering a pact with those who supported the IRA. The DUP indicated that it would refuse to talk to the SDLP for as long as such contacts continued. Nonetheless, it was also obvious that criticism was muted reflecting a growing acceptance that somehow or other Sinn Fein would have to be involved if the search for a lasting solution was to be successful. The need to accept Sinn Fein's involvement was reinforced when the party gained its twelve per cent share of the poll at the district council elections just several weeks after word of its renewed contacts with the SDLP became public.

The months that followed were full of anticipation as some form of response from the British and Irish became inevitable, a response that might open the way to an IRA ceasefire and to a more inclusive political process. The response took some six months to formulate but when it came it did not disappoint either in terms of its immediate significance or in terms of its impact on subsequent developments.

NINE

AN INCLUSIVE PROCESS: FROM DOWNING STREET TO SUBSTANTIVE TALKS

On the 15 December 1993 the Irish and British Prime Ministers, Albert Reynolds and John Major, issued a Joint Declaration which was primarily intended to respond to what appeared to be a significant shift in Sinn Fein's position on the prospects for a peaceful resolution.[1] The declaration dealt essentially with the following: the 'right to self-determination' of the people living in Ireland; the conditions under which the status of Northern Ireland might change to become part of a separate and sovereign united Ireland and the terms by which those political parties currently supporting the use of violence for political ends would be admitted to negotiations with other parties and with both governments in the search for new political institutions, North and South.[2] These were the issues upon which Sinn Fein had claimed, in its various contacts with both governments, that it needed clarification and reassurance so that it might present the IRA with a convincing case for a ceasefire in order to allow inclusive negotiations to commence.

Throughout 1993 and especially in the months following the revelation that Hume and Adams had resumed contact, several drafts of a possible declaration containing a British-Irish response to Sinn Fein's request were prepared and rejected before the Joint Declaration was eventually agreed.[3] The period was also one in which some horrific terrorist atrocities were perpetrated giving rise to the largest death toll for a single month since 1976. The bombing by the IRA of a fish shop on Belfast's Shankill Road, the centre of a large loyalist area, in October, left ten dead, including one of the bombers. The whole unionist-loyalist community was enraged that such an attack would be mounted against a civilian target on a busy Saturday afternoon. Dire threats against the political leadership of the nationalist community followed as Loyalists claimed that Sinn Fein-IRA and the SDLP were now very visibly acting together.[4]

But it was not political leaders upon whom vengeance was wreaked. A week after the Shankill bombing eight customers in a Catholic-owned public house in the County Derry village of Greysteel were shot dead by members of a loyalist gang and many others seriously injured. The atmosphere throughout the whole of Northern Ireland became extremely tense and full of foreboding, no doubt adding a spur to both governments in their search for the words that might break the cycle of violence. The Joint Declaration was to contain those words, though their effect was not to achieve their desired objective immediately.

In this chapter the central issues in that declaration are examined together with the developments which flowed from it and which led to the IRA's ceasefire at the end of August 1994, to be followed soon afterwards by that of the loyalist paramilitaries.

ROOTS OF THE DECLARATION

Judged in its historical context the Joint Declaration, while marking a highly significant development in Anglo-Irish diplomacy, had its roots very firmly in the Anglo-Irish Agreement. The declaration was effectively an elaboration and development of key concepts and commitments contained in that agreement, some of which had previously found expression in the report of the New Ireland Forum. As discussed in Chapter 7 the Forum parties formally acknowledged that only a balanced approach which took account of the fears, aspirations and rights of both communities in Northern Ireland could achieve the widespread acceptance necessary for success. Paramilitary violence, or any other form of coercion was rejected by these same parties as means whereby Irish unity should be achieved. The Anglo-Irish Agreement had built on this statement by formally committing both the Irish and the British governments to recognize, reconcile and acknowledge 'the rights of the two major traditions that exist in Ireland, represented on the one hand by those who wish for no change in the present status of Northern Ireland and on the other hand by those who aspire to a sovereign united Ireland achieved by peaceful means and through agreement'.[5]

Of the three commitments, that of reconciling both sets of rights posed the greatest challenge. Recognizing and acknowledging two sets of rights as legitimate does not automatically reconcile them, at least not in the political and constitutional sense. Recognition and acknowledgement can be afforded in a variety of ways, none of which might directly impinge on the major problem of how to reconcile two mutually exclusive aspirations, one of which is also a reality, i.e. the unionist aspiration to maintain Northern Ireland as part of the United Kingdom. In the Anglo-Irish Agreement, this central problem of reconciliation had been addressed in Article One by affirming the principle of consent as the only possible basis for constitutional change in the status of Northern Ireland and by formally recognizing and accepting the region's *present* status and the *possibility* of it becoming part of a united Ireland. So, while the agreement did not explicitly use the classic language of self-determination, it did so implicitly.

SELF-DETERMINATION AND IRISH UNITY

In their declaration the two Prime Ministers repeated these commitments, but, in addition, went beyond the actual terms of the agreement by explicitly referring to the need for an *all-Ireland* framework to a solution and by pledging themselves 'to foster agreement and reconciliation, leading to a new political framework founded on consent and encompassing arrangements within Northern Ireland, for the whole of the island and between these islands'.[6] This common pledge was followed by a commitment on the part of the British Prime Minister, on behalf of his government, first, 'to uphold the democratic wish of a greater number of the people of Northern Ireland on the issue of whether they prefer to support the Union or a sovereign united Ireland' but also 'to work together with the Irish government to achieve such an agreement, which will embrace the totality of relationships. The role of the British Government will be to encourage, facilitate and enable the achievement of such agreement . . . They accept that such an agreement may, as of right, take the form of a united Ireland achieved by peaceful means'.[7] Placed alongside the statement, in the same paragraph, that the British government had 'no selfish strategic or economic interest in Northern Ireland', it is difficult to interpret this commitment other than as the door being clearly opened, as far as the British were concerned, to a united Ireland. The invitation to go through that door was left to be issued by those who believed it to be in the best interests of the Irish people that all should enter. Meantime, however, the British committed themselves to *encouraging*, *facilitating* and *enabling* agreement between the people of Ireland. If, in seeking agreement, the Irish people decided to unite, it is clear from the declaration that this wish would be respected. In the event of a united Ireland being agreed then, as the Anglo-Irish Agreement had stated, both governments 'will introduce and support in their respective Parliaments legislation to give effect to that wish'.[8]

It can be argued that by these commitments the British government put itself into the ranks of the *persuaders*, as Sinn Fein had demanded, if not for a united Ireland then at least for *agreement* between the unionist and nationalist traditions in Ireland. For its part, the Irish government reiterated its previous acceptance, in the Anglo-Irish Agreement, of the principle of consent to constitutional change by stating that 'it would be wrong to impose a united Ireland, in the absence of the freely given consent of a majority of the people of Northern Ireland' and 'that the democratic right of self-determination by the people of Ireland as a whole must be achieved and exercised with and subject to the agreement and consent of a majority of the people of Northern Ireland'.[9] The principles upon which a united Ireland would be established were listed in this paragraph. In many respects they were similar to those endorsed by the Anglo-Irish Agreement where their explicit focus was Northern Ireland, rather than the island as a whole. Essentially these principles were the fundamental rights which appear in the United Nations International Charter of Human Rights: the right to freedom of thought, to freedom of religion, to political action within the law, to live without hindrance, to equal treatment in social and economic activity, etc.

Furthermore, the Irish government indicated what it believed should be the initial stages of a process for promoting better relationships between the people of the nationalist and unionist traditions in Ireland as a whole. These included examining 'any elements in the democratic life and organisation of the Irish State that can be represented to the Irish Government . . . as a real and substantial threat to their (the unionist) way of life and ethos, or that can be represented as not being fully consistent with a modern democratic and pluralist society, and undertakes to examine any possible ways of removing such obstacles'.[10] This commitment reiterated the expressed desire of the New Ireland Forum parties, quoted above, that respect for both traditions should be upheld not just in Northern Ireland, but throughout the whole island. As a contribution to the dialogue of reconciliation, the Irish Government undertook to set up a Forum for Peace and Reconciliation 'to make recommendations on ways in which agreement and trust between both traditions can be promoted and established'.[11]

IMMEDIATE AIMS

While the declaration dealt quite extensively with self-determination and the conditions under which a united Ireland could be brought into existence, such an eventuality was not seen as likely in the immediate future.

The declaration dealt, therefore, with the pressing need for political dialogue 'to create institutions and structures which, while respecting the diversity of the people of Ireland, would enable them to work together in all areas of common interest'. Such structures were regarded as essential in building the trust necessary to end past divisions, leading to an agreed and peaceful future. They would, 'include institutional recognition of the special links that exist between the peoples of Ireland as part of the totality of relationships, while taking account of newly forged links with the rest of Europe'.[12]

While this paragraph does not refer explicitly to new institutions in Northern Ireland, it is clear that this is what was intended as one element in addressing 'the totality of relationships' between Ireland and Britain. In effect, this part of the declaration was an endorsement of the agenda set for the inter-party and inter-government talks initiated by Secretary of State Peter Brooke in 1991. That agenda specified the elements which make up this totality by requiring that new structures would have to address relationships within Northern Ireland, between North and South and between Ireland and Britain. So, while the talks had been in abeyance for more than a year, both governments clearly envisaged their relaunch in some form or other. Furthermore, the governments indicated that if Sinn Fein accepted the terms of the declaration and the IRA ceased its campaign of violence, the former would be 'free to participate fully in democratic politics and join in dialogue in due course between the Governments and the political parties on the way ahead'.[13]

RESPONSES

Although the primary target of the declaration was, undoubtedly, Sinn Fein and the IRA, it is important to note the responses to it of other sections of opinion in Ireland, in Britain and elsewhere before turning to consider how it was received in those two quarters. In terms of general responses to an Anglo-Irish initiative on Northern Ireland, it is probably true to say that seldom did such an initiative receive so widespread and so enthusiastic a response. In the Irish and British parliaments both Prime Ministers received overwhelming support. In the Irish parliament, members from all sides loudly applauded Reynolds and his Deputy, Dick Spring, when they returned to report on the declaration. In the British Parliament, only Ian Paisley and his two colleagues from the DUP expressed dissent arguing, in an open letter to John Major, that it was in effect 'a tripartite agreement between Reynolds, the IRA and you'.[14] John Hume described the declaration as 'one of the most comprehensive declarations that has been made about British-Irish relations in the past seventy years' and urged that all parties to the conflict should now come to the negotiating table 'armed only with the strength of their convictions, and not with any form of coercion or physical force'.[15]

The response of the Ulster Unionist Party is of particular note since the position of Unionists was the second major concern of the two Prime Ministers. Given the commitments by the British Prime Minister to respect the wishes of 'the greater number of the people of Northern Ireland' and of the Irish Premier to respect the will 'of a majority of the people of Northern Ireland', James Molyneaux, Leader of the Ulster Unionist Party, felt able to extend a cautious welcome to the declaration and to indicate, later, that 'Ulster Unionists are content to work in harmony with all who subscribe to that principle'.[16]

Outside the political parties the declaration was widely endorsed in Ireland, North and South by the main churches, trade unions, employers organizations and many others. In the US where interest in Northern Ireland was quickening in official circles, President Bill Clinton, and leading members of the US Congress warmly welcomed the declaration. A majority of members of the European Parliament and later the Council of Ministers of the European Union signalled Europe's welcome. Support for the declaration also came, surprisingly to some, from loyalist paramilitaries, another audience at whom it had been carefully directed. The scale of the welcome was such that hopes were high that Sinn Fein and the IRA would soon express a limited welcome for aspects of the declaration, if not for it all.

SINN FEIN'S HESITATION

Initial comments from various sources within Sinn Fein, including such leading figures as Gerry Adams and his deputy Martin McGuinness indicated considerable unease about the declaration and a tendency towards a negative judgement of it. Reports from a meeting of IRA prisoners, paroled for the Christmas period, revealed very negative attitudes. According to one reporter present, the overall mood of the meeting was in favour of continuing the struggle because it was being claimed that the declaration had offered nothing which could be regarded as coming close to the Sinn Fein-IRA position. One participant was reported as saying, 'they haven't given us what we want yet, but they will if we use all the forces at our command'.[17] Martin McGuinness made what appeared to be the most hardline and negative comment to be issued by a leading figure in Sinn Fein when he was reported as saying that 'anything short of a British government decision to withdraw from Northern Ireland'[18] was unacceptable and that direct talks between Sinn Fein, Albert Reynolds and John Major were essential to any further progress in the peace talks.

In his first detailed comment on the Joint Declaration Gerry Adams identified five points which he claimed were essential to any new agreement:[19] (i) that the Irish people as a whole had the right to self-determination; (ii) that an internal settlement would not be a solution; (iii) that the Unionists could not have a veto over British policy, but that the consent and allegiance of Unionists, expressed through an accommodation with the rest of the Irish people, were essential ingredients if a lasting peace was to be established; (iv) that the British government had to become a 'persuader' for an agreement; (v) that the two governments had the responsibility to secure political progress. While the Sinn Fein President claimed that these principles had not been addressed to Sinn Fein's satisfaction in the declaration, he did not point to any specific sections of the latter to support his claim. Of the five issues identified, only two appeared to be of overriding importance to Sinn Fein, self-determination and the so-called unionist veto. The question of an internal settlement could hardly have been described as a significant issue given the set of relationships which had formed the agenda of the inter-party talks of 1991-92 and which were implicit in the declaration. That agenda had clearly indicated that any settlement would have to go beyond simply providing new arrangements for the government of Northern Ireland and also deal with the other key relationships. The question of the British government joining 'the ranks of the persuaders' has already been discussed above to indicate the extent to which it is likely that any British government would go in this respect. As for the two governments taking 'responsibility for securing political progress' the Joint Declaration was in itself clear evidence as to how that responsibility was being met.

Sinn Fein's initial response also attempted to suggest, notwithstanding the SDLP's clear support for the declaration, that Nationalists generally had found it disappointing. Nevertheless, despite these negative comments it soon became evident that a debate of considerable intensity was taking place within the ranks of Sinn Fein-IRA as to the formal response that the whole movement should make to the declaration. As that debate intensified it also became clear that Sinn Fein-IRA would not endorse the declaration in full and, in particular, would reject its acceptance that the primary condition for any change in the constitutional position of Northern Ireland hinged on the will of a majority in Northern Ireland. Sinn Fein continued to interpret this condition as a 'unionist veto' on constitutional change, a veto that they had traditionally objected to and to which they continued to show no signs of accommodating themselves. Added to this was their demand that the British government should 'join the ranks of the persuaders', in other words that the British government should use all its influence to persuade Unionists to accept and negotiate a place for themselves within a united Ireland. Neither position found any support within the declaration.

The much heralded special delegate conference which Sinn Fein convened at the end of July 1994 to adopt its formal response did not produce any significant change in the party's publicly declared position. The communique issued after the close of that conference stated that while the Joint Declaration contained several positive statements, it failed to address the unionist veto in terms which Sinn Fein could endorse.[20] In fact, the declaration was explicitly described by Sinn Fein as contradictory on the issue of self-determination because of the conditions it contained regarding any change in the status of Northern Ireland. Sinn Fein's tactic was to place the larger part of the onus for moving the situation forward on the British government. This was evident from its attempts to suggest that it was the British government alone which endorsed the key condition for change in Northern Ireland, ignoring the fact that Irish governments, both in the Anglo-Irish Agreement and in the Joint Declaration, had explicitly accepted the very same condition. Furthermore, Sinn Fein suggested that if only the British government would try to persuade Unionists that a united Ireland would be preferable to the present situation, then Unionists could be persuaded. Such a suggestion naively ignored the lessons of unionist determination not to be persuaded, either by coercion or otherwise to accept a united Ireland.

UNIONIST VETO

On the twin issues of self-determination and the unionist veto, the position of Sinn Fein now lacked clarity. The Hume-Adams statement of April 1993 had indicated that Sinn Fein had accepted the need for the allegiance of all traditions to any new arrangement but had not made clear whether allegiance implied consent or not. It would seem that it did not, at least as far as Sinn Fein was concerned. Sinn Fein continued to argue as it had consistently done that the people of Ireland as a whole constitute 'a people' in the sense intended by the UN; that the country had been partitioned in 1921 by a treaty imposed by Britain to serve its (Britain's) own strategic interests and as a response to the demands of the unionist minority in the north-east of Ireland. Partition, according to

Sinn Fein, had effectively denied the Irish people as a whole their right to self-determination and had granted Unionists a veto not only over constitutional change in Northern Ireland, but also over any form of political change there as well. Only a decision by a British government to restore that right and to treat with the people of Ireland as a whole could, therefore, undo the injustice that had been done.

As has been pointed out several times in this discussion this thesis no longer enjoyed much support outside the ranks of Sinn Fein. In the light of international understanding of the right to self-determination and especially in light of the commitments entered into in the Anglo-Irish Agreement, no Irish government was ever likely to change its stand on the manner in which self-determination would be exercised with respect to the Northern Irish problem. As to the question of the 'unionist veto', Sinn Fein's understanding was long since out of line with events. In terms of any veto on political, as opposed to constitutional, development it can be argued that unionist hegemony had been successfully challenged, first by the civil rights movement, and then subsequently in a series of developments involving the British and Irish governments and the SDLP. As a result, any unionist capacity to prevent such developments had been gradually diluted and then eventually removed, first by the 1972 decision to prorogue the parliament and government of Northern Ireland and impose direct rule. Finally, it was signalled when the Anglo-Irish Agreement provided the Irish government with a consultative role in the affairs of Northern Ireland. Since then, Unionists were no longer in a position to dictate terms to the British government on matters affecting the administration of Northern Ireland. The clearest example of this was unionist failure to achieve either a restoration of 'Stormont', or a return of any significant powers to local authorities, also removed in the early 1970s.[21]

This interpretation of developments since the early 1970s does not mean that Unionists had been left without influence. As representatives of the larger of the two main communities in Northern Ireland they continued to exercise considerable influence and, as their voting strength at Westminster was able to demonstrate whenever the government party's own position was weakened, they could use that influence to considerable effect. The decision, in 1994, to proceed with the establishment of a House of Commons Select Committee to oversee the conduct of affairs in Northern Ireland, long a unionist demand, was clear evidence of that influence and a form of *quid pro quo* from a Conservative government that was being criticized by Unionists as too anxious to concede to nationalist demands.

In general terms, of course, a unionist veto on political change in Northern Ireland remained, but only in the sense that a nationalist veto also exists. Since the stability of any new institutions of government for Northern Ireland would require the cooperation of significant sections of both communities, their establishment was unlikely without their joint consent. As for the veto on constitutional change, it is not strictly a unionist veto. As the Anglo-Irish Agreement and the Joint Declaration both clearly imply, this veto is only exercisable by a majority of the electorate in Northern Ireland and is not exclusive to the unionist community. At present the majority of that electorate clearly favours retaining Northern Ireland's position within the United Kingdom and as long as that remains the position it will be respected. It is also clear that any change is unlikely for a considerable time given the present composition of the electorate. Only in this pragmatic sense can the conditions for constitutional change be understood as amounting to a unionist veto. Nevertheless, even with respect to constitutional change, it is not true to say that no change had taken place. It can be argued with some validity that the Irish government's consultative role under the terms of the Anglo-Irish Agreement represents a dilution of British sovereignty over Northern Ireland and as such amounted to a form of constitutional change. Indeed, unionist reaction to this role since 1985 was clear evidence that Unionists acknowledged it in those terms.

DEMOCRATIC RESPONSIBILITY

It is difficult to understand, in the light of the above, what possible reason of principle Sinn Fein had for not immediately accepting the terms of the Downing Street Declaration particularly if, as they seemed to have been saying, or at least implying, that they now accepted the need for unionist consent to new political arrangements. The Joint Declaration clearly stated the limits to which the Irish government believed that it was possible to go on the question of self-determination without resorting to forms of coercion which would not be effective anyway and which clearly would not enjoy a level of support amounting to a democratic mandate. On this point, the Declaration clearly rejected the Sinn Fein-IRA case for the use of violence and challenged the right of Sinn Fein to arrogate to itself and to the IRA the right to decide how self-determination should be exercised. It was a case that Sinn Fein continued to ignore.

Despite the negative responses from Sinn Fein some signs of a positive approach had also emerged even at a early stage. The first came at the party's annual conference at the end of February when some leading members described the Declaration as an important contribution to peace, even if it was still far from being sufficient. Gerry Adams spoke of it as marking 'a stage in the slow and painful process of England's disengagement from Ireland', while Martin McGuinness acknowledged that the British were 'tentatively grappling with new realities'.[22] Such comments suggested that Sinn Fein members like McGuinness were also grappling with new realities. However, while the conference took place under the slogan of 'Peace through Self-determination' there was no acknowledgement that the Irish people had the right not just to determine their constitutional future, but also the right to determine *how* they might effect that future. The debate continued and, as noted earlier, despite Sinn Fein's eventual rejection of the Declaration, the commitments contained in it were such as to enable the IRA to announce not just a ceasefire, but 'a complete cessation of military operations' on 31 August 1994. The purpose of this cessation was, as the IRA stated, 'to enhance the democratic process'.[23] A month later the loyalist paramilitaries followed suit and also announced a ceasefire. For the first time in nearly twenty-five years Northern Ireland began to enjoy freedom from the bomb and bullet and the whole community hoped that the democratic process would indeed be enhanced. It was to be a more tortuous process than most people imagined on that beautiful August day when relief and joy spread across and far beyond Northern Ireland. The second ceasefire only added to the sense that a new dawn was breaking. But there were dark clouds and these were not slow to make their appearance, however delayed their impact would be on the ceasefires themselves.

ENHANCING THE DEMOCRATIC PROCESS

Deep suspicion characterized unionist reaction to the IRA's 'cessation of military activities'. On the one hand unionist politicians claimed that the ceasefire had only been declared in order to allow a broad nationalist alliance to be consolidated, an alliance which would inevitably follow Sinn Fein's agenda and so be profoundly ominous for Unionists. On the other hand they claimed that the cessation would not endure, that it would end within a few months, by the following January according to one unionist MP. For Ian Paisley the ceasefire meant that Protestants in Northern Ireland faced 'the worst crisis in Ulster's history since the setting up of the state'.[24] The British authorities were also circumspect and suspicious. They demanded proof that the cessation was 'permanent', a word that became the focus of considerable debate until the government eventually announced that it was making 'a working assumption' that the cessation would endure.[25]

Anxious to consolidate what it believed the cessation signified in terms of the major changes in the IRA's and Sinn Fein's political agenda and buoyed up with the expectation of the advances that might now be possible, the Irish government shared none of this suspicion or caution, at least not openly. Gerry Adams was very publicly received by Albert Reynolds, in the company of John Hume, in Dublin and all three declared themselves to be 'totally and absolutely committed to demo-cratic and peaceful methods of resolving our political problems'.[26] In Dublin's view a new and more hopeful day had really dawned.

FORUM FOR PEACE AND RECONCILIATION

As he had indicated in the Joint Declaration, Taoiseach Albert Reynolds moved swiftly to establish a new forum, open to all parties with public representation, North and South, to discuss all aspects of relationships affecting the people of Ireland. This forum, the Forum for Peace and Reconciliation, convened for its opening meeting in Dublin at the end of October 1994. All of the southern parties with representation in the Irish parliament together with most northern parties, the unionist parties excepted, agreed to participate. For Sinn Fein, membership of the Forum marked its first experience of a broad based consultative process. Operating through a process of internal and external consultation, the Forum began to address a wide agenda of issues, constitutional, politi-cal, social, economic and cultural. Its deliberations continued until it was suspended in February 1996 following the breakdown of the IRA's ceasefire.

What was of most significance in the Forum were the public signs of a shift in Sinn Fein's approaches to a number of key issues, most notably those relating to the principle of consent and to possible political struc-tures in Northern Ireland as part of an overall agreement. While the party formally remained totally opposed to the application of the prin-ciple of consent as enunciated in the Joint Declaration, i.e. in a manner which would allow for a distinct voice to the Northern Irish electorate on the question of any constitutional change, it became clear that Sinn Fein was gradually moving towards a compromise. Such a compromise would most likely be found in a formula by which Sinn Fein would accept that Irish unity in the traditional territorial sense was not presently attainable, not because Britain was opposed to it, but rather because a sufficient majority of Irish people were not yet in favour of it. Furthermore, references by Sinn Fein delegates to a willingness on their part to consider 'interim' (i.e. interim to a united Ireland) political structures for Northern Ireland marked another shift by their party towards the position endorsed by both governments and most of the other major parties, North and South.

POSSIBLE STRUCTURES

In the spring of 1995 both governments published a set of consultative documents on possible political arrangements. Preparation of these documents had first been decided in response to requests by the parties at the Brooke-Mayhew talks for the governments to do just that. Entitled *Frameworks for the Future*, the documents outlined the shape which both governments believed that new structures might take, structures which in all their essentials would be based on the principles discussed above.[27] Firstly, such structures would have to be provided to enable representatives from all sections of society in Northern Ireland to co-operate in governing and administering the affairs of the region. Essentially, this would mean building into the very fabric of future governmental arrangements provisions for power-sharing between Nationalists and Unionists as well as mechanisms for safeguarding human and civil rights. The precise nature of such arrangements as well as the powers which they would exercise would be a matter for negotiation between the parties and the two governments. Nonetheless, it was clear that future institutions could include a parliamentary type body and a politically controlled administration in which representatives from both communities would be involved.

Secondly, to address North-South and all-island relationships, new structures involving representatives from both parts of the island would have to be established. This requirement was based on the need to express in institutional form the affinity which people in Northern Ireland, especially those of the nationalist tradition, have with the people in the rest of Ireland. These structures would 'help heal the divisions among the communities on the island of Ireland; provide a forum for acknowledging the respective identities and requirements of the two major traditions . . . and promote understanding and agreement among the people and institutions in both parts of the island'.[28]

The SDLP was the northern party most anxious to see such structures in place and had envisaged them being modelled in general terms, account taken of scale, on the institutions of the European Union.[29] In other words, ministers or political heads of departments from both North and South would meet in council to discuss and agree matters of mutual concern while a parliamentary type body could provide a broad political and consultative base for such matters. North-South structures could also have a special role with respect to relationships with the European Union, many of whose initiatives had a cross-border and all-Ireland remit. Such structures could ensure effective consultation within Ireland on these initiatives as well as providing common representation on specific issues to the European Union.

Thirdly, and in recognition of the fact that the historic and geo-political framework of the problems to be resolved was the British-Irish framework, the establishment of British-Irish structures was also proposed. In this respect the Anglo-Irish Agreement had already put in place the Inter-Governmental Ministerial Council and the Inter-Parliamentary Body. Further development of such structures to include representation from Northern Ireland, especially from Unionists who had boycotted any dealings with both, were not seen to be problematic.

The challenge in agreeing the kind of structures outlined above revolved around the age-old fears of both communities. On the one hand, unionist fears that such structures, particularly those addressing North-South relationships, could become a 'Trojan horse' wheeling them into a united Ireland, would have to be allayed as well as ensuring that their sense of Britishness was being satisfactorily recognized. On the other hand and in mirror image of these fears and expectations, Nationalists had to be convinced that new structures would not pose a threat to their identity within Northern Ireland and would satisfactorily express their affinity with people in the rest of Ireland.

PROCESS

As the broad principles upon which a settlement could be based were becoming clearer, the stumbling blocks along the road to that settlement became much more process-related. In other words, the crises which arose over the period following the ceasefires in 1994, derived from a failure to agree such matters as the timing and nature of negotiations, such as who should be present and by what means should they be empowered to participate, rather than the issues to be addressed when negotiations would actually take place. The essence of this impasse lay primarily in unionist attitudes to Sinn Fein and the IRA and in the atti-tudes of the latter towards the British government.

Both of the main unionist parties, with some support from the British government, insisted that Sinn Fein, because of its association with the IRA, had to clearly demonstrate its commitment to the democratic process before they would agree to enter negotiations with that party. A clear commitment would, in the view of the unionist parties, be made evident by decommissioning IRA arms and by Sinn Fein receiving a fresh, post-ceasefire electoral mandate. Sinn Fein regarded such demands as unacceptable pre-conditions and began to suspect that the British government, with unionist connivance, was deliberately trying to undermine its position. The resultant logjam created by these demands prevented the immediate opening of all-party negotiations following the ceasefires in 1994 and produced a protracted process of pre-negotiation talks between Sinn Fein and the British government. Mistrust and suspicion mounted as these talks failed to break the impasse on disarmament. The ensuring logjam was to lead to the ending of the IRA ceasefire in early February 1996 when a massive bomb was exploded in London's dockland.

Meantime the increasingly significant role of the United States government, a role which the SDLP, through John Hume, had long cultivated and encouraged, was now more evident than ever. The most practical expression of this role was the invitation extended by both governments to President Clinton's emissary ex-Senator George Mitchell to chair a commission on how paramilitary arms might be decommissioned and on the linkage between this issue and the commencement of all-party talks. In its report the commission recommended that all parties subscribe to a set of six principles termed 'Principles for Democracy and Non-Violence' as a test of their *bona fides* before entering such talks and that the disarmament of paramilitary forces take place in parallel with negotiations.[30] While some parties declared their willingness to accept these principles, the unionist parties would not agree that IRA disarmament should not commence prior to Sinn Fein's entry to negotiations. Sinn Fein, while not rejecting the Mitchell principles, appeared to equivocate and made it clear that, in its view the IRA would not consent to any disarmament until an agreement had been reached.

To break the logjam and to provide what it claimed would be a democratic base for negotiations the British government announced that elections would have to held before parties could be admitted to the negotiating table. Both governments also agreed that a new IRA ceasefire would have to be in place before Sinn Fein would be admitted. A fixed date for the commencement of negotiations was agreed, 10 June 1996, with the Irish government and elections to determine party participation took place at the end of May. Meantime the IRA continued to explode bombs in British cities and at British army bases in Germany. For the May elections the electoral system employed required votes to be cast for parties rather than for individual candidates with the ten parties receiving most votes being invited to nominate delegates to the negotiations. The decision to allow ten parties to participate arose from a desire to include parties associated with loyalist paramilitaries despite their rather low level of electoral support. In the event two such parties, the Ulster Democratic Party (UDP) and the Progressive Unionist Party (PUP), succeeded in gaining a place amongst the top ten, as did the Northern Ireland Women's Coalition (NIWC), an all-female group which was set up virtually on the eve of the elections, and a loose grouping under the banner of Northern Ireland Labour.

The most notable outcome from the elections was the increased support registered for both Sinn Fein and the DUP. The former increased its share of the votes to almost sixteen per cent against twenty-two per cent for the SDLP while the DUP received almost nineteen per cent against twenty-four per cent for the UUP. Of the top ten parties those which could be safely described as sharing the 'middle ground', i.e. UUP, SDLP, APNI, NIWC and Labour, their share of the total vote amounted to only just over fifty-four per cent The more extreme parties in this group of ten, Sinn Fein, the DUP and the UKUP together accounted for almost thirty-eight per cent of the votes. This marked a significant decrease in support for the moderates, from sixty-three per cent in 1992, and an increase in support for the extremists, from approximately twenty-five per cent in the same year. From these percentages, it would appear that as Sinn Fein moved, however slowly, closer to the centre of Northern Irish politics following the IRA ceasefire in 1994 and, notwithstanding the ending of that ceasefire five months prior to the elections, many Nationalists no longer held reservations about giving it electoral support. Conversely, the more Sinn Fein moved into the realm of constitutional politics, the greater the fear of its presence many Unionists began to feel. Hence their need to seek the protection of Ian Paisley's DUP, as always the more strident expression of unionism's siege mentality. Once again, barely concealed fears and expectations in both communities were being ominously revealed in these results, fears of what a more confident and aggressive form of Irish nationalism might demand and expectations that it could achieve more than realistically appeared to be on offer. Just how ominous this revelation was would become evident in the following few weeks.

ANOTHER WICKED SUMMER

The negotiations which commenced on 10 June 1996 were intended to be as inclusive as it was possible and practicable. However, with Sinn Fein excluded until a new ceasefire would be declared by the IRA, the negotiations started in the absence of the party around which much of process leading to the negotiations had been woven. Sinn Fein protested that its electoral mandate was as real and as democratic as that of the other nine parties, that it had no formal links with the IRA and did not speak for that organization. Such claims had no effect. Both governments had long indicated their conviction that Sinn Fein did have close, organic links with the IRA and it was these links, not any question about its electoral mandate, which precluded them from issuing it with an invitation to the negotiations.

For seven weeks until the end of July the negotiations were completely ensnared in procedural matters, i.e. the rules by which the negotiations would proceed and the agenda which would be followed. Underlying the wrangling was a determination by the main unionist parties, ever suspicious of any 'imposition', to wrest control over the negotiations from what they regarded as the manipulations of both governments. To signal this intent they opposed the procedural guidelines and agenda proposals drawn up by the governments, thus ensuring only tediously slow progress in the opening months of the talks. Meantime, events on streets in the cities, towns and villages of Northern Ireland sketched a fraught, tense and, at times, brutal mirror image of the logjammed negotiations.

Another marching season was underway and nationalist opposition to local branches of loyalist organizations, the Orange Order, the Apprentice Boys and the Royal Black Preceptory, holding parades close to areas where considerable numbers of Nationalists lived was already being expressed in increasingly trenchant tones. At issue was the right to march versus the claim that such a right should not be exercised without the consent of residents wherever the latter might take objection to particular parades. As the summer of 1996 progressed, the number of incidents surrounding parades increased with politicians on both sides inevitably drawn into the controversies.

On the nationalist side, controversies and conflict over parades suited Sinn Fein's style of confrontational politics much more than they did the SDLP. Excluded from the political negotiations, Sinn Fein discovered a popular cause which could be exploited to reinforce its view that the unionist community was still intent on harassing and intimidating

Nationalists. Measures taken by the RUC to ensure that marches did take place despite such protests, only strengthened Sinn Fein's argument that Northern Ireland was still an inherently Protestant-unionist state. Notwithstanding that police action in several incidents was taken to protect nationalist communities and that some objections to parades were not well founded and quite obviously tendentious, nursing a sense of grievance which fitted into a pattern of historic wrongs seemed more important than efforts to resolve the issues by genuine discussions.

Unionist politicians found it necessary to defend the Loyal Orders' right to march claiming that the parades did not intend to cause offence and that those who took offence did so deliberately. Since such parades celebrated the very essence of Protestant-culture in Ireland, the achievement of civil and religious liberties during the Grand Revolution of 1689-90, protests against parades were represented as evidence of hostility towards these liberties and, more significantly, of the permanent siege under which Protestants and Unionists had been living for generations in Ireland from a hostile Catholic-Nationalist people. The offence which the Catholic-nationalist community took at parades because of their celebration of Protestant victories over them, was not regarded as at all well founded.

In the summer of 1996 controversies over parades climaxed at the small country church of Drumcree near Portadown where the Orange Order was founded in 1795. There a stand was made against a police order rerouting an Orange Order parade away from passing close to a mainly nationalist residential area. The Orangemen's defiance of this order produced a wave of support and protest throughout the unionist community. Huge crowds gathered at Drumcree itself demanding that the order be revoked. A five-day stand-off with the police who barred the way ensued. Across the North protests, road-blocks and riots occurred in predominantly unionist areas threatening to bring life to a stand-still, almost in a repeat of the events of May 1974. Faced with this show of might the police relented and forced the parade through the nearby, predominantly nationalist area. What was for Unionists a vindication of their right to march on the public highway was seen by Nationalists as another victory for unionist might.

There was a sense of the wheel coming full circle, from the civil rights protest over housing when it was Catholics and Nationalists who had felt discriminated against to a situation in which Protestants and Unionists were taking to the streets to protest against their right to march being impeded. The combination of such protests with a renewed IRA campaign meant that in coming full circle the wheel was precipitating

Northern Ireland into one of its most dangerous periods since the hunger strikes.

Reaction within the Catholic and nationalist community was profound. Gangs took to the streets in nationalist areas to add to the destruction caused earlier in the same week by loyalist gangs. A sense that might alone would prevail and that at least the IRA offered some form of redress, if not a solution, took hold amongst people who previously would never have countenanced violence. Expressing some of this frustration and anger, the SDLP members of the Northern Ireland Forum, a consultative body consisting of all those elected in May 1996, resigned from that body, but were careful to emphasize that they would remain part of the separate negotiating process.[31]

Throughout the remainder of the summer tensions were high as other key events in the marching orders' calendar, such as the Apprentice Boys' commemoration of the siege of Derry, approached. Even in small, rural communities where, previously, demonstrations by the marching orders had passed off with little or no controversy, there was no escaping the effects of what had transpired at and around Drumcree. Communal strife mounted as attempts were made, on the one hand, to prevent parades taking place and, on the other, to insist that the right to parade was above question. Schools, churches and other property clearly associated with either community became regular targets for arsonists. In North Antrim, protests by supporters of the Orange Order gained international headlines when several Catholic churches were picketed at mass times and church-goers subjected to physical and verbal abuse.[32]

Wherever parades were prevented from taking place and, particularly, whenever this involved police decisions to prohibit parades, the sense of loss amongst many Protestants was profound. Territory where once they had marched with impunity was seen as lost, not just to the ancient foe, but worse to that foe with the connivance of the police service over which they once had control and which still consisted, overwhelmingly, of members drawn from their own community. Adding further to this loss was yet again a deep sense of betrayal by the British. While Drumcree had been a victory of sorts for Unionists and provided compensation for losses elsewhere, it was a victory which carried a heavy price. Like 1974, essentially it only proved that by exercising their might Unionists could gain an immediate victory but they could not thereby sustain their position in the longer term, nor could they hope to guarantee their security without a more positive engagement with their nationalist neighbours.

As the marching season drew to its close tensions eased somewhat and the threat of falling into the abyss receded. However, with the IRA continuing its violence, albeit at a considerably reduced level, those tensions remained and when the Stormont negotiations resumed in mid-September their lack of progress failed to inspire any hope that therein lay the way forward. The nationalist community too had a choice to make, more precisely that section of it represented by Sinn Fein and which continued to lend support of a greater or lesser kind to the IRA. The prospect of a place at the negotiating table still required restoring the IRA's ceasefire.

Throughout the autumn and winter of 1996-7 negotiations remained virtually logjammed – the procedural rules having been agreed by the end of July, the parties then failed to make any progress on the question of arms decommissioning. Unionists insisted that following a ceasefire they would only negotiate with Sinn Fein if the IRA had already commenced disarming, a position that seemed to be in contradiction to that adopted towards the parties associated with loyalist paramilitaries. The loyalist ceasefire not having been broken, these parties were at the negotiating table without their associated paramilitaries being required to disarm.

BREAKING THE LOGJAM

The logjam both within the talks and without proved unbreakable until the summer of 1997. Against the background of a Conservative government in Britain whose majority in Parliament continued to erode through a series of by-election defeats and itself bitterly divided on vital policy matters arising from membership of the European Community, there was little willingness to risk further division by appearing to engage too closely with Sinn Fein to achieve a new ceasefire. Using the argument that all of the reassurances necessary had already been given to Sinn Fein and that the initiative was exclusively with the latter to persuade the IRA to restore its ceasefire, the government rejected requests for precise guarantees as to when Sinn Fein would be permitted entry to negotiations following such a ceasefire. In February 1997 with a general election imminent in Britain and local government elections scheduled for May in Northern Ireland, the negotiations adjourned until early June. When they resumed the political scene had been transformed in a number of crucial respects.

The British general election held in early May swept the Conservative party out of power with one of the greatest defeats in British parliamentary history and returned the Labour Party under Tony Blair with one of the largest parliamentary majorities ever.[33] In Northern Ireland Sinn Fein achieved a significant increase both in its overall support and in its representation. Winning sixteen per cent of the vote and two MPs, it appeared to be seriously threatening the SDLP at whose expense it won one of those two seats, the seat in West Belfast where Gerry Adams once again became the MP. In Mid-Ulster Sinn Fein won the seat previously held by William McCrea of the DUP. However, despite this loss the SDLP recorded its highest vote ever, over 190,000, and twenty-four per cent of the votes cast. These results meant that the combined nationalist vote had now reached forty per cent for the first time. The UUP also achieved a good result winning an extra seat in the newly created constituency of West Tyrone while the DUP lost one of its three seats to Sinn Fein, that for the constituency of Mid-Ulster. Results from the local government elections, held three weeks later, also reflected Sinn Fein's advance.[34] In the South a general election took place resulting in a change of government when a Fianna Fail-Progressive Democrats coalition replaced the Fine Gael-Labour-Democratic Left coalition which had been in power since 1994.

With its increased mandate, achieved notwithstanding the continuation of the IRA's campaign, Sinn Fein was in a much stronger political position than ever before. Consequently, pressure on both new governments mounted to ease Sinn Fein's entry into negotiations so that the latter could influence the IRA to restore its ceasefire. The effects of this pressure came quicker than many had anticipated, particularly in light of renewed tensions over parades at Drumcree and elsewhere in early July. The British government made it clear that entry to negotiations could follow as soon as six weeks after a renewed ceasefire provided the ceasefire appeared to be meaningful. This was the guarantee John Major had been unable to give. On 19 July, therefore, the IRA announced that it would restore its ceasefire at noon the following day using language which complied with the requirements of the British legislation governing entry to the negotiations.[35] With both governments having made it clear that negotiations would commence on 15 September and that they would have to be concluded by May 1998, the momentum seemed to be building towards a crucial phase in the whole process.

Reaction to the pace of developments, especially amongst the unionist parties, once again underlined the depth of their fears and apprehensions. A British government determined to force the pace in negotiations in which Sinn Fein would participate so soon after an IRA ceasefire and with no prior requirement that the latter disarm, raised the spectre of further and imminent betrayal. Ian Paisley declared that his party would no longer participate in the negotiations and was joined by Robert McCartney of the UKUP in a joint walk-out. Only the UUP and the loyalist parties remained on the unionist side. On this occasion the UUP determined rather than walk away to stand its ground and test Sinn Fein's credibility and on this decision it had considerable support from a wide section of public opinion.[36]

TEN

TRANSFORMING THE CONFLICT

Following Sinn Fein's entry to the multi-party talks in September 1997, negotiations proceeded with increasing intensity, through many difficult moments, to end with an historic agreement the following April, on Good Friday. That agreement, now known as the Good Friday Agreement, confounded popular expectations. Public response was, nonetheless, extremely positive and the sense of relief that at last a political agreement had been achieved was obvious in many quarters. The result was that the referenda held at the end of May to endorse it, North and South, resulted in overwhelming majorities in both jurisdictions, seventy-two voting in favour in the North and ninety-five per cent in the South.

In this final chapter we examine how the agreement was achieved and the extent to which its underlying principles, as well as the influences which worked to make it possible, relate to the approach outlined in our discussion. From the beginning, we have been arguing that the conflict could not be transformed unless there were changes in key relationships. Such changes could only occur if one or more of the major parties moved to a more differentiated, neutral position, accepting responsibility for its own interpretation, and inviting all others to do the same. Increased differentiation, we have maintained, on the part of the governments set in motion a long process of change within both republican and unionist ranks. The Good Friday Agreement is the result of this long and difficult process.

ORGANIZING THE NEGOTIATIONS

In organizational terms the negotiations were conducted in three key committees and two sub-committees. Unlike the arrangements followed during the Brooke-Mayhew talks, on this occasion a parallel, rather than a sequential approach to all aspects of the negotiations, was adopted.

This meant that negotiations on new arrangements for Northern Ireland proceed alongside similar negotiations for North-South and for new British-Irish arrangements. Each of the three committees focused on one of the three sets of relationships which had formed the agenda for the Brooke-Mayhew talks. The first, or Strand 1 committee, dealt with relationships between the communities in Northern Ireland and proposals for new political institutions there. The second, the Strand 2 committee, dealt with North-South, i.e. all-island relationships and proposals for political institutions which would link both parts of the country. The third, the Strand 3 committee, dealt with East-West, i.e. British-Irish relationships, and proposals for institutional links between both parts of Ireland and Britain. Two sub-committees also operated. One committee considered arrangements for the decommissioning of paramilitary weapons with members of the International Body on Decommissioning established by both governments to advise and oversee the process in attendance. The second had a broader remit which was to consider what were termed 'confidence building measures', i.e. initiatives in such areas as the treatment of prisoners, equality of job opportunity, culture and language, economic development and human rights, all of which could contribute to the confidence of both communities in the whole negotiating process itself and whatever agreements might emerge from it.

The overall chair of the negotiations was former US Senator George Mitchell, assisted by former Finnish Prime Minister Harri Holkeri and the Canadian General John de Chastelain. In deference to unionist sensitivities about 'outside' involvement in matters affecting the administration of Northern Ireland, the Strand 1 committee was chaired by the new Secretary of State, Dr Marjorie Mowlam, assisted by the Minister for Political Development, Paul Murphy. Senator Mitchell took particular responsibility for Strand 2 and the confidence building measures committee, while Strand 3 was jointly chaired by both governments. The decommissioning sub-committee was chaired by General de Chastelain who was also the head of the International Body on Decommissioning.

Following Sinn Fein's entry and the immediate departure of the DUP and UKUP, the political party composition of the talks was, from a community representation perspective, quite unbalanced. While the overwhelming majority of the nationalist community in Northern Ireland was represented through the combined presence of the SDLP and Sinn Fein, the same was by no means true of the unionist community. Using the May 1996 election returns, the basis upon which negotiating mandates were established, just slightly above fifty per cent of Unionists were represented through the UUP and the two small loyalist parties, the UDP and PUP. The balance, represented by the DUP and McCartney's UKUP, was now outside the process and decidedly hostile to the whole enterprise. Adding to these divisions were those within the UUP itself, several of whose parliamentary members were strongly opposed to the party remaining in the talks once Sinn Fein had entered. To this imbalance was also added the fact that northern nationalism was strengthened by the presence of the Irish government's delegation whose approach was always very close to that of the SDLP.

Throughout the autumn and early winter of 1997 the negotiations consisted of a series of party presentations outlining their respective analyses of the problems together with the principles and requirements which each believed necessary in order to achieve a settlement. While some presentations repeated what the parties present at the 1991-2 talks had argued, there were shifts in emphasis. Not surprisingly, considerable attention focused on the position and proposals of the newly arrived Sinn Fein, and on how the UUP would react to its presence.

SINN FEIN – UNAPOLOGETICALLY REPUBLICAN

In its submission entitled *Principles and Requirements*[1], Sinn Fein argued that it was entering the talks fully committed to its republican position. Asserting that 'partition had failed', Sinn Fein ruled out as unacceptable any 'internal six-county settlement' and described the maintenance of the union between Britain and Northern Ireland as 'a direct impediment to and interference with the right of the people of Ireland alone to determine their development'.[2] While the submission stressed the need for accommodation, agreement and consent involving 'the two main traditions', Sinn Fein was careful to couch such references in an exclusively all-Ireland context, making no concession, as the Downing Street Declaration had, to any separate consideration for the wishes of the people living in Northern Ireland. The political framework which Sinn Fein regarded as 'the best and most durable basis for peace and stability', was 'a sovereign, united and independent Irish state'.[3] Achieving that goal required that the British government accept 'the right of the Irish people to national self-determination' and 'the right of the Irish nation to sovereignty and independence'.[4]

For Sinn Fein, therefore, the case for 'a sovereign, united and independent Irish state' was simply self-evident. Despite unionist opposition in principle and practice, Irish unity did not need to be argued for. Being so self-evidently right and just, achieving Irish unity merely required a

British initiative because, in Sinn Fein's analysis, it was British sovereignty over Northern Ireland that was the essential barrier to unity, not unionist opposition. It also followed that how Unionists might become involved in persuading the British to move to such a position, or any sense of what might be the consequences of a British government adopting such a position in the absence of significant unionist assent, did not require immediate consideration. Only after a British initiative along the lines suggested would these questions become relevant. The approach was, despite all of the references to agreement, accommodation and consent, based on a very traditional republican analysis. Britain had to move first on the question of sovereignty after which an accommodation and agreement with Unionists could be determined. As listed in its submission, the issues which Sinn Fein claimed the negotiations needed to address pointedly revealed this sequence:

1   Sovereignty;
2   The constitutional status of the northern statelet and the constitutional legislation which underpins it;
3   Britain's policy on this core issue;
4   Unionist participation, involvement and agreement;
5   The exercise of national self-determination by the people of Ireland.

Sinn Fein clearly viewed the negotiations as an opportunity to put its case in the first instance to the British government rather than to any of the other participants. With no support for its analysis from any of the other participants, nor for the proposals based on it, the case was simply heard and noted. Neither the Irish government nor the SDLP offered any support, nor could they give the analysis and the approach which had been argued for and accepted by both since the New Ireland Forum in 1984 and, even more significantly, since the Anglo-Irish Agreement in 1985. The practical consequences of Sinn Fein's approach within the negotiations was that the UUP simply refused to engage directly with its delegation. Sinn Fein's failure to accept the principle of consent to constitutional change allowed the UUP to claim that the Sinn Fein approach simply had nothing to offer them, except in the extremely unlikely event of a British initiative in favour of Irish unity.

Notwithstanding its fundamentalist position there was evidence suggesting a willingness on Sinn Fein's part to accept, or at least acquiesce, in arrangements that would fall far short of its declared goal. The party's very presence at the negotiations was part of that evidence. It was, in effect, an acknowledgement of the need to argue, to persuade and, probably, to compromise. Violence was no longer instrumental. Furthermore, in a negotiating process where its approach was not shared by either the SDLP or the Irish government, it must have been clear to Sinn Fein that its goal of a united Ireland was not going to be achieved. More significantly, in its own submission Sinn Fein highlighted issues on which progress could be made separately. These issues included what Sinn Fein termed its 'equality agenda', issues like fair employment, greater recognition and support for the Irish language and especially, the treatment of prisoners. While many of these issues were already being positively addressed, further progress could be represented as advances which Sinn Fein had helped to achieve, the case for Irish unity notwith-standing. With respect to the broader political agenda, Sinn Fein's stress on no 'internal settlement' and its reference to the need for a 'democ-ratic accommodation of the differing views of the two main traditions, which takes full account of the conflicting identities',[5] contained hints that the party was prepared to be more flexible than at first seemed likely.

UUP – RELUCTANT TO PROPOSE

Having made its decision to remain at the talks, surprisingly the Ulster Unionist Party adopted a rather reluctant approach to announcing firm proposals in any of the strands. For a considerable period the UUP concentrated on defending its fundamental constitutional position rather than on advancing any detailed proposals for a settlement. In its submis-sion on principles and requirements the party offered a trenchant defence of the union with Britain which effectively served as a rebuttal of the Sinn Fein analysis. Rejecting any suggestion that the union was imposed on Unionists, the UUP argued that:

The Union with Great Britain is a Union in the hearts and minds of the Unionist people. This feeling of Britishness is not a device or artifice which has been imposed on an unsuspecting people by successive British governments. Britishness is at the heart of Unionist philosophy, the feeling of belonging; the feeling of sharing with our fellow citizens in Great Britain in great national events; of being part of something larger than simply the six counties in the north-eastern corner of our island.[6]

Unlike the bland approach to identity in UUP submissions to the Brooke-Mayhew talks, this argument had more power and vibrancy. Its analysis and logic were remarkably similar to that which underlay the SDLP's approach. Basing its case on the sense of identity of the unionist community rather than on references to the 'greater number' or to the 'majority of the people' in Northern Ireland as in the Brooke-Mayhew submissions, the UUP now explicitly acknowledged that what was at issue was the need to politically accommodate people of two different identities and two different national allegiances, both of which transcended the confines of Northern Ireland. Indeed, as the UUP submission went on to argue, Unionists did not reject the 'legitimacy of Irish nationalism'.[7] What they rejected was the argument that Irish unity was the *only* legitimate answer to the conflict in Northern Ireland. It therefore followed that an acceptable answer had to acknowledge, as fundamental, the consent of the people of Northern Ireland. Making that consent only operative following a British decision to abandon sovereignty, as Sinn Fein seemed to suggest, was, not surprisingly, totally unacceptable to Unionists.

While rejecting as still unacceptable the role afforded the Irish government by the Anglo-Irish Agreement, the UUP did indicate that it was prepared to consider a 'special relationship' with the Irish Republic, but only if Articles 2 and 3 of the Irish Constitution were first removed. The preferred nature of that relationship was hinted at in the first of what were to be frequent references to the manner in which minority problems elsewhere in Europe were being dealt with in the aftermath of the break-up of the Soviet Union. Referring to recent developments under the auspices of the Organisation for Security and Co-operation in Europe, the UUP pointed to the kind of benevolent role which Hungary was playing on behalf of the Hungarian minority in Romania, as an example of the kind of role which the Irish Republic might play vis-à-vis the nationalist community in Northern Ireland.[8] Such a role is purely consultative and involves no mechanisms such as those which had been provided by the Anglo-Irish Agreement. However, given the twelve-year existence of the Anglo-Irish Agreement, the obvious value of it to both governments and its significance to the nationalist community, it was highly unlikely that any new agreement could contain the kind of minimalist role for the Irish government suggested by the UUP. The UUP were probably fully aware of this and were preparing for a much stronger and more structured outcome.

SDLP – STEADFAST ON RELATIONSHIPS

Once again the SDLP emphasized the New Ireland Forum's position on the rights of both Unionists and Nationalists 'to effective political, symbolic and administrative expression of their identity, ethos and way of life' as 'key to the success of the negotiations'.[9] This position, the SDLP reiterated, meant that the negotiations would have to 'be focused within the framework which embraces and addresses the key political, social, economic and cultural relationships between the communities within the North, between communities North and South and, thirdly, on relationships between Ireland and Britain'.[10] Given the structure and agenda for the negotiations, this focus had already been adopted and no longer had to be argued for in any essential manner.

OTHER PARTIES

Among the minority parties there tended to be less analysis and more a 'wait and see' approach at this stage. Brief submissions from the two loyalist parties stressed Northern Ireland's place within the UK and the principle of consent; likewise the Labour Group also emphasized the importance of North-South relationships. In addition to also acknowledging the importance of the consent principles and the British-Irish framework, the Alliance Party[11] and the Northern Ireland Women's Coalition[12] both highlighted the need for an inclusive approach to an agreement and to its institutional implementation. In other words, an agreement should make it possible for all shades of political opinion with an effective mandate to be represented at all levels of any new institutions.

BRITISH AND IRISH GOVERNMENTS

Both governments stressed the three-fold set of relationships outlined by the SDLP and, not surprisingly, also placed considerable emphasis on the principles of consent and self-determination as expressed in the 1993 Joint Declaration.[13] With their common concerns about paramilitaries in mind, they reminded participants in the talks of the commitments in the Mitchell Principles to abide by any agreement reached and to use only democratic means in pursuit of any changes which they might subsequently want to achieve to an agreement. Decommissioning paramilitary weapons and disbanding paramilitary organizations had not gone away as issues, however much they had been pushed down the immediate agenda.

UUP-SINN FEIN STAND OFF

Dominating proceedings in the period prior to Christmas was the UUP's refusal to engage directly with Sinn Fein. This refusal did not mean, as many outside the talks seemed to interpret it, that UUP representatives did not respond to Sinn Fein submissions or to the latter's questions.

Essentially it meant the UUP's refusal of Sinn Fein's requests for bi-lateral meetings in which Gerry Adams might have the opportunity of directly addressing David Trimble. The UUP argued that since Sinn Fein's proposals dismissed the case for Northern Ireland remaining part of the UK, the foundation stone in the UUP's case, the potential for agreement in bi-lateral meetings between both parties simply did not exist. Sinn Fein stressed that such bi-lateral meetings would at least signal a step towards mutual understanding. However, within the formal sessions of the talks themselves engagement of a sort between both parties did take place as each responded to comments and questions by the other. In time, this engagement intensified, though no bilateral meeting between Sinn Fein and the UUP ever did take place.

THREATS TO THE PROCESS

As 1997 drew to a close, attempts to persuade the parties to accept 'a heads of agreement' document that would allow detailed negotiations to commence in the new year failed.[14] Coinciding and combining with this failure, renewed paramilitary activity placed the whole process under severe pressure. The fractious loyalist paramilitaries, some connected with political parties involved in the talks and some not, embarked on a campaign of targeted and random killings of Catholics which reached a high point over the Christmas and New Year period. Republican groups like the INLA and the newly formed CAC (Continuity Army Council – an IRA splinter group) countered by murdering loyalists and placing bombs in predominantly Protestant towns.[15] The IRA itself was accused of breaching its ceasefire following the murder of a prominent loyalist in late January 1998. Across the countryside churches, schools and community halls serving both communities were once again attacked and some destroyed throughout the same period.

As a result of this violence two parties were expelled from the negotiations for short periods when their paramilitary associates were found to have breached their ceasefires and thereby the 'Principles on Democracy and Non-Violence'.[16] The Ulster Democratic Party was expelled when one of its associates, the Ulster Freedom Fighters, openly admitted to having been responsible for the killing of Catholics. Sinn Fein was expelled in very controversial circumstances when police intelligence alleged IRA involvement in two killings in Belfast. Although both expulsions were for short durations, they added further to tension within the talks and above all to delay. While the violence remained at a relatively low level compared to previous periods, it served, nonetheless, as a sharp reminder of the parameters within which a political settlement could be reached. The newly-emerged Loyalist Volunteer Force which was centred on the County Armagh town of Portadown, the scene of the controversial Drumcree parades, was an expression of extreme unionist disaffection with the talks process, as well as a violent threat to an outcome which was bound to contain features which would be deemed unacceptable by some Unionists. On the republican side violence was being carried out by CAC and suspicions were strong that assistance of a kind was being provided by the IRA itself, given the type of weapons used in a number of incidents. A further threat to republican solidarity was the emergence of a lobby group under the label 32-County Sovereignty Committee consisting of other dissident Sinn Fein and IRA members who accused former colleagues of betraying the 'cause' by not insisting on a British declaration of withdrawal before entering negotiations.

GOVERNMENTS ACCELERATE PACE

From late January to mid-February during which time sessions of the negotiations were held in London and Dublin, very little progress was made due to the indictment proceedings affecting the UDP and Sinn Fein. Nevertheless, two significant joint documents from the governments did lay down more precise parameters for the rest of the negotiations. The first, issued in early January and entitled 'Propositions for Heads of Agreement' outlined, in summary terms, the framework for an agreement.[17] The second, issued the following month, dealt more specifically with North South arrangements.[18]

In a joint statement on the first document the governments indicated that their propositions derived 'from views of all parties on the various issues which arise in the talks' and that they represented their 'best guess at what could be a generally acceptable outcome'.[19] Not surprisingly the kind of outcome foreseen was one which would include: a new Northern Ireland assembly and administration; a North-South Ministerial Council; a British-Irish Council; provisions to safeguard human, social, economic and cultural rights; and constitutional change based on the principle of consent.

Together with the second document which detailed key features of North-South structures as the two governments saw them, the parties now had outline proposals to which they were invited to respond. From mid-February onwards the negotiations focused, therefore, with increasing detail on proposals which addressed the substance of both documents. Unionists who had expressed considerable satisfaction with the first document because it made no reference to the Framework Documents and included what they regarded as a significant reference to the role of the proposed British-Irish Council were clearly disappointed with the second because of the decision-making powers envisaged for the North-South Council. Dissatisfaction for the very opposite reasons was expressed by Sinn Fein which claimed that the 'Propositions' document envisaged the establishment of a scarcely-concealed version of the old Stormont regime which would inhibit and frustrate from the outset any degree of discretion vested in the North-South council.

The atmosphere surrounding the talks was once again heavy with accusations and fears of betrayal. Divisions in unionist ranks increased and intensified. Within the UUP's own negotiating team, differences emerged which seemed to threaten David Trimble's determination to keep his party at the negotiating table.[20] From without, UUP politicians opposed to the talks increasingly added their voices to those of the DUP and UKUP in calling upon Trimble to withdraw. Sinn Fein, which had submitted no proposals of its own for new northern institutions within Northern Ireland, accused the SDLP of accepting the case for a new assembly and administration which, it alleged, with an inevitable unionist majority would restore a pre-1972 Stormont regime. How a North-South council could function without an elected administration in the North from which to draw its northern membership, nor how trust might be developed between Unionists and Nationalists without an institution based on partnership, Sinn Fein did not explain. While the legacy of unionist rule could explain Sinn Fein's deep-seated mistrust and suspicion of Unionists, the failure of a party committed to Irish unity to acknowledge the need to create political partnerships in which responsibility could be shared and trust develop, was difficult to understand.

However deeply felt, neither sets of fears were, in fact, sustainable. It was clear that, in the case of a North-South council, it would not be an independent, stand-alone body. Although provided with some decision-making powers the council would not be directly elected and, therefore, had to be accountable to the sources from which its members would acquire their authority. This authority would be derived both from the new northern assembly and from the southern parliament and it would be to both that the members would be accountable. Unionist concerns that a North-South council would be an embryonic and independent all-Ireland parliament, were therefore, unfounded. As for the new northern institutions, neither the assembly nor its administration would mark a return to the old Stormont. Requirements that a new administration be cross-community and that there be safeguards against abuse built into the decision-making process, signalled an institution very different to that of the unionist-dominated regimes of the past. Sinn Fein's allegations were, also, clearly without foundation.

INTO ENDGAME

Since the two governments had declared the previous September that the deadline for the negotiations would be May 1998, pressure mounted for an earlier conclusion to allow, in the case of an agreement, for referenda, North and South, to be held before the summer and its potentially disruptive marching season. In the event of a positive outcome to the referenda, it was also hoped that elections to the new northern assembly could also be held within the same period. With these considerations in mind and the fact that eighteen months had elapsed since the negotiations had commenced, Chairman George Mitchell announced at the end of March that the talks would close, with or without agreement, in ten days, on 9 April.[21]

An intense round of bilateral contacts followed during which the direct involvement of both Prime Minister Tony Blair and Taoiseach Bertie Ahern became crucial to the agreement that emerged a day late, on 10 April, Good Friday.[22] Late night and all-night sessions marked the closing days of the negotiations much of which focused on the details of the proposed northern and North-South institutions, as well as on three critical issues in the confidence-building area: police reform, decommissioning and the early release of paramilitary prisoners held in both the British and Irish jurisdictions. Given the very immediate sensitivities surrounding these three matters, it was not surprising that they, rather than the institutional arrangements, became the focal points for dissension in post-agreement debates. Indeed, in the final hours of negotiations divisions within the UUP's own delegation on these matters delayed the formal adoption of the agreement by the last plenary session.

THE GOOD FRIDAY AGREEMENT

Institutionally the Good Friday Agreement was a realisation of what the negotiations' three-stranded agenda and the relationships analysis underlying it, had long predicted. There never had been any prospect of an alternative outcome and within the negotiations it had been more a question of parties attempting to strengthen or weaken proposals for its different aspects than of seriously expecting to achieve a different outcome. Unionists were fully aware that North-South arrangements would have to entail considerable discretion with respect to decision making, if the SDLP was to be satisfied. Conversely the SDLP was fully aware that such arrangements would have to include accountability by the northern members of a North-South council to an assembly in Belfast, if the council was to be acceptable to Unionists. Sinn Fein must also have been fully aware that its proposals for an end to British sovereignty and the creation of a form of Irish unity had no chance of acceptance and that it would have to accommodate itself to the kind of outcome implied by the three-stranded agenda. Sinn Fein's main aims were, therefore, to ensure that the agreement included provisions for the early release of prisoners and for police reform, together with the strongest possible commitments on human, cultural and civil rights. The agreement did contain such provisions, notably a review of the sentences of those held for terrorist offences and associated with paramilitary groups on ceasefire, with the intention of securing releases within two years. A special commission would review the whole structure, organization and ethos of the police. Other provisions included commitments to enhance the status of the Irish language and to reinforce existing provisions, aimed at guaranteeing fair employment and an end to discrimination.

Constitutional changes, as long predicted, included a declaration on the Irish government's part to amend Articles 2 and 3 of the Republic's constitution, first, to remove the section implying a territorial claim on Northern Ireland and, second, to include the principle of consent as the only basis upon which Irish unity could be achieved. On the British government's part, it was agreed that the Government of Ireland Act (1920) would be repealed in its entirety and subsequent legislation would include the principle of consent. Finally, upon entering into force the Good Friday Agreement would mean that the 1985 Anglo-Irish Agreement would be replaced by a new British-Irish Agreement. The catalyst for all of the political developments over the intervening twelve and a half years would be replaced by its more comprehensive and far-reaching successor.

REACTION – YES AND NO

The considerable local and international media presence ensured attention to the agreement on a scale unrivalled by any other single event over the preceding decades and the message was, the predictable exceptions apart, an extremely positive one. Civic society in Northern Ireland itself expressed general pleasure that at last the politicians had managed to reach agreement.[23] In the rest of Ireland a similar welcome was widely expressed. Abroad, the US administration which had kept in close touch with the negotiations, especially in their final stages, expressed considerable satisfaction.[24] From throughout the European Union came a chorus of welcomes and promises of further support once the agreement was implemented.[25]

However, there were critical hurdles to be crossed before the agreement could be said to have really begun effecting the changes it was intended to achieve. Joint referenda had to be held in the North and in the South by the end of May. Even before then, as the UUP and Sinn Fein had made clear, final acceptance of the agreement by their respective parties would have to await the outcome of internal party consultative processes.

The UUP was the first to complete this process when at meetings of its executive committee and of its governing council, significant votes in favour of the agreement were cast.[26] However, notwithstanding such support, divisions within the party were not healed and a section of the UUP, led by several of the party's MPs and other prominent members, emerged to join an alliance opposed to the Agreement which also consisted of Ian Paisley's DUP and Robert McCartney's UKUP. Betrayal of the union with Britain was once again the main banner raised as this opposition characterized the agreement as weakening the Union and increasing the influence of the Irish government in the affairs of Northern Ireland. Echoing statements made following the Anglo-Irish Agreement, the DUP claimed that 'The Union is fundamentally weakened by this deal'.[27] The agreement, it stated, gave nationalist parties a veto, would place Sinn Fein leaders in government without any decommissioning of the IRA's arsenal of weapons being insisted upon, would destroy the RUC, and provide an amnesty for terrorist prisoners. Such arguments touched deep emotional chords within the unionist psyche.

Reform of the RUC, an institution which for so long represented the unionist state would affect large numbers of people within that community, taking account of families and friends of each of the force's approximately 12,000 members. Secondly, notwithstanding the fact that loyalist prisoners would also benefit, the early release of prisoners, many sentenced for the killing of RUC members and of other members of the unionist community and for destroying unionist owned businesses, was viewed as deeply offensive. Furthermore, the absence of any progress on the decommissioning of paramilitary weapons and a statement from the IRA that there 'will be no decommissioning by the IRA'[28] except in accordance with its own determination, offered little reassurance to Unionists fearful of change. Finally, there was, in the weeks following the agreement, the evidence of on-going, albeit low level, terrorist activity by dissident IRA groups to strengthen those fears.[29]

As the referendum campaign commenced, all of the above dramatically increased the pressures upon the UUP and reinforced the case being made by Unionists opposed to the agreement. However, the weakness in the latter's case was that while they were able to identify what they opposed, they had no viable alternative to offer that would jointly address unionist and nationalist aspirations. They could only offer an exclusively unionist solution, one to which there was not the remotest possibility of recruiting any nationalist support whatsoever. On the contrary, the UUP could point to several features of the agreement which were major achievements as far as Unionists were concerned: the removal of Articles Two and Three of the Irish Constitution; the inclusion of the principle of consent in the same constitution; the establishment of a British-Irish Council to strengthen political, social and economic links across the Irish Sea, and accountability by North-South Council members to the new assembly. Above all, the agreement was one which had the full support of the SDLP, considerable support from Sinn Fein and the support of the loyalist and other minor parties within the negotiations. To this local support was added that of the Republic's government and opposition parties, as well as of the British government and opposition. UUP dissidents, together with the Paisley-McCartney alliance, had no prospect of achieving anything quite so substantial as the Good Friday Agreement, nor as widely supported.

For the SDLP the agreement represented broad acceptance of its three-fold 'relationship' analysis, for its emphasis on a British-Irish framework and on the need for both governments to jointly create the circumstances and lay down the parameters within which an agreement could be reached. In essence, by providing the means and the opportunity for new political relationships within the North, between North and South and between Ireland and Britain, the agreement vindicated what had very explicitly been the SDLP's approach from the late 1970s.

Sinn Fein's initial responses were cautious as it set about consulting its membership before determining a definitive position on the agreement. In a speech to the Dail, in Dublin, the Sinn Fein representative, Caoimhin O Caolain, stressed that Sinn Fein did not regard the Good Friday document as a settlement. However, he added that 'we do believe that the new political scenario which it creates can provide a basis for advancement'.[30] As expected, the measures against which Sinn Fein

Transforming the Conflict

would assess immediate gains from the agreement was the extent to which its 'equality' agenda and such other matters as policing, prisoners etc. would be delivered upon. As Ó Caoláin indicated,

the emergence of a new policing service, the release of all political prisoners, the demilitarization of the Six Counties and the withdrawal of the British Army, the ending of sectarian discrimination in employment, the repeal of repressive legislation, full and equal status for the Irish language – these are now awaited and demanded.[31]

On the fundamental goal of Irish unity the chief Sinn Fein negotiator at the talks, Martin McGuinness, admitted to his party's annual conference, two weeks after the agreement, that 'A united Ireland was not attainable in this phase, not because of unionist opposition but because of all the participants, only Sinn Fein was advocating and promoting that objective'.[32] This admission was almost an open acknowledgement that Sinn Fein's approach to Irish unity had not been shared by the other nationalist participants. Sinn Fein's subsequent decision, taken with open IRA approval, to support a 'yes' vote in both referenda and to allow members elected to a new northern assembly to take their seats, was an even more open acknowledgement that the traditional Sinn Fein-IRA approach to unity was being transformed.[33] The new phase of the struggle for unity would be an exclusively democratic one, one in which unionist views would, by virtue of entering common institutions, have to be taken into account and not relegated to a secondary position as previously was the case.

Notwithstanding the considerable support for the agreement within the ranks of Sinn Fein and the IRA, opposition within republican ranks did exist, though in a somewhat disjointed form. As we have already noted dissident IRA members, who had withdrawn from the movement at the time of the 1994 ceasefire, had constituted themselves into the Continuity Army Council (CAC) under which umbrella terrorist attacks and killings had been taking place for some time. Following the agreement, CAC continued to engage in terrorist activity and found itself joined by more recent dissidents operating under the same umbrella, or none. Politically two republican groups led opposition to the agreement: Republican Sinn Fein led by the former Sinn Fein President, Ruairi O Bradaigh,[34] allegedly with links to the CAC; the second group, the 32-County Sovereignty Committee, was of more recent origin consisting as it did of Sinn Fein members opposed to the agreement, led by Bernadette Sands-McKevitt, a sister of the first hunger-striker to die.

The political case of these republican groups was that the agreement reinforced partition and the so-called unionist 'veto' on Irish self-determination. The proposed new northern institutions would, they argued, reinstate unionist domination, while the North-South Council was mere window-dressing. The Sinn Fein argument that the agreement provided a transition phase to Irish unity was dismissed as without foundation. 'There is no dynamic in this process to lead to a British withdrawal and a New Ireland' was how one of the groups characterized the agreement.[35] Instead the new arrangements would achieve the exact opposite because the new northern administration 'will seek to involve as much of the nationalist population as possible and will be a barrier administration between the Irish people and the imperialist British government. Such a new, reinforced Stormont will be much more difficult to remove than the old corrupt regime which was brought down by the people's struggle in 1972'.[36] The message was the pure, undiluted traditional republican message from the logic of which Sinn Fein was, after the failure of that struggle, now extricating itself.

The political threat posed by such groups to Sinn Fein was minimal. More significantly, suspicion of some IRA collusion with dissident groups only reinforced unionist fears that Sinn Fein would not live up to the commitments on decommissioning contained in the Good Friday Agreement. The terrorist threat was, therefore, the more problematic. Considerable stocks of explosives and arms were obviously under the control of some dissident IRA members, to judge from the actual attacks carried out and the supplies intercepted by police on both sides of the Irish border in the first six months of 1998. As the IRA had demonstrated throughout the previous decades, even a small number of well armed activists could pose a very serious security threat and, consequently, a political threat as well.

BEYOND THE REFERENDA

Despite the significance of the referenda results, questions remained as to the durability of the Good Friday Agreement and its more general acceptance as a way forward. Opposition to it remained significant in the unionist community and was not completely insignificant amongst nationalists, more precisely those who deemed themselves traditional republicans. Unionist opposition to the implementation of the agreement posed the greater danger and was starkly revealed in the election campaign for the new assembly which followed in the month after the referendum. Fuelling unionist opposition, most significantly within the UUP, were fears that the IRA had no intention to decommissioning any of its considerable store of arms. As a result, the UUP was not able to maintain a united front against internal opposition mobilized on the issue of decommissioning and only managed to obtain twenty-one per cent of the vote, putting it in second position to the SDLP which gained twenty-two per cent. This was the first time in Northern Ireland's history that a party of the nationalist tradition emerged from any election as the single most popular party.[37]

The age-old fears of abandonment and betrayal by Britain and of encroachment by, and enforced assimilation into, the ethos of a Catholic-nationalist Ireland persisted within sections of the unionist community. Worse was the sense of betrayal from within. For those who held these fears the Good Friday Agreement encapsulated them all. Britain's betrayal, long anticipated, had been at its most profound in the Anglo-Irish Agreement, and could not get worse. On this occasion, however, it was David Trimble's betrayal which was the more profound. A leader who, in his younger days, had strenuously opposed the 1974 Sunningdale arrangements, who had campaigned against the Anglo-Irish Agreement and who had been elected leader of the UUP because of his strong, determined defence of unionism, had accepted an agreement which seemed to forebode nothing but dangers for the unionist community. The future was ominous for those who held such views. Their immediate hope was that in the elections to the new assembly they would be able, following the precedent of unionist opposition in 1973-4, to return a sufficiently strong anti-agreement representation to make the new arrangements unworkable. While they did not immediately succeed in this objective, a strong anti-agreement block of assembly members was elected with a capacity to cause considerable difficulties for the operation of all of the new arrangements. The extent to which they were able to cause such difficulties was to become evident in the first phase of the implementation of the agreement. Combined with other factors, the anti-agreement unionist block was sufficiently influential to inhibit progress on a considerable number of elements in the agreement.[38]

With minimum popular support, the opposition within nationalism had no prospect of mounting any successful political campaign against the agreement. Politically it would have to await the outcome of the struggle within unionism where a victory for opponents to the agreement could threaten the broad nationalist consensus which had emerged once Sinn Fein had declared its acceptance. More immediately, its various paramilitary associates could only attempt to create instability, adding to unionist fears and hence strengthen unionist opposition.

Despite these dark possibilities, the strong endorsement which the agreement received in both parts of the country strengthened the mood of optimism and raised hopes for a more peaceful and stable future across both the nationalist and unionist communities. A bridge had been crossed by large sections of both those communities and there could be no turning back. Their future now lay inexorably together and, whatever the difficulties and delays in implementing the Good Friday Agreement, its achievement indicated a recognition by the people of Northern Ireland that they could no longer continue living apart.

EPILOGUE

What is it, despite the apparent simplicity of the problems to be resolved, despite the relative sophistication of the people and despite their closeness to each other, that continued to make the Northern Ireland problem apparently so intractable for so long? Our analysis and perspective have attempted to show the significant influence which the 1980s shifts in both the British and Irish approaches made to the provision of a context in which both communities could begin to have faith in the guarantorship roles of their respective external referents. These shifts representing as they did a psychological withdrawal by Britain and a redefinition by the main elements of nationalist Ireland of the conditions under which Irish unity could be achieved injected a new flexibility into the situation. No longer were the claims of the 'parent' states irredentist; instead they focused on the need to address fundamental relationships and to establish political institutions which would effectively represent both communities in the North in their relationships with each other as well as with their external referents. Northern Ireland was no longer just another region of the UK, nor was it a part of Ireland 'unjustly' separated from the rest of the island for whose 'liberation' people should kill and be killed.

The effects of such shifts were slow to influence events on the ground. Unionists and Loyalists saw in the British shift the kind of betrayal which traditionally they were almost programmed to expect and reacted accordingly. Republicans were at best suspicious and more likely to be dismissive, sensing a degree of unacceptable compromise of the hallowed goal of an independent Ireland.

The search for a settlement to Northern Ireland's political crisis lasted for over thirty years. A whole generation of politicians and policy makers in Northern Ireland applied themselves to the task. More than 3,000 people were killed, thousands more injured and millions of pounds worth of property destroyed and rebuilt in the course of the violence which marked these years. The mobilization of resources and effort by both the

Irish and British governments together with the support provided internationally by the US and other governments as well as the European Union was probably unprecedented in the case of a conflict which did not threaten international stability, nor even the likelihood of conflict between the two 'parent' states, Ireland and Britain.

Many people are justifiably perplexed that it took so long, that a tragedy of such proportions had to be enacted and that so much effort and resources had to be invested before the Good Friday Agreement provided a basis for a resolution.

> History says Don't hope
> On this side of the grave.
> But then, once in a lifetime
> The longed for tidal wave
> Of justice can rise up
> And hope and history rhyme.
>
> So hope for a great sea-change
> On the far side of revenge
> Believe that a further share
> Is reachable here.
> Believe in miracles
> And cures and healing wells.

From *The Cure at Troy* by Seamus Heaney

SIGNIFICANT DATES
AND DEVELOPMENTS

1601   Defeat of the Gaelic and Catholic chiefs of Ulster at the Battle of Kinsale; political domination of Ireland by England completed.

1609   First Plantation of Ulster.

1641   Catholic rebellion and massacre of Protestants at Portadown.

1690-92   Williamite War; Treaty of Limerick and Protestant Settlement.

1795   Foundation of the Orange Order.

1798   Rebellion by United Irishmen in Leinster and Ulster.

1801   Act of Union unites Britain and Ireland under the London Parliament.

1828   Catholic Emancipation.

1845-47   The potato famine devastates rural Ireland and intensifies emigration.

1886   First Home Rule Bill defeated; foundation of Ulster Unionist Council.

1893   Second Home Rule Bill defeated.

1912-14   Third Home Rule Bill enacted; unionist resistance to Home Rule in Ulster produces a constitutional crisis and plans for the partitioning of Ireland; outbreak of World War I delays implementation of Home Rule legislation.

1916   Easter Rising in Dublin organized by the secret Irish Republican Brotherhood; execution of its leaders evokes considerable anti-British feelings.

1918   General election in December; Sinn Fein displaces the Irish National Party as the main political voice of Irish nationalism.

1919   Sinn Fein MPs declare Ireland to be an independent republic and refuse to take their seats at Westminster; instead a parliament (Dail Eireann) is convened in Dublin attended only by Sinn Fein members; IRA campaign against British forces and the police commences.

1920   Atrocities by Irish and British forces throughout the country; communal rioting and disturbances in Belfast and other northern centres; Government of Ireland Act establishes Northern Ireland as a separate entity with its own parliament and administration and control of the six north-eastern counties.

1921   Northern Ireland parliament and government take office with jurisdiction over the six north-eastern counties; in the South truce arranged in July and negotiations between the British government and Sinn Fein open; Anglo-Irish Treaty in December establishes the Irish Free State with sovereignty over the other twenty-six counties of Ireland.

1922-3   Civil war in the Irish Free State between those who support the Anglo-Irish Treaty and those opposed to it.

1925   Irish and British governments confirm the border between Northern Ireland and the Irish Free State.

1937   New constitution adopted in the South which contains articles claiming jurisdiction over Northern Ireland.

1939   South declares neutrality on the outbreak of the Second World War; North placed on war footing.

1941   Belfast suffers from severe German bomb attacks.

1949   The South formally declares itself a Republic and withdraws from the British Commonwealth.

1956   IRA commences a campaign of bombing and shooting in Northern Ireland.

1958   Sean Lemass succeeds Eamon de Valera as Taoiseach of the Irish Republic.

1962   IRA ends its campaign.

1963   Terence O'Neill elected Prime Minister of Northern Ireland.

1967-69   Civil rights campaign for social, political and electoral reform; rioting widespread.

1969   Terence O'Neill resigns as Prime Minister; succeeded by James Chichester-Clark.

1970   Alliance Party and SDLP founded; IRA (Provos) campaign commences.

1971   Brian Faulkner succeeds Chichester-Clark as Prime Minister; internment without trial of alleged IRA members and sympathizers introduced.

1972   Thirteen men shot dead by British Army in Derry (Bloody Sunday); Northern Ireland Parliament prorogued and Direct Rule introduced.

1973   Northern Ireland Assembly elected; successful negotiations on a cross-community, power-sharing form of government; Sunningdale Agreement on a Council of Ireland.

1974   'Power-sharing' Executive elected from within the Northern Ireland Assembly takes office; Ulster Workers Council strike against Sunningdale agreement forces collapse of Executive and closure of Assembly.

1975-76   Northern Ireland Constitutional Convention elected to agree new forms of government; unsuccessful and so terminated.

1977   Prison protests, the 'dirty' protests, commence.

1979   First direct elections to the European Parliament; John Hume (SDLP), Ian Paisley (DUP) and John Taylor (UUP), elected to represent Northern Ireland.

1980   Secretary of State Atkins convenes multi-party talks to agree new political structures, but the initiative collapses; a new Anglo-Irish process of consultation commences between Prime Minister Thatcher and Taoiseach Charles Haughey.

1981   Hunger strikes commence; election of Bobby Sands as MP shortly before he dies on hunger strike.

1982   Following the deaths of ten prisoners hunger strikes end; Secretary of State Prior proceeds with proposals for a new Northern Ireland Assembly; SDLP and Sinn Fein members abstain.

1983   New Ireland Forum of the main nationalist parties (Sinn Fein excepted) in Ireland deliberates in Dublin; John Hume elected to Westminster; Gerry Adams also elected, but declines to take his seat.

1994   New Ireland Forum publishes its report; Mrs Thatcher rejects its main constitutional recommendations.

1985   Anglo-Irish Agreement signed and a consultative mechanism established between both governments, the Anglo-Irish Conference; Unionists embark on campaign of non-cooperation with British government, the 'Ulster Says NO' campaign.

1986   Northern Ireland Assembly prorogued.

1987   Enniskillen Remembrance Sunday massacre.

1988   SDLP – Sinn Fein talks initiate a process of persuading Sinn Fein-IRA to take an exclusively political approach.

1990   Secretary of State Peter Brooke launches new initiative aimed at political dialogue.

1991-92   Inter-party and inter-government talks in Belfast, London and Dublin; Sinn Fein excluded because of continuing IRA campaign; secret talks between Sinn Fein and various groups, including the SDLP and the London and Dublin governments.

1993   Joint Declaration by the Taoiseach and British Prime Minister on the principle of self-determination in Ireland, in December.

1994   IRA and Loyalist ceasefires; Forum for Peace and Reconciliation convened by the Irish government commences its deliberations in Dublin.

1995   'A New Framework for Agreement' document outlines both governments' views on a possible way forward; preliminary talks open between Sinn Fein and British government; President Clinton visits Northern Ireland; International Commission on Decommissioning of Paramilitary Arms established by Irish and British governments and chaired by former US Senator George Mitchell.

1996   IRA ceasefire ends and bombing campaign recommences in Britain; British and Irish governments agree inclusive, all-party talks to open on 10 June following elections to determine each party's delegates and to establish a new Northern Ireland Forum; elections take place on 30 May; negotiations commence on 10 June with Senator George Mitchell as Chair; Sinn Fein excluded because of ongoing IRA campaign.

1997   IRA declares a new ceasefire in July; Sinn Fein enter the negotiations in September; DUP and UKUP withdraw.

1998   Good Friday Agreement signed by both governments and the eight parties that remained in the negotiations; the agreement is endorsed by large majorities in referenda North and South in May; elections follow in June to new Northern Ireland Assembly.

BIBLIOGRAPHY

Adams, Gerry. *Falls Memories*. Belfast: Brandon, Dingle, 1982.

Akenson, Donald Harman. *God's People: Covenant and Land in South Africa, Israel and Ulster*. Ithaca: Cornell University Press, 1992.

Amnesty International. *Political Killings in Northern Ireland*. London: Amnesty International British Section, 1994.

Anderson, Benedict. *Imagined Communities: Reflections on the Origin and Spread of Nationalism*. London: Verso, rev. edn., 1991.

Arthur, Paul. *Government and Politics of Northern Ireland*. Harlow: Longman, 1980.

— *The People's Democracy 1968–1973*. Belfast: Blackstaff Press, 1974.

Arthur, Paul and Keith Jeffery. *Northern Ireland Since 1968*. Oxford: Basil Blackwell, 1988.

Aughey, Arthur. *Under Siege: Ulster Unionism and the Anglo-Irish Agreement*. Belfast: Blackstaff, 1989.

Bardon, Jonathan. *A History of Ulster*. Belfast: Blackstaff Press, 1992.

Barber, Benjamin. *Strong Democracy: Participatory Politics for a New Age*, Berkeley: University of California Press, 1984.

Barritt, D.P. and Charles F. Carter *The Northern Ireland Problem: A Study in Group Relations*. Oxford: Oxford University Press, 1962.

Beckett, J.C. *The Anglo-Irish Tradition*. London: Faber and Faber, 1976.

Bell, J. Bowyer. *The Secret Army*. London: Sphere, 1972.

— *The Irish Troubles*. Dublin: Gill and Macmillan, 1993.

Beresford, David. *Ten Men Dead: The Story of the 1981 Irish Hunger Strike*. London: Grafton, 1987.

Bew, Paul, Peter Gibbon and Henry Patterson. *The State in Northern Ireland 1921–71: Politica Forces and Social Classes*. Manchester: Manchester University Press, 1979

Bew, Paul and Gordon Gillespie. *Northern Ireland: A Chronology of the Troubles 1968–1993*. Dublin: Gill and Macmillan, 1993.

Bingham, S. and J.R. Powell. *Contemporary Democracies: Participation, Stability and Violence*. Cambridge: Harvard University Press, 1982.

Bishop, Patrick and Eamonn Mallie. *The Provisional IRA*. London: William Heinemann, 1987.

Bloomfield, David. *Political Dialogue in Northern Ireland: The Brooke Initiative*, 1989–92. London: Macmillan, 1998.

Bloomfield, Ken. *Stormont in Crisis: A Memoir*. Belfast: Blackstaff, 1994.

Boal, Fred, John A. Campbell and David Livingstone. 'The Protestant Mosaic: A Majority of Minorities', Patrick J. Roche and Brian Barton, eds., *The Northern Ireland Question: Myth and Reality*. Aldershot: Avebury, 1991, pp. 99–129.

Bolton, Roger. *Death on the Rock*. London: W.H.Allen, 1990.

Bowen, Murray, 'A family Concept of Schizophrenia'. *Etiology of Schizophrenia*, D.D. Jackson, ed., New York: Basic Books, pp. 346–72.

Bowen, Murray. *Family Therapy in Clinical Practice*. New York: Jason Aronson, Inc., 1978.

Boyle, K., and Tom Hadden. *Ireland: A Positive Proposal*. Harmondsworth: Penguin Books, 1985.

Brown, Terence. *Ireland: A Social and Cultural History 1922–79*. Glasgow: Fontana, 1981.

— *The Whole Protestant Community*. Derry: Field Day Publications, 1985.

— 'British Ireland', Edna Longley, ed., *Culture in Ireland: Division or Diversity?* Belfast: Institute of Irish Studies, 1991, pp. 72–83.

Bruce, Steve. *God Save Ulster: The Religion and Politics of Paisleyism*. London: Clarendon Press, 1986.

— *The Edge of the Union: The Ulster Loyalist Political Vision*. Oxford: Oxford University Press, 1994.

— 'The Politics of the Loyalist Paramilitaries', Brian Barton and Patrick J. Roche, eds., *The Northern Ireland Question: Perspectives and Policies*. Aldershot: Avebury, 1994, pp. 103–20.

Bryson, Lucy and Clem McCartney. *Clashing Symbols*. Belfast: Institute of Irish Studies, 1994.

Buckland, Patrick. *A History of Northern Ireland*. Dublin: Gill and Macmillan, 1981.

Budge, Ian and Cornelius O'Leary. *Belfast: Approach to Crisis: A Study of Belfast Politics 1613–1970*. London: Macmillan, 1973.

Cahill, Thomas. *How the Irish Saved Civilization*. London: Hodder and Stoughton, 1995.

Cairns, Ed. 'Political Violence, Social Values and the Generation Gap', Peter Stringer and Gillian Robinson, eds., *Social Attitudes in Northern*

Ireland: The Second Report. Belfast: Blackstaff, 1992, pp. 149–61.

Clarke, Liam. *Broadening the Battlefield.* Dublin: Gill and Macmillan, 1987.

Compton, Paul. 'The Changing Religious Demography of Northern Ireland: Some Political Considerations', *Studies*, 78, 312, 1989, pp. 389–402.

— 'Employment Differentials in Northern Ireland and Job discrimination: A Critique', Patrick J. Roche and Brian Barton, eds., *The Northern Ireland Question: Myth and Reality.* Aldershot: Avebury, 1991, pp. 40–76.

Conlon, Gerry. *Proved Innocent.* London: Penguin, 1993.

Conroy, John. *War as a Way of Life: A Belfast Diary.* London: Heinemann, 1988.

Coogan, Tim Pat. *Ireland Since the Rising.* London: Pall Mall, 1966.

— *On the Blanket.* Dublin: Ward River, 1980.

— *The IRA: A History.* Boulder: Roberts Rinehart, 1994.

— *Michael Collins.* London: Roberts Rinehart, 1996.

— *The Troubles.* London: Roberts Rinehart, 1996.

Cormack, R.J., A.M. Gallagher and R.D. Osborne. *Fair Enough? Religion and the 1991 Population Census.* Belfast: Fair Employment Commission, 1993.

Crapanzano, Vincent. *Waiting: The Whites of South Africa.* New York: Random House, 1985.

Crozier, Maurna, ed. *Cultural Traditions in Northern Ireland: Varieties of Irishness.* Belfast: Institute of Irish Studies, 1989.

— *Cultural Traditions in Northern Ireland: Varieties of Britishness.* Belfast: Institute of Irish Studies, 1990.

— *Cultural Traditions in Northern Ireland: All Europeans Now?* Belfast: Institute of Irish Studies, 1992.

Daly, Archbishop Cahal B. *The Price of Peace.* Belfast: Blackstaff, 1991.

Darby, John. *Conflict in Northern Ireland.* Dublin: Gill and Macmillan, 1976.

— *Northern Ireland: the Background to the Conflict.* Syracuse: Syracuse University Press, 1983.

— *Intimidation and the Control of Conflict in Northern Ireland.* Syracuse: Syracuse University Press, 1984.

— *What's Wrong with Conflict?* Coleraine: Centre for the Study of Conflict, University of Ulster, 1991.

— 'Northern Ireland: The Persistence and Limitatons of Violence', J.V. Montville (ed.), *Conflict and Peacemaking in Multiethnic Societies.*

Lexington, MA: Lexington Books, 1991, pp. 151–59.

Dangerfield, George. *The Strange Death of Liberal England*. Palo Alto: Stanford University Press, 1997.

Deane, Seamus (general ed.). *Field Day Anthology of Irish Writing Vol. 1*. Derry: Filed Day Publications, 1991.

De Paor, Liam. *The Peoples of Ireland*. Notre Dame: Notre Dame University Press, 1986.

De Rosa, Peter. *Rebels: The Irish Rising of 1916*. New York: Fawcett Columbine, 1992.

Devlin, Bernadette. *The Price of My Soul*. London: Andre Deutsch, 1969.

Devlin, Paddy. *The Fall of the Northern Ireland Executive*. Belfast: Published by the author, 1975.

Dillon, Martin. *The Dirty War*. London: Arrow Books, 1990.

Donoghue, Denis. 'The Hunger Strikes', *New York Review of Books*, November, 1981: 25: pp. 28–31.

Dunn, Seamus, ed. *Facets of the Conflict in Northern Ireland*. London: Macmillan, 1995.

Dunn, Seamus and Valerie Morgan. *Protestant Alienation in Northern Ireland: A Preliminary Survey*. Coleraine: Centre for the Study of Conflict, 1994.

Edgerton, Robert. *Alone Together: Social Isolation on a California Beach*. Berkley: University of California Press, 1986.

Elliott, Marianne. *Watchmen in Sion: the Protestant Idea of Liberty*. Derry: Field Day Publications Pamphlet, 1985.

Farrell, Michael. *Northern Ireland: The Orange State*. London: Pluto, 1980.

— *Arming the Protestants*. Dingle: Brandon, 1983.

Farren, Sean. 'The Anglo-Irish Agreement and the Protection of Minority Rights in Northern Ireland', *Etudes Irlandaises*, XIV, 1991, pp. 141–59.

— 'Addressing Northern Ireland's Political Crisis within a British-Irish Framework', *Southeastern Political Review*, 21(3), 1993, pp.737–61.

— *The Politics of Irish Education 1920–1965*. Belfast: Institute of Irish Studies, 1994.

Farren, Sean, Tom Kirk and Joanne Hughes. *Students Together – Students Apart*. Coleraine: University of Ulster, 1992.

Farren, Sean and Robert Mulvihill. 'Beyond Self-determination towards Co-determination', *Etudes Irlandaises*, 21–1, 1996, pp. 183–94.

Faulkner, Brian. *Memoirs of a Statesman*. London: Weidenfeld and Nicolson, 1978.

Ferrera, Stephanie J. *Neutrality in a Violent World*. Unpublished paper, Center for Family Consultation, Chicago, Illinois, (n.d.).

Finnegan, Richard B. *Ireland: The Challenge of Conflict and Change*. Boulder: Westview Press, 1983.

— 'The United Kingdom's Security Policy and IRA Terrorism in Ulster', *Eire-Ireland*, Spring, 1988.

Fitzduff, Mari. 'Move Sideways to Progress? Mediation Choices in Northern Ireland'. Paper presented to the First Meeting of the Ethnic Studies Network, Portrush, Northern Ireland.

FitzGerald, Garret. *All In A Life*. Dublin: Gill and Macmillan, 1991.

Flackes, W.D. and Sydney Elliott. *Northern Ireland: A Political Directory*. Belfast: Blackstaff Press, 1994.

Foster, R.F. *Modern Ireland 1600–1972*. London: Allen Lane: Penguin Press, 1988.

Friedman, Edwin H. 'Bowen Theory and Therapy', Gurman and Kniuskern, eds., *The Handbook of Family Therapy, Vol. II*. New York: Brunner and Mazel, 1981.

Gallagher, A.M. 'Community Relations', Peter Stringer and Gillian Robinson, eds., *Social Attitudes in Northern Ireland: The Third Report*. Belfast: Blackstaff, 1993, pp. 33–48.

— 'Psychological Approaches to the Northern Ireland Conflict', *The Canadian Journal of Irish Studies*, 12,2, 1987, pp. 21–32.

— 'Social Identity and the Northern Ireland Conflict', *Human Relations*, 42,10, 1989, pp. 917–35.

Gallagher, Michael. 'Do Ulster Unionists Have a Right to Self-Determination?', *Irish Political Studies*, 5, 1990, pp. 11–30.

Gallaher, John F. and Jerry DeGregory. *Violence in Northern Ireland: Understanding Protestant Perspectives*. Dublin: Gill and Macmillan, 1985.

Gamba, Stonehouse. *Signals of War: The Falklands Conflict of 1982*. London: Faber, 1991.

Gellner, Ernest. *Nations and Nationalism*. Oxford: Basil Blackwell, 1983.

Gilbert, Roberta M., M.D. *Extraordinary Relationships: A New Way of Thinking About Human Interactions*. Minneapolis, MN: Chronimed Publishing, 1992.

Gilomee, H. and J. Gagiano (eds). *Peace: South Africa, Israel, Northern Ireland*. Capetown: Oxford University Press, 1990.

Goldring, Maurice. *Faith of Our Fathers: The Formation of Irish Nationalist Ideology*. Dublin: Repsol, 1982.

Guelke, Adrian. *Northern Ireland: The International Perspective*.

Dublin: Gill and Macmillan, 1988.

— 'The Political Impasse in South Africa and Northern Ireland: A Comparative Perspective', Paper presented to the 1988 Annual Meeting of the American Political Science Association, September 1988, pp. 1–4.

Gulliver, P.H. *Disputes and Negotiation: A Cross-Cultural Perspective.* New York: Academic Press, 1979.

Hadden, Tom, Kevin Boyle and Colin Campbell, 'Emergency Law in Northern Ireland: The Context', A. Jennings, ed., *Justice Under Fire: The Abuse of Civil Liberties in Northern Ireland.* London: Pluto, 1988, pp. 1–26.

— *The Anglo-Irish Agreement.* London: Edwin Higel Ltd. and Sweet and Maxwell, 1989.

Hamill, Desmond. *Pig in the Middle: The Army in Northern Ireland 1969–1985.* London: Methuen, 1985.

Hamilton, Andrew, Clem McCartney, Tony Anderson and Ann Finn. *Violence in the Communities: The Impact of Political Violence in Northern Ireland on Intra-community, Inter-community and Community-State Relationships.* Coleraine: Centre for the Study of Conflict, 1990.

Hardy, Henry, (ed.). *Against the Current: Isaiah Berlin-Selected Writings.* London: Hogarth Press, 1979. New York: The Viking Press, 1980.

Harris, Rosemary. *Prejudice and Tolerance in Ulster: A Study of Neighbours and 'Strangers' in a Border Community.* Manchester: Manchester University Press, 1972.

Hopkinson, Michael. *Green Against Green: The Irish Civil War.* Dublin: Gill and Macmillan, 1988.

Horowitz, Donald L. *Ethnic Groups in Conflict.* Berkeley: University of California Press, 1985.

Hume, John. 'The Irish Question: A British Problem', *Foreign Affairs*, 58, pp. 300–13.

Hume, John. 'Europe of the Regions', Richard Kearney, ed., *Across the Frontiers: Ireland in the 1990s.* Dublin: Wolfhound, 1988, pp. 45–57.

Hume, John. *Personal Views: Politics, Peace and Reconciliation in Ireland.* Dublin: Town House, 1996.

Ireland. *The Constitution of Ireland.* Dublin: Stationery Office, 1937.

— *The Anglo-Irish Agreement.* Dublin: Stationery Office, 1985.

— *Review of the Workings of the Anglo-Irish Agreement.* Dublin: Stationery Office, 1989.

— *Joint Declaration by the Taoiseach and the British Prime Minister.* Dublin: Stationery Office, 1993.

— *A New Framework for Agreement (Joint Framework Document)*. Dublin: Stationery Office, 1995.

— *Report of the International Body*. Dublin: Stationery Office, 1996.

Kee, Robert. *Ireland: A History*. London: Abacus, 1993.

Kelman, Herbert. 'Israelis and Palestinians: Psychological Prerequisites for Mutual Acceptance', *International Security*, 3, 1978, pp. 255–78.

Kenna, G.B. *The Belfast Pogroms 1920–22*, Dublin: The O'Connell Publishing Company, 1922 (reprinted in a special edition, editor Thomas Donaldson, 1997).

Kennedy, Dennis. *The Widening Gulf*. Belfast: Blackstaff Press, 1988.

Kenny, Anthony. *The Road to Hillsborough*. London: Pergamon Press, 1986.

Keogh, Dermot and Michael H. Hatzel. *Northern Ireland and the Politics of Reconciliation*. Cambridge: Cambridge University Press, 1996.

Kerr, Michael E. 'Chronic Anxiety and Defining a Self', *The Atlantic Monthly*, September, 1988.

Kriesberg, Louis, Terrell A. Northrup and Stuart J. Thorson (eds.). *Intractable Conflicts and their Transformation*. Syracuse: Syracuse University Press, 1989.

Larson, Deborah Welch. *Origins of Containment: A Psychological Explanatiion*, Princeton: University of Princeton Press, 1989.

Lebow, Richard Ned. *Black Ireland and White England: The influence of Stereotypes on Colonial Policy*. Philadelphia: Institute for the Study of Human Issues, 1976.

Lee, J.J. *Ireland 1912–1985: Politics and Society*. Cambridge: Cambridge University Press, 1989.

LeVine, Robert A. and Donald T. Campbell. *Ethnocentrism*. New York: John Wiley and Sons, 1972.

Lipset, Seymour Martin and Earl Raab. *The Politics of Unreason:* Right-Wing Extremism in America 1790–1970, New York: Harper and Row, 1970.

Litton, Helen. *The Irish Famine*. Dublin: Wolfhound, 1994.

Longley, Edna. 'From Cathleen to Anorexia: the Breakdown of Irelands', Edna Longley, ed., *The Living Stream: Literature and Revisionism in Ireland*. Newcastle upon Tyne: Bloodaxe Books, 1994, pp. 173–95.

Lustick, Ian S. *State-Building Failure in British Ireland and French Algeria*. Berkeley: University of California Press, 1985.

— *Unsettled States, Disputed Lands: Britain and Ireland, France and Algeria, Israel and the West Bank-Gaza*. Ithaca: Cornell University Press, 1993.

Lyons, F.S.L. *Ireland Since the Famine.* London: Collins, Fontana, 1973.
— *Culture and Anarchy in Ireland 1890–1930.* Oxford: Oxford University Press, 1982.
MacAllister, Ian. *The Northern Ireland Social Democratric and Labour Party.* London: Macmillan, 1977.
MacBarry, John. 'The Anglo-Irish Agreement and the Unlikely Prospects for Power-Sharing in Northern Ireland', *Eire-Ireland*, Spring, 1988.
McCann, Eamonn. *War in an Irish Town*, 2nd edn., London: Pluto, 1980.
McCluskey, Conn. *Up Off Their Knees.* Galway: Conn McCluskey and Associates, 1989.
MacDonagh, Oliver. *Ireland: The Union and its Aftermath.* London: George Allen and Unwin, 1977.
MacDonald, Michael. *Children of Wrath: Political Violence in Northern Ireland.* New York: Blackwell, 1966.
McGarry, John and Brendan O'Leary. *Explaining Northern Ireland: Broken Images.* Oxford: Basil Blackwell, 1995.
— eds. *The Future of Northern Ireland.* Oxford: Clarendon, 1990.
MacManus, Seamus. *The Story of the Irish Race.* Old Greenwich: C.T. Devin-Adair, 1983.
Mack, J.E. 'The Enemy System', V.D.Volkan, D.A. Julius and J.V. Montville, eds., *Psychodynamics of International Relationshiops*, vol. 1, MA: Lexington Books, 1990, pp. 57–69.
Mallie, Eamon and David McKitterick. *The Fight for Peace.* London: William Heinemann, 1996.
Mansergh, Martin. 'The Peace Process in Historical Perspective', *Etudes Irlandaises*, 21–1, 1996, pp.195–211.
Mansfield, Michael. *Presumed Guilty.* London: Heinemann, 1993.
Marrinan, Patrick. *Paisley, Man of Wrath.* Tralee: Anvil, 1973.
Miller, David W. 'One Nation vs. Two: The Debate', *The Irish Literary Supplement*, Spring 1989, pp. 46–47.
— *Queen's Rebels: Ulster Loyalism in Historical Perspective.* Dublin: Gill and Macmillan, 1978.
Moody, T.W. and Martin, F.X., eds. *The Course of History History.* Cork: Mercier Press, 1967.
Moloney, Ed and Andy Pollak. *Paisley.* Swords Co., Dublin: Poolbeg Press, 1986.
Morrow, Duncan. *The Churches and Inter-Community Relationships.* Coleraine: Centre for the Study of Conflict, University of Ulster, 1991.
— 'Warranted Interference? The Republic of Ireland in the Politics of

Northern Ireland', *Etudes Irlandaises*, 20,1,1995, pp. 125–47.

Moxon-Browne. 'National Identity in Northern Ireland', Peter Stringer and Gillian Robinson, eds., *Social Attitudes in Northern Ireland*. Belfast: Blackstaff, 1991, pp. 23–30.

Mullin, Chris. *Error of Judgment: The Truth About the Birmingham Bombings*. Dublin: Poolbeg, 1980.

Mulvihill, Robert. *Attitudes Towards Political Violence: A Survey of Catholics and Protestants in Derry*. Doctoral dissertation presented at the University of Pennsylvania. Philadelphia: University of Pennsylvania, 1979.

— 'Family Systems Theory and Ethnic Conflict Management', Paper presented to the First Ethnic Studies Network Conference, Portrush (Northern Ireland), 1992.

— and Sean Farren. *The Anglo-Irish Agreement of 1985. Pew Case Studies in International Affairs, 459*. Georgetown: Institute for the Study of Diplomacy, Georgetown University, 1993.

— and Marc Howard Ross. 'Theories of Conflict, Conflict Management and Peacemaking in Northern Ireland', Paper presented to the North American Conference on Conflict Resolution and Peacemaking, Montreal, 1989.

Mulvihill, Robert, March Howard Ross and Victor L. Shermer. 'Psychocultural Interpretations of Ethnic Conflict in Northern Ireland: Family and Group Systems', Mark F. Ettin, Jay W. Fidler and Bertram D, Cohen, eds., *Group Process and Political Dynamics*. Madison: International Universities Press, 1995, pp. 255–78.

Nagel, Jack. *Participation*. Englewood Cliffs: Prentice Hall, 1987.

Nelson, Sarah. *Ulster's Uncertain Defenders: Loyalists and the Northern Ireland Conflict*. Belfast: Appletree, 1984.

New Ulster Political Research Group. *Beyond the Religious Divide*. Belfast: NUPRG, 1979.

Noone, Robert. 'Systems Thinking and Differentiation of Self', *CFC Review*, 1,1, January 1989.

Nordlinger, Eric A. *Conflict Regulation in Divided Societies*. Cambridge, MA: Center for International Affairs, Harvard University, 1972.

Northern Ireland. *Disturbances in Northern Ireland: Report of the Committee Appointed by the Governor of Northern Ireland (The Cameron Report)*. Belfast: HMSO, 1969.

— *Report of the Advisory Committee on Policing in Northern Ireland (The Hunt Report)*. Belfast: HMSO, 1970.

— *Report of the Tribunal Appointed to Inquire into the Events on*

Sunday 30th January 1972, which led to the loss of life in connection with the procession in Londonderry on that day. (Widgery Report). Belfast: HMSO, 1972.

— *The Future of Northern Ireland.* Belfast: HMSO, 1972.

— *Northern Ireland Constitutional Proposals.* Belfast: HMSO, 1973.

Northrup, Terrell A. 'The Dynamics of Identity in Personal and Social Conflict', Louis Kriesberg, Terrell A. Nortrup and Stuart J. Thorson eds., *Intractable Conflicts and Their Transformation*, Syracuse University Press, 1989.

O'Brien, Conor Cruise. *States of Ireland*. London: Panther, 1974.

— 'Ireland: The Mirage of Peace', *New York Review of Books*. 24 April 1986: pp. 40–45.

— *The Great Melody: A Thematic Biography of Edmund Burke.* London: Sinclair-Stevenson, 1992.

O'Brien, Conor Cruise and Maire. *Ireland, A Concise History*. London: Thames and Hudson, 1992.

O'Brien, Jack. *British Brutality in Ireland*. Dublin: Mercier Press, 1989.

O'Connor, Fionnuala. *In Search of a State: Catholics in Northern Ireland*. Belfast: Blackstaff, 1993.

O'Faolain, Sean. *The Irish*. London: Penguin, 1969.

O'Leary, Brendan. 'Public Opinion and Northern Irish Futures', *The Political Quaterly*, 63,2, 1992, pp. 143–70.

O'Malley, Padraig. *The Uncivil Wars: Ireland Today.* Boston: Houghton Mifflin, 1983.

— 'Ulster – the Marching Season', *The Atlantic Monthly*, May 1986, pp. 28–34.

— 'The Anglo-Irish Agreement: Placebo or Paradigm', H. Gilomee and J. Gagiano, eds., *The Elusive Search for Peace: South Africa, Israel, Northern Ireland*. Capetown: Oxford University Press, 1990.

— *Biting at the Grave: The Irish Hunger Strikes and the Politics of Despair*. Belfast: Blackstaff, 1990.

O'Neill, Terrence. *Ulster at the Crossroads.* London: Faber and Faber,1969

— *The Autobiography of Terence O'Neill.* London: Rupert Hart-Davis, 1972.

Pakenham, Thomas. *The Year of Liberty: The History of the Great Irish Rebellion of 1798.* New York, 1993.

Phoenix, Eamon. *Northern Nationalism 1890–1939.* Belfast: Ulster Historical Foundation, 1994.

Piller, Paul. R. *Negotiating Peace: War Termination as a Bargaining Process*. Princeton: Princeton University Press, 1983.

Probert, Belinda. *Beyond Orange and Green: The Political Economy of the Northern Ireland Crisis*. London: Zed Press, 1976.

Pruitt, D.G. and Rubin, J.Z. *Social Conflict: Escalation, Stalemate and Settlement*. Englewood Cliffs: Prentice-Hall, 1986.

Purdie, Bob. *Politics in the Streets: The Origins of the Civil Rights Movement in Northern Ireland*. Belfast: Blackstaff, 1990.

Rauseo, Louise. 'Differentiation of Self as Social Action: Standing Alone for the Common Good', Paper presented at the Conference on Theology, Washington Theological Union, July 1992.

Rose, Richard. *Governing Without Consensus: An Irish Perspective*. London: Faber and Faber, 1971.

Ross, Marc Howard. 'The Limits to Social, Structural and Psychological Explanations for Political Action and Violence', *Anthropological Quarterly*, 59, 1986, pp. 171–76.

— 'The Language of Success and Failure in Ethnic Conflict Management', Paper presented to the First Ethnic Studies Network Conference, Portrush (Northern Ireland), 1992.

— *The Culture of Conflict: Interpretations, Interests and Disputing in Comparative Perspective*. New Haven: Yale University Press, 1993.

Rowthron, Bob and Naomi Wayne. *Northern Ireland: The Polical Economy of Conflict*. Boulder: Westview Press, 1988.

Roy, James Charles. *The Road Wet, the Wind Close*. Dublin: 1986.

Ruane, Joseph and Jennifer Todd. *The Dynamics of Conflict in Northern Ireland: Power, Conflict and Emancipation*. Cambridge: Cambridge University Press, 1996.

Sennett, Richard. *Authority*. New York: W.W. Norton, 1993.

Sinn Fein. *Sinn Fein-SDLP Talks*. Belfast: Sinn Fein, 1988.

Smith, B. and T. Layne. 'Recruiting Serjeant or Solution ? Internment in Northern Ireland', Paper presented at Earlham College, No. 17, 1993.

Smith, David J. *Equality and Inequality in Northern Ireland, Part 3, Perceptions and Views*. London: Policy Studies Institute, 1987.

Social Democratic and Labour Party. *Towards a New Ireland*. Belfast: SDLP, 1972.

— *Assembly Elections Manifesto*. Belfast: 1973.

— *Towards a New Ireland – A Policy Review*. Paper presented to the Annual Conference, 1979

— *Northern Ireland – A Strategy for Peace*. Paper presented to the Annual Conference, 1980.

Stewart, A.T.Q. *The Narrow Ground: Aspects of Ulster 1609–1969*. London: Faber and Faber, 1977.

Tajfel, H. and Turner, J.C. 'The Social Identity Theory of Intergroup

Behaviour', S. Worchel and W.G. Austine (eds.), *Psychology of Intergroup Relations*. Chicago: Nelson-Hall, 1986.

Todd, Jennifer. 'Two Traditions in Unionist Political Culture', *Irish Political Studies*, 2,1987, pp. 1–26

— 'Northern Irish Nationalist Political Culture', *Irish Political Studies*, 5, 1990, pp. 31–44.

— 'Unionist Political Thought 1920–1970', D.G. Boyce, R. Eccleshall, and V. Geoghegan, eds., *Political Thought in Ireland Since the Seventeenth Century*. London: Routledge, 1993, pp.190–211.

— 'Beyond the Community Conflict: Historic Compromise Or Emancipatory Process?', *Irish Political Studies*, 10, 1995, pp.161–78.

— 'Equality, Plurality and Democracy: Justifications of Proposed Constitutional Settlements of the Northern Ireland Conflict', *Ethnic and Racial Studies*, 18, 4, 1995, pp. 818–36.

Toolis, Kevin. *Rebel Hearts: Journeys Within the IRA's Soul*. New York: St. Martin's Press, 1996.

Urban, Mark. *Big Boys's Rules: The SAS and the Secret Struggle Against the IRA*. London: Faber, 1992.

Volkan, V.D. *The Need to Have Enemies and Allies, From Clinical Practice to International Relationships*. Northvale, NJ: Jason Aronson, 1988.

White, Barry. *John Hume: Statesman of the Troubles*. Belfast: Blackstaff Press, 1984.

White, Ralph. *Fearful Warriors: A Psychological Profile of US-Soviet Relations*. New York: The Free Press, 1984.

Whyte, J.H. *Interpreting Northern Ireland*. Oxford: Clarendon Press, 1990.

Wichert, Sabine. *Northern Ireland Since 1945*. New York: Longman.

Wilson, Des. *An End to Silence*. Cork: Royal Carbery, 1985.

Wright, Frank. *Northern Ireland: A Comparative Analysis*. Dublin: Gill and Macmillan, 1987.

— *Two Lands on One Soil*. Dublin: Gill and Macmillan, 1998

NOTES

CHAPTER ONE

DIVISIVE THEMES

1   John Darby, ed., *Northern Ireland: The Background to the Conflict*, Belfast: Appletree, 1983.
2   John Whyte, *Interpreting Northern Ireland*, Oxford: Clarendon Press, 1990, chs.1, 2.
3   John Darby, *op. cit.*
4   R.F. Foster, *Modern Ireland 1600–1972*, Allen Lane: Penguin Press, 1988, pp. 585–86.
5   Padraig O'Malley, *The Uncivil War Ireland Today*, Boston: Houghton Mifflin, 1983.
6   Robert Edgerton, *Alone Together: Social Isolation on a California Beach*, Berkeley: University of California Press, p. 18.
7   Ian Lustick, *State-Building Failure in British Ireland and French Algeria*, Berkeley: University of California Press, 1985, p. 6.
8   Foster, *op. cit.*, p. 63ff.
9   *Ibid.*
10 *Ibid.*
11 D.H. Akenson, *God's People: Covenant and Land in South Africa, Israel and Ulster*. Ithaca: Cornell University Press, 1992, p. 110.
12 David Miller, *Queen's Rebels: Ulster Loyalism in Historical Perspective*, Dublin: Gill and Macmillan, 1978, p. 25.
13 Conor Cruise O'Brien, *States of Ireland*, London: Hutchinson, 1972.
14 Richard Ned Lebow, *White Britain, Black Britain: the Influence of Stereotypes on Colonial Policy*, Philadelphia: Institute for the Study of Human Issues, 1976.
15 Padraig O'Malley, 'Ulster The Marching Season.'*The Atlantic Monthly*, May 1986, p. 30.
16 Seamus Deane (general ed.), *The Field Day Anthology of Irish Writing Vol.1*, Derry: Field Day Publications, 1991, pp. 830–50.
17 Liam de Paor, *The Peoples of Ireland*, Notre Dame: Notre Dame University Press, 1986, p. 212.
18 Foster, *op. cit.*, p. 225.
19 Lustick, *op. cit.*, p. 10.
20 Foster, *op. cit.*, p. 104.

21 Miller, *op. cit.*, p. 85.
22 Lustick, *op. cit.*, p. 2.
23 Miller, *op. cit.*, pp. 85–86.
24 Lustick, *op. cit.*, p. 2.
25 de Paor, *op. cit.*, p. 110.
26 Lustick, *op. cit.*, p. 8.
27 *Ibid.*, p. 9.
28 Foster, *op. cit.*, p. 257.
29 *Ibid.*, p. 29.
30 Lustick, *op. cit.*, p. 9.
31 F.S.L. Lyons, *Culture and Anarchy in Ireland 1890–1930,* London and New York: Oxford University Press, 1979, p. 30.
32 Foster, *op. cit.*, p. 244.
33 Lustick, *op. cit.*, p. 8.
34 Ralph White, *Fearful Warriors: A Psychological Profile of U.S–Soviet Relations,* New York: The Free Press, 1984, p. 139.
35 Foster, *op. cit.*, p. 251.
36 Lustick, *op. cit.*, p. 82.
37 Foster, *op. cit.*, p. 251.
38 *Ibid.*, p. 254.
39 Akenson, *op. cit.*, p.13.
40 *Ibid.*, p. 115.
41 *Ibid.*
42 Deborah Welch Larson, *Origins of Containment: A Psychological Explanation,* Princeton: University of Princeton Press, 1989, p. 49.
43 Miller, *op. cit.*, p. 28.
44 *Ibid.*, p. 37.
45 *Ibid.*, p. 56.
46 *Ibid.*, p. 61.
47 *Ibid.*, p. 64.
48 Seymour Martin Lipset, *The Politics of Unreason: Right-Wing Extremism in America 1790–1970*, New York: Harper and Row, 1970, p. 87.
49 Akenson, *op. cit.*, p. 186.
50 George Dangerfield, *The Strange Death of Liberal England*, Palo Alto: Stanford University Press, 1997, p. 18.
51 Paddy Devlin, *The Fall of the Northern Ireland Executive*, Belfast: (published by the author), 1975, ch. 8.
52 Miller, *op. cit.*, p. 120.
53 *Ibid.*, p. 103.
54 Akenson, *op. cit.*, p. 21.
55 Vamik Volkan, *The Need for Enemies and Allies: From Clinical Practice to International Relationships,* Northvale, New Jersey: Jason Aronson, 1988, (p. 301 in Marc Ross).
56 Isaiah Berlin, 'Nationalism: Past Neglect and Present Power', *Against the Current: Isaiah Berlin – Selected Writings*, ed. Henry Hardy, New York: The Viking Press, 1980, p. 341.
57 Miller, *op. cit.*
58 *Ibid.*
59 A.T.Q. Stewart, *The Narrow Ground: Aspects of Ulster 1609–1969.*

London: Faber and Faber, 1977.
60 Akenson, *op. cit.*, p. 12.
61 G.B. Kenna, *The Belfast Pogroms 1920–22*, Dublin: The O'Connell Publishing Company, 1922 (reprinted in a special edition, editor Thomas Donaldson, 1997).
62 Akenson, *op. cit.*, p. 150.
63 Eamon Phoenix, *Northern Nationalism 1890–1940*, Belfast: Ulster Historical Foundation, 1994, chs. 8–10.
64 Patrick Buckland, *A History of Northern Ireland*, Dublin, Gill and Macmillan, 1980, ch. 6.
65 *Ibid., passim.*
66 Dennis Kennedy, *The Widening Gulf*, Belfast: Blackstaff, 1988.
67 Joseph Lee, *Ireland 1912–1985*, Cambridge: Cambridge University Press, 1989.
68 Phoenix, *op. cit.*, ch. 10.
69 W.D. Flackes and Sydney Elliott, *Northern Ireland: A Political Directory*, Belfast: Blackstaff Press, 1994, pp. 219–20.
70 A referendum to delete this article was carried with an overwhelming majority, 7 December 1972.
71 Sean Farren, *The Politics of Irish Education 1920–1965*. Belfast: Institute of Irish Studies, 1994.
72 Census returns have continuously revealed a high degree of residential segregation along denominational lines, a feature exacerbated when intercommunal tension has been high, see *Northern Ireland Census of Population 1990*, Belfast: HMSO, 1991.
73 On Good Friday 1998, after almost two years of negotiation, a new agreement was signed by representatives of the main unionist party, the Ulster Unionist Party, together with the two main nationalist parties, the SDLP and Sinn Fein, a number of smaller parties and the British and Irish governments. A month later it was endorsed by significant majorities in both parts of Ireland.

CHAPTER TWO

SIMMERING CONTENTION:
THE O'NEILL PERIOD

1 Donald Horowitz, *Ethnic Groups in Conflict*, Berkeley, University of California Press, 1985, p. 290.
2 Bob Purdie, *Politics in the Streets: The Origins of the Civil Rights Movement in Northern Ireland*, Belfast: Blackstaff Press, 1990.
3 *Ibid.*
4 Terence O'Neill, *Ulster at the Crossroads*, London: Faber and Faber, 1969, pp. 113–16
5 *Ibid.*
6 *Ibid.*
7 Berlin, *op. cit.*, p. 340.
8 Eric A. Nordlinger, *Conflict Regulation in Divided Societies*, Cambridge: Center for International Affairs, Harvard University, 1972, p. 114.
9 Horowitz, *op. cit.*, p. 22.

10   Speech to the Oxford Union, *Irish Times*, 15 October 1959.
11   Terence O'Neill, *The Autobiography of Terence O'Neill*, London: Rupert Hart-Davis, 1972, pp. 68–75.
12   S. Wichert, *Northern Ireland Since 1945*, Harlow: Longman, 1991, pp. 94–96: Ian Paisley then a forty-year-old fundamentalist preacher and moderator of the Free Presbyterian Church, which he had founded; later to become a very significant figure in Northern Irish politics as founder and leader of the Democratic Unionist Party.
13   Purdie, *op. cit.*, p. 82–83.
14   *Ibid.*
15   *Ibid.*, pp. 82–102.
16   Conn McCluskey, *Up Off Their Kneees,* Galway: Conn McCluskey and Associates, 1989.
17   Purdie, *op. cit.*, pp. 14 and 35.
18   *Ibid.*, p. 165.
19   Ed Moloney and Andy Pollak, *Paisley*, Swords: Poolbeg Press, 1986, p. 115.
20   Purdie, *op. cit.*, p. 30.
21   *Ibid.*
22   *Ibid.*
23   O'Neill, *Autobiography*, *op. cit.*, p. 121.
24   *Irish News*, 24 October 1967.
25   *Newsletter*, 25 October 1967.
26   Wichert, *op. cit.*, pp. 104–12.
27   O'Neill, *op. cit.*, p. 99.
28   Purdie, *op. cit.*, p. 100.
29   *Ibid.*, p. 213.
30   *Belfast Telegraph*, 12 December 1968.
31   Flackes and Elliott, *op. cit.*, p. 2.
32   O'Neill, *Autobiography*, *op. cit.*, p. 106–07.
33   *Ibid.*, ch. 5
34   O'Neill, *Crossroads*, pp. 140–46.
35   Paul Arthur, *The People's Democracy 1968–1973*, Belfast, 1974, 23ff.
36   Flackes and Elliott, *op, cit.*, p. 306.
37   O'Neill, *Autobiography*, *op. cit.*, p. 112.
38   Wichert, *op. cit.*, pp.122, 206.
39   *Ibid.*, p. 122.
40   O'Neill, *Autobiography*, *op. cit.*, p. 122.
41   *Ibid.*, pp. 122–23.
42   *Ibid.*, p. 127.

CHAPTER THREE

ESCALATING FEARS AND HOPES:
FROM STREET RIOTS TO DIRECT RULE

1   *Disturbances in Northern Ireland: Report of the Committee appointed by the Governor of Northern Ireland*, (Cameron Report), Belfast: HMSO, 1969, Cmd 532, p. 14.
2   *Report of the Advisory Committee on the Police in Northern Ireland, (Hunt*

Report), Belfast: HMSO, 1969, Cmd 535, p. 210.
3 Todd, *op. cit.*, 1987, p. 9.
4 Buckland, *op. cit.*, p. 130.
5 Paul Arthur, *Government and Politics of Northern Ireland*, Harlow: Longman Press, 1980, p. 45.
6 Flackes and Elliott, p. 212.
7 O'Neill, *Autobiography, op. cit.*, p. 35.
8 Wichert, *op. cit.*, p. 120.
9 Flackes and Elliott, pp. 129–30 & 349–50.
10 Timothy Pat Coogan, *The IRA: A History*, Boulder: Roberts Rinehart Publishers, 1994, chs. 18 and 19.
11 J. Bowyer Bell, *The Irish Troubles*, Dublin: Gill and Macmillan, 1993, pp. 162–63.
12 *Ibid.*
13 Wichert, *op. cit.*, p. 140.
14 *Ibid.*, p. 156.
15 *Ibid.*, p. 148.
16 Flackes and Elliott, *op. cit.*, pp. 78–80.
17 Wichert, *op. cit.*, p. 139–40.
18 Arthur, *op. cit.*, pp. 98, 104.
19 Faulkner, *op. cit.*
20 Northern Ireland Parliament, *Commons Debates,* vol. 82, col. 93. Belfast: HMSO, 1972.
21 Bell, *op. cit.*, chs. 5 and 6.
22 G. Bingham Powell, *Contemporary Democracies: Participation, Stability, and Violence*, Cambridge: Harvard University Press, 1982, p. 161.
23 Powell, *op. cit.*, p. 167.
24 Beth Smith and Tobey Layne, 'Recruiting Sergeant or Solution? Internment in Northern Ireland', paper presented at Earlham College, November 17, 1993, pp. 6–7.
25 *Irish Times*, 10 August 1971.
26 Miller, *op. cit.*, p. 37.
27 Arthur, *op. cit.* p. 113.
28 Flackes and Elliott, *op. cit.*, p. 466.
29 Faulkner, *op. cit.*
30 *Ibid.*
31 Organized by Bill Craig and later transformed into the Vanguard Movement.
32 Arthur, *op. cit.*, pp. 117, 121.
33 Coogan, *op. cit.*, pp. 572–73.
34 *Report of the Tribunal appointed to inquire into the events on Sunday, 30th January 1972, which led to loss of life in connection with the procession in Londonderry on that day* (Widgery Report), London: HMSO, 1972.
35 Sarah Nelson, *Ulster's Uncertain Defenders: Loyalists and the Northern Ireland Conflict*, Belfast: Appletree, 1984, p. 104.
36 *Ibid.*, pp. 108–16.
37 Faulkner, *Memoirs of a Statesman*, London, Weidenfeld and Nicolson, 1978, pp. 151–53.
38 *Ibid.*, pp. 151–53.
39 *Ibid.*

CHAPTER FOUR

COMMUNITIES AT RISK: FROM DIRECT
RULE TO POWER-SHARING

1   Ross, *The Culture of Conflict: Interpretations, Interests and Disputing in Comparative Perspective*, New Haven: Yale University Press, 1993, p. 156.
2   *Ibid.*, p.157; see also Robert Mulvihill and Marc Howard Ross, 'Theories of Conflict, Conflict Management and Peacemaking in Northern Ireland', a paper presented at the National Conference on Peacemaking and Conflict Resolution, Montreal, 1989, p. 3.
3   The Sunningdale Agreement of December 1973 was concluded by the UUP, the SDLP and the Alliance Party together with the Irish and British governments.
4   Flackes and Elliott, *op. cit.*, p. 351.
5   Nelson, *op. cit.*, ch. 7.
6   J. White, *John Hume,* Belfast: Blackstaff, 1984, p. 125.
7   Bell, *op. cit.*, p. 319.
8   Merlyn Rees, *Northern Ireland, a Personal Perspective*, London: Methuen, 1985, p. 14.
9   Coogan, *op. cit.*, pp. 606–08.
10 Bell, *op. cit.*, pp. 332–34.
11 Coogan, *op. cit.*, p. 610.
12 The term constitutional came to be applied to those parties and those politicians who eschewed violence as a political weapon and normally, included the following: the Ulster Unionist Party, Democratic Unionist Party, Alliance Party, Social Democratic and Labour Party as well as several minor parties but not Sinn Fein nor those parties which came to be associated with loyalist paramilitary forces.
13 Flackes and Elliott, *op. cit.*, p. 8.
14 A research group within the UDA, the New Ulster Political Research Group, prepared models of government for an independent Northern Ireland and actively lobbied the main political parties on its prospects; see *Beyond the Religious Divide*, Belfast: NUPRG, 1979.
15 O'Malley, *op. cit.*, pp. 490–91; McGarry and O'Leary, pp. 371–73.
16 Arthur, *op. cit.*, p. 14.
17 Bell, *op. cit.*, pp. 1–22.
18 Wichert, *op. cit.*, p. 147.
19 *Ibid.*, p. 150.
20 White, *op. cit.*, p. 135.
21 *Ibid.*
22 *Ibid.*
23 *Ibid.*
24 *Ibid.*
25 SDLP, *Towards a New Ireland*, Belfast: SDLP, 1972.
26 *Ibid.*
27 *Ibid.*
28 I. McAllister, *The Northern Ireland Social Democratic and Labour Party*, London: Macmillan, 1977, p. 122.
29 Northern Ireland Office, *The Future of Northern Ireland*, Belfast: HMSO,

1972.
30 *Ibid.*
31 *Ibid.*
32 *Ibid.*
33 *Ibid.*
34 *Ibid.*
35 *Ibid.*
36 *Ibid.*
37 *Ibid.*
38 *Ibid.*
39 Powell, *op. cit.*, p. 157.
40 Arthur, *op. cit.*, p. 116.
41 Northern Ireland, *Northern Ireland – Constitutional Proposals*, Belfast: HMSO, 1973.
42 Flackes and Elliott, p. 163 and 250.
43 *Northern Ireland Office – Constitutional Proposals*, Belfast: HMSO, 1973.
44 *Ibid.*
45 *Ibid.*
46 Faulkner, *op. cit.*
47 Flackes and Elliott, *op. cit.*, p. 369–72.
48 *Ibid.*
49 McGarry and O'Leary, *op. cit.*, pp. 104, 124.
50 *Ibid.*
51 *Irish Times*, 22 November 1973.
52 SDLP, *Assembly Election Manifesto*, 1973.
53 Faulkner, *op. cit.*
54 Alliance Party of Northern Ireland, *Assembly Election Manifesto*, 1973.
55 SDLP, *op. cit.*
56 Flackes and Elliott, *op. cit.*, pp. 316–17.
57 *Ibid.*
58 McGarry and O'Leary, *op. cit.*, pp. 94, 125ff; Akenson, p. 283.
59 Faulkner, *op. cit.*
60 Bell, *op. cit.*,
61 Wichert, *op. cit.*, pp. 165–68.
62 *Ibid.*
63 *Ibid.*
64 Nelson, *op. cit.*, p. 155ff.
65 Devlin, *op. cit.*, ch. 8.
66 Flackes and Elliott, *op. cit.*, pp. 377–80.
67 *Ibid.*
68 *Ibid.*, p. 101.
69 One hundred and one people were killed in the period January–June 1974, ninety in the preceding six months.
70 Flackes and Elliott, *op. cit.*, pp. 325–29.
71 Bell, *op. cit.*, p. 437.
72 *Ibid.*
73 Flackes and Elliott, *op. cit.*, p. 468.
74 *Ibid.*, p. 125.
75 McGarry and O'Leary, *op. cit.*, pp. 144, 203.

76 Bell, *op. cit.*, chs. 14 and 15.
77 At the 1978 annual conference, SDLP delegates overwhelmingly endorsed a motion calling for British withdrawal in the context of an overall settlement.
78 SDLP, *Towards a New Ireland – A Policy Rreview*, paper presented to the 1979 annual conference; *Northern Ireland – A Strategy for Peace*, paper presented to the 1980 annual conference.

CHAPTER FIVE
SOURCES OF STRUCTURAL FAILURE

1 Marc Howard Ross, *op. cit.*, p. 156; Ed Cairns, 'Intergroup Conflict in Northern Ireland', in Henri Tajfel, ed., *Social Identity and Intergroup Relations*, Cambridge, England, 1982, pp. 277–97.
2 Ross, *op. cit.*, p. 38.
3 *Ibid.*, p. 39.
4 Kevin Boyle and Tom Hadden, *Northern Ireland: The Choice*, London: Penguin Books, 1994, ch. 2.
5 O'Malley, *The Uncivil Wars, Ireland Today*, chs. 4, 5.
6 John Darby, *Intimidation and the Control of Conflict in Northern Ireland*, Syracuse: Syracuse University Press, 1984.
7 Nelson, *op. cit.*, ch. 4.
8 Horowitz, *op. cit.*, p. 97.
9 Darby, *op. cit.*
10 Horowitz, *op. cit.*, p. 97.
11 Bell, *op. cit.*, p. 387.
12 Dangerfield, *op. cit.*, p. 37.
13 Nelson, p. 158.
14 Jennifer Todd, 'Two Traditions in Unionist Political Culture', *Irish Political Studies*, 2, 1987.
15 O'Malley, *op. cit.*, pp. 133–68.
16 *Ibid.*, p. 201.
17 DUP, website: http://www.dup.org.uk.
18 Rose, *op. cit.*, p. 33.
19 Miller, *op. cit.*, p. 85.
20 O'Malley, *op. cit.*, p. 191.
21 Horowitz, *op. cit.*, p. 347.
22 Flackes and Elliott, *op. cit.*, pp. 359–412.
23 Horowitz, *op. cit.* p. 346.
24 *Ibid.*
25 *Ibid.*
26 *Ibid.*
27 David J. Smith, *Equality and Inequality in Northern Ireland. Part 3: Perceptions and Views*, London: Policy Studies Institute, 1987, table 119.
28 Powell, *op. cit.*, pp. 155–57.
29 *Ibid.*, p. 161.
30 *Ibid.*, p. 167.
31 Miller, *op. cit.* pp. 83ff.

32 Several leading nationalist politicians had participated in delegations which had sought arms for defensive purposes from the Irish government, see Kelly, *Orders for the Captain,*
33 Foster, *op. cit.*, pp. 403–05.
34 Richard Ned Lebow, *Black Ireland and White England – the Influence of Stereotypes on Colonial Policy,* Philadelphia: Institute for the Study of Human Issues, 1976.
35 Dermot P.J. Walsh, *The Use and Abuse of Emergency Legislation in Northern Ireland,* London: The Cobden Trust, 1983.
36 Bell, *op. cit.*, pp.158–59.
37 The data in this table are drawn from Tables V.4 and V.5 in Rose, *op. cit.*
38 Robert F. Mulvihill, *Attitudes Towards Political Violence: A Survey of Catholics and Protestants in Derry,* Doctoral Dissertaton presented at the University of Pennsylvania, 1979.
39 Conversation with Fr. Raymond Murray, July 12 1987.
40 Volkan, *op. cit.*, p. 5.
41 Quoted from the television documentary *Northern Irelandf: at the Edge of the Union,* London: BBC, 1990.
42 Robert Mulvihill and Marc Howard Ross, 1989, 'Theories of Conflict, Conflict Management and Peacemaking in Northern Ireland', paper presented to North American Conference on Conflict Resolution and Peacemaking, Montreal, p. 3.
43 Ross, *op. cit.*
44 Nordlinger, *op. cit.*; Horowitz, *op. cit.*
45 Horowitz, *op. cit.*
46 Boyle and Hadden, *op. cit.*, p. 82
47 Horowitz, *op. cit.*

CHAPTER SIX
PSYCHOCULTURAL THEORIES OF CONFLICT

1 Henri Tajfel and John C. Turner, 'An Integrative Theory of Intergroup Conflict', in *The Social Psychology of Intergroup Relations*, eds., William G. Austin and Stephen Worchel, Monterey, California: Brooks/Cole Publishers, 1979.
2 Volkan, *op. cit.*, p. 23.
3 Mulvihill and Ross, *op. cit.* p. 4.
4 *Ibid.*, p. 5; for a full discussion of these issues see Marc Howard Ross (1993), *op. cit.*, ch.4.
5 Ross, *op. cit.*, pp. 10–11.
6 Horowitz, *op. cit.*, pp. 179, 201.
7 Moloney and Pollak, *op. cit.*, p. 216.
8 Conversation with DUP councillor in Derry, Gregory Campbell.
9 Terrell Northrup, 'The Dynamics of Identity in Personal and Social Conflict', Louis Kriesberg, Terrell A. Northrup and Stuart J. Thorson, eds., *Intractable Conflicts and Their Transformation,* Syracuse: Syracuse University Press, 1989, p. 65.

10 *Ibid.*, p. 65.
11 *Ibid.*, p. 68.
12 *Ibid.*, p. 97.
13 *Ibid.*
14 Roy F. Foster, *Cultural Traditions in Northern Ireland: Varieties of Irishness,* ed. Maurna Crozier, Belfast: Institute of Irish Studies; 1989, pp. 5–24.
15 Vincent Crapanzo, *Waiting: The Whites of South Africa,* New York: Random House, 1985.
16 Boyle and Hadden, *op. cit.*, ch. 2.
17 Fionnuala O'Connor, *In Search of a State: Catholics in Northern Ireland,* Belfast, Blackstaff, 1993, p. 167.
18 Volkan, *op. cit.*, p. 222.
19 Northrup, *op. cit.*, p. 1982.
20 Cairns, *op. cit.*, p. 105.
21 Northrup, *op. cit.*, p. 50.
22 Berlin, *op. cit.* p. 342.
23 Volkan, *op. cit.*, p. 230.
24 Todd (1990), *op. cit.*, p. 34.
25 Robert A. Le Vine and Donald Campbell, *Ethnocentrism: Theories of Conflict, Ethnic Attitudes and Group Behaviour,* New York: John Wiley, 1972.
26 Todd (1987), *op. cit.*, p. 35.
27 Goldensen, ed., *Longman Dictionary of Psychiatry and Psychology,* New York: Longman Press, 1984, p. 357.
28 Northrup, *op. cit.*
29 *Ibid.*, p. 68.
30 dePaor, *op. cit.*, p. 212.
31 O'Connor, *op. cit.*
32 Terence Brown, *The Whole Protestant Community: the Making of a Historical Myth,* Derry: Field Day Theatre, 1985, p. 8.
33 Marianne Elliott, *Watchmen in Sion: the Protestant Idea of Liberty,* Derry: Field Day Theatre, 1985, p. 15.
34 Foster, *op. cit.*, p. 275; dePaor, *op. cit.*, p. 219.
35 Todd (1990), p. 11.
36 Crapanzano, *op. cit.*, p. 21.
37 Todd (1990), *op. cit.*, p.3.
38 Elliott, *op. cit.*, p.
39 Todd (1990), *op. cit.*, p.
40 Jervis, *op. cit.*, p. 94.
41 *Ibid.*, p. 94.
42 Crapanzano, *op. cit.*, p. 21.
43 Benjamin Barber, *Strong Democracy: Participatory Politics for a New Age,* Berkeley: University of California Press, 1984, p. 202.
44 Crapanzano, *op. cit.*, p. 21.
45 Volkan, *op. cit.*, p.174.
46 J.E.Mack, 'The Enemy System', *Psychodynamics of International Relationships,* Vol.1, eds., V.D. Volkan, D.A. Julius and J.V. Montville, Lexington, MA: Lexington Books, pp. 57–69.

47 *Ibid.*
48 *Ibid.*
49 Volkan, *op. cit.*
50 O'Malley, *Biting at the Grave,* Belfast: Blackstaff, p. 44.
51 Volkan, *op. cit.*, p. 155.
52 O'Malley, *op. cit.*, p. 44.
53 Herbert Kelman, 'Israelis and Palestinians: Psychological Rerequisites for Mutual Acceptance', *International Security*, 3, 1978, pp. 162–86.
54 Volkan, p. 155.
55 Todd (1990), *op. cit.*
56 Elliott, *op. cit.*
57 O'Malley, *op. cit.*, pp. 13–14.
58 *Ibid.*, p. 56.
59 Foster, *op. cit.*, p. 486.
60 Northrup, *op. cit.*, p. 70.
61 Akenson, *op. cit.*, p. 184.
62 Foster, *op. cit.*, p. 99.
63 Boyle and Hadden, *op. cit.*, p. 34.
64 Northrup, *op. cit.*, p.71.
65 Ross, *op. cit.*, p.172.
66 Mulvihill, Ross and Shermer, *op. cit.*, p. 266.

CHAPTER SEVEN

FORGING NEW RELATIONSHIPS: THE ANGLO-IRISH AGREEMENT

1 The talks were convened by Secretary of State Atkins and were mainly focused on possible arrangments for the government of Northern Ireland; at the SDLP's insistence parallel talks focused on North-South relations.
2 *Anglo-Irish Agreement 1985,* Dublin: The Stationery Office, 1985.
3 Jack Nagel, *Participation*, Englewood Cliffs, New Jersey: Prentice Hall, 1987, p. 14.
4 Northrup, *op. cit.*, pp. 77–81.
5 *Ibid.*, p. 77.
6 *Ibid.*, p. 77.
7 Todd (1987), p. 1.
8 Todd, *op. cit.*, p. 20.
9 Nelson, *op. cit.*, ch. 11.
10 Todd, *op. cit.*, p. 21.
11 Northrup, *op. cit.*, p. 64.
12 Boyle and Hadden, *op. cit.*, p. 86.
13 Edwin H. Friedman, 'Bowen Theory and Therapy', in *Handbook of Family Therapy, Vol. II*, p.150.
14 Paul R. Pillar, *Negotiating Peace: War Termination as a Bargaining Process*, Princeton: Princeton University Press, 1983, p. 246.
15 David Beresford, *Ten Dead Men: The Story of the 1981 Irish Hunger Strike*, London: Grafton Press.

16 O'Malley (1990a), *op. cit.*, p. 22.
17 R. Mulvihill and S. Farren, *The Anglo-Irish Agreement*, PEW Case Studies in International Affairs, Washington: Georgetown University, 1993, p. 5.
18 O'Malley, *op. cit.* pp. 28–34.
19 Organized by two Belfast women following a number of killings in the city; the *Peace People* movement rapidly gained popular support in the late seventies by organizing mass rallies against violence but almost as rapidly lost momentum.
20 Denis Donoghue, 'The Hunger Strikers', *The New York Review of Books*, 22 October 1981, p. 30.
21 O'Malley, *op. cit.*,p. 176.
22 Flackes and Elliott, *op. cit.*, pp. 337–43.
23 Pruitt and Rubin, *op. cit.*, p. 126.
24 *Ibid.*, pp. 152ff.
25 Boyle and Hadden, *op. cit.*, p. 70.
26 Dermot Keogh and Michael H. Haltzel, eds., *Northern Ireland and the Politics of Reconciliation*, Cambridge, Mass.: Woodrow Wilson Center Press, 1993, p. 108.
27 Northern Ireland Census data for 1971, 1981, 1991.
28 *Report of the New Ireland Forum*, Dublin: Stationery Office, 1984, ch. 5.
29 J. Darby: *What's Wrong with Conflict*, Coleraine: Centre for the Study of Conflict, University of Ulster, 1991.
30 Boyle and Hadden, *op. cit.*, p. 105.
31 Stephanie J. Ferrera, 'Neutrality in a Violent World', unpublished paper, pp. 9ff.
32 Pruitt and Rubin, p. 122.
33 Ferrera, *op. cit.*, p. 10.
34 Bowen, *op. cit.*
35 *Ibid.*
36 *Report of the New Ireland Forum*, Dublin: Stationery Office, 1984.
37 *Ibid.*
38 At a press conference following a meeting with Taoiseach Garret FitzGerald, Mrs. Thatcher indicated in very emphatic terms that each of these three proposals was 'out of the question'.
39 Mulvihill and Farren, *op. cit.*, p. 6.
40 David Bloomfield, *Political Dialogue in Northern Ireland: The Brooke Initiative*, 1989–92. London: Macmillan, 1998, ch. 1.
41 Keogh and Haltzel, *op. cit.*, p. 9.
42 Mulvihill and Farren, *op. cit.*, p. 9.
43 *Ibid.*, p. 9.
44 Boyle and Hadden, *op. cit.*, pp. 70–71.
45 Richard Sennett, *Authority*, New York: W.W. Norton, 1993, p. 42.

CHAPTER EIGHT

DIFFICULT RELATIONSHIPS:
FROM HILLSBOROUGH TO STORMONT

1 McGarry and O'Leary, *op. cit.*, pp. 126–28.
2 Joseph Ruane and Jennifer Todd, *The Dynamics of Conflict in Northern*

Ireland: Power, Conflict and Emancipation, Cambridge: CUP, 1996, pp. 114, 135.

3   Mulvihill and Farren, *op. cit.*, p. 9.
4   Flackes and Elliott, *op. cit.*, pp. 346–47.
5   Boyle and Hadden, *op. cit.*, pp. 128–30.
6   Sean Farren and Bob Mulvihill, 'Beyond Self-Determination Towards Co-determination', *Etudes Irlandaises*, Printemps, 1996, no. 21–1, p. 184.
7   *Ibid.*, p. 185.
8   *International Covenant on Civil and Political Rights,* New York: United Nations and the *International Covenant on Economic Social and Cultural Rights,* New York
9   United Nations, *Declaration on Principles of International Law Concerning Friendly Relations and Co-operation Among States in Accordance with the Charter of the United Nations,* New York: United Nations.
10 Martin Mansergh. 'The Peace Process in Historical Perspective', *Etudes Irlandaises*, Printemps, 1996, no. 21–1, p. 195–211.
11 O'Malley, *op. cit.*, p. 126.
12 Mulvihill and Farren, *op. cit.*, p. 9.
13 Heavy patrolling by security forces in nationalist areas; the use of plastic bullet rounds for riot control; allegations of a continuing 'shoot-to-kill' policy – all reinforced mistrust of the security forces.
14 Persons arrested on extradition warrants frequently had their appeals against extradition upheld in the Irish courts on grounds that their alleged crimes had a 'political' motivation.
15 Boyle and Hadden, p. 118.
16 Statement by Secretary of State Brooke to the House of Commons, 26 March 1991. *Irish Times*, 27 March 1991.
17 DUP submission to the Brooke-Mayhew talks.
18 *Ibid.*
19 *Ibid.*
20 Farren and Mulvihill, *op. cit.*, p. 184.
21 DUP, *op. cit.*
22 *Ibid.*
23 Ruane and Todd, pp. 49–50.
24 UUP submission to the Brooke-Mayhew talks.
25 *Ibid.*
26 Ruane and Todd, *op. cit.*, p. 51.
27 UUP, *op. cit.*
28 Ruane and Todd, *op. cit.*, pp. 198–99.
29 UUP, *op. cit.*
30 Alliance Party submission to the Brooke-Mayhew talks.
31 *Ibid.*
32 SDLP submission to the Brooke-Mayhew talks.
33 *Ibid.*
34 Horowitz, *op. cit.*, p. 197.
35 Flackes and Elliott, *op. cit.*, pp. 408–10.
36 SDLP, *op. cit.*
37 Mallie and McKitterick, *The Fight for Peace in Northern Ireland*, ch. 7.
38 *Ibid.*, p. 171.

234 *Notes to pages 158–179*

39 Statement by J. Hume and G. Adams, *Irish Times*, 26 April 1993.
40 *Ibid.*

CHAPTER NINE

INCLUSIVE NEGOTIATIONS:
FROM DECLARATION TO CEASEFIRE

1 Mallie and McKitterick, *op. cit.*, detail the background to this shift.
2 The Joint Declaration of the Taoiseach, Mr. Reynolds and the British Prime Minister, Mr. John Major (The Downing Street Declaration), 15 December 1993.
3 Mallie and McKitterick, *op. cit.*, chs. 9–13.
4 *Ibid.*, p. 204.
5 Preamble to *Anglo-Irish Agreement, op. cit.*, 1985.
6 *Joint Declaration, op. cit.*, para. 2.
7 *Ibid.*, para. 4.
8 *Anglo-Irish Agreement, op. cit.*, Art. 1(c).
9 *Joint Declaration., op. cit.*, par. 5.
10 *Ibid.*, par. 6.
11 *Ibid.*, par. 11
12 *Ibid.*, par. 9.
13 *Ibid.*, par. 10.
14 *Irish Times*, 16 December 1993.
15 *Ibid.*
16 *Belfast Telegraph*, 7 January 1994.
17 *Irish Times*, 30 December 1993.
18 *Sunday Business Post*, 2 January 1994.
19 *Irish News*, 14 January 1994.
20 *Irish Times,* 25 July 1994.
21 Local government reforms in the early 1970s removed a wide range of powers over such controversial matters as public housing, public planning and education from local councils and placed them in the control of nominated boards.
22 *Irish Times*, 28 February 1994.
23 *Irish Times*, 1 September 1994.
24 *Ibid.*
25 *Ibid.*, 7 September 1994.
26 *Ibid.*
27 *A New Framework for Agreement (Joint Framework Document),* February 1994.
28 *Ibid.*, par. 38.
29 SDLP submission on North-South structures to the Forum for Peace and Reconciliation, 1995.
30 *Report of the International Body,* January 1996.
31 Statement issued by the SDLP members of the Northern Ireland Forum, 13 July 1996.
32 A Saturday night picket by a group of loyalists at the Catholic church at

Harryville in Ballymena lasted almost two years, from September 1996–May 1998.

33 The Labour Party was returned with a majority over the Conservatives of 172.

34 Sinn Fein increased their percentage of the vote slightly to seventeen per cent but gained many more council seats than the party had previously held, seventy-four compared with fifty-one in 1993.

35 *Irish Times*, 22 July 1997.

36 The UUP had announced that it would be sounding opinion within its own community during August as to whether it should remain in the talks or not. The outcome of this consultation contributed to the decision to remain.

CHAPTER TEN
TRANSFORMING THE CONFLICT

1 *Peace in Ireland – Principles and Requirements*, Sinn Fein submission to the multi-party talks, 14 October 1997.

2 *Ibid.*

3 *Ibid.*

4 *Ibid.*

5 *Ibid.*

6 Submission by the UUP to Strand 2 of the multi-party-talks, *Principles and Requirements,* 7 October 1997.

7 *Ibid.*

8 *Ibid.*

9 Submission by the SDLP to the multi-party talks, *Principles and Requirements,* 13 October 1997.

10 *Ibid.*

11 Submission by the Alliance Party of Northern Ireland to the multi-party talks *Principles and Realities,* 13 October 1997.

12 Submission by the Northern Ireland Women's Coalition to the multi-party talks *Principles and Requirements*, 13 October 1997.

13 Submission by the British Government to Strand 2 of the multi-party talks *Principles and Requirements,* 10 October 1997; submission by the Irish Government to Strand 2 of the multi-party talks, *Principles and Requirements,* 10 October 1997.

14 Statement by the Independent Chairmen of the multi-party talks, 16 December 1997.

15 The towns of Moira and Portadown suffered severe bomb damage in February.

16 The 'Principles of Democracy and Non-Violence' were contained in the *Report of the International Body on Decommissioning,* 22 January 1996.

17 *Propositions on Heads of Agreement,* 12 Jan. 1998.

18 *North-South Structures – a paper to facilitate discussion presented by the British and Irish Governments,* 27 January 1998.

19 *Joint Statement by the British and Irish Governments, 12 January 1998.*

20 One of Trimble's closest associates at the talks, Jeffrey Donaldson MP,

called upon his colleagues to reconsider the party's participation in the talks, *Irish News*, 20 December 1997.

21 Statement by Chairman George Mitchell, *Irish Times*, 31 March 1998.

22 Both prime ministers were present and devoted themselves exclusively to the talks during the last three days of negotiations.

23 The Northern Committee Irish Congress of Trade Unions and the Confederation of British Industry (Northern Ireland) issued statements welcoming the agreement and urging support for it in the referenda.

24 Statement by President Clinton, *Washington Post*, 11 April 1998.

25 At a special meeting of the European Parliament in Brussels on 2 May overwhelming support was given to the agreement.

26 Meetings of the UUP executive on 11 April and of the Ulster Unionist Council on 18 April strongly endorsed the agreement.

27 Statement by the DUP on the Good Friday Agreement, http://www.org.uk/.

28 Statement by the IRA, *Irish Times,* 30 April 1998.

29 A number of failed attacks on police stations in the North and the interception of large caches of bomb-making material in the South was evidence of this activity.

30 Address by Caoimhin O Caolain to Dail Eireann, 21 April 1998, *Irish Times*, 22 April 1998.

31 *Ibid.*

32 *Irish Times*, 27 April 1998.

33 The agreement was endorsed by ninety-six per cent of the delegates at the special convention on 10 May 1998, *Irish Times*, 11 May 1998.

34 Ruairi O Bradaigh, a former President of Sinn Fein who, in 1986 after the party had decided to allow members elected to Dail Eireann to take their seats, resigned to form Republican Sinn Fein.

35 Editorial comment in *Saoirse* (newspaper of Republican Sinn Fein), April 1998.

36 *Ibid.*

37 In terms of assembly seats the UUP obtained twenty-eight, the SDLP twenty-four, the DUP twenty, Sinn Fein eighteen, Alliance six, UKUP five, PUP two, Independent Unionists three, Women's Coalition two; these results provided an overall majority for parties in favour of the Good Friday Agreement but, within the unionist block, only thirty pro-agreement against twenty-eight anti-agreement.

38 At the time of completion, July 1999, such parts of the agreement as the Assembly's Executive and the North-South Ministerial Council had not been formed and no progress at all had been achieved on the decommissioning of paramilitary arms. A review of those aspects of the agreement not implemented was scheduled to commence in September 1999 with Senator George Mitchell once again in the chair.

INDEX

Page numbers in **bold** refer to complete chapters